Traumatic Events and Ethnic Diasporas

Dorie G. Taylor

ABSTRACT

This research examines how ethnic diaspora communities perceive and respond to "traumatic events" in the homeland and evaluates the capacity of these events to act as catalysts to mobilize diasporas in support of co-ethnic separatist movements. Although other factors help to shape perceptions and influence the relative effectiveness of mobilization, the purpose of this research is to develop a clearer understanding of how a single violent event can have a grave and unique impact on diaspora views of a homeland separatist movement and help lead to the mobilization of its supporters. To gain these insights and analyze diaspora perceptions and ensuing forms of mobilization, the research entails both an in-depth single case study and a multi-case comparative approach. For the single case study, I use structured interviews conducted with Sikh diaspora members living in the United States to examine the perceptions and ensuing actions of these Sikhs to a controversial 1984 Indian military operation codenamed Operation Blue Star. For the multi-case study, I analyze the response of the Irish and Uyghur ethnic diasporas to three homeland traumatic events: the 1972 Bloody Sunday killings and 1981 Irish hunger strike in Northern Ireland, and the 2009 Urumqi riots in Xinjiang. Based on the results of these comparative case examinations, I argue that traumatic events affect ethnic members symbolically and emotionally, leading to a process of "event galvanization" where diaspora opinions shift in favor of the separatist movement, increasing the likelihood of mobilization among diaspora members to take actions in support of the separatist movement.

Key Words: diaspora, ethnic conflict, ethnonationalism, traumatic events, symbolism, emotion, Punjab, Sikhs, Northern Ireland, Irish America, Xinjiang, Uyghurs

TABLE OF CONTENTS

PART I

TRAUMATIC EVENTS AND DIASPORA RESPONSES

1

INTRODUCTION

How do "traumatic events" — by which I mean an episode in the homeland that ethnic group members view as physically or symbolically threatening to the survival of the ethnic group — alter perceptions in the ethnic diaspora? This research examines how relevant and threatening traumatic events that take place in the homeland are perceived and defined within diasporic communities. The main focus of this study is to examine the relationship between diasporas and ethnic separatist movements in the homeland. It considers if there is capacity for traumatic events to act as a catalyst for mobilization among members of the diaspora to begin to support, or increase support for co-ethnic separatist movements. By helping to clarify these relationships, this study attempts to serve as a resource for those seeking to reduce or contain separatist violence and insurgency.

In this research, through the trial of several hypotheses, I test the strength of an explanatory model for diaspora perception creation and ensuing mobilization in response to a traumatic event. This research argues traumatic events influence ethnic members symbolically and emotionally, and that these processes "galvanize" diaspora opinions in favor of separatist movements, increasing the likelihood of mobilization among some diaspora members to take actions in support of the separatist movement. The explanatory model that I have developed relies in part on the scholarly literature on "contentious politics," or social movements (Tarrow

1998, 2011; McAdam, Tarrow, and Tilley, 2001; Wayland 2004; Tsutsui 2004), but is also steeped in several works examining ethnic identity, nationalism, and ethnic conflict (Anderson 1983; Calhoun 1993; Sewell 1996; Motyl 1999; Horowitz 2000; Eriksen 2002; Varshney 2002, 2003, Behdad 2005; Barreto 2009). There is general agreement among scholars of contentious politics that framing processes — attempts to influence group members' worldview, establish a set of common grievances, and provide justification for action — help drive groups to engage in collective action. As a framing process, a traumatic event can provide a crucial opportunity for a separatist movement to set or reset perceptions of the conflict, attract attention to its cause, win new supporters to its side, and increase the overall involvement of some members in the ethnic group. In addition to framing processes, the literature on contentious politics conceptualizes mobilizing structures and political opportunities as crucial determinants of mobilization, and this research without losing its main focus will therefore also take into account other mobilization influences within these latter two dimensions, including: (i) the strength of diaspora organizations, (ii) the role of communications and technology, (iii) overall foreign policy trends dictating what political opportunities exist, and (iv) the nature of the relationship between the homeland ethnic group and the diaspora.

<u>The Structure of this Dissertation:</u>

The study of ethnic conflict and diasporas calls for comparison, and I have adopted a comparative case study approach to guide this research and develop a suitable way of testing my explanatory model. This research entails both a single case study and multi-case approach to understanding and analyzing diaspora perceptions and ensuing forms of mobilization after a traumatic event. The more comprehensive single case study allows the research to focus more intensively on the dynamics of how perceptions are created in response to a traumatic event, while comparison across cases is particularly helpful in yielding a clearer assessment of the relative strength of mobilization for each case in response to a traumatic event. By synthesizing these two approaches, this research attempts to facilitate a comparative explanation combining the detailed exploration of a single case study with the more structured analysis of cross-national comparison.

As a single case study, I examine the perceptions and mobilization responses of diaspora Sikhs in the United States to a 1984 Indian government military operation known as Operation Blue Star, in which Indian military forces stormed the Golden Temple in Amritsar to drive out Sikh militants who had sought refuge. This examination of the Sikh diaspora relies on structured interviews that I conduct with diaspora members regarding their memories of the attack and the Sikh response. Overall, this part of the research affords a more exploratory and comprehensive examination of an ethnic diaspora community's response to a traumatic event than other approaches might allow.

As a multi-case study, I bring in the Irish and Uyghur ethnic diasporas for the sake of comparison with the Sikhs, and examine the role of these diasporas in supporting separatist movements in their respective homelands. I analyze the response of these groups to homeland traumatic events comparable to Blue Star — two in the case of Northern Ireland, one in the case of Xinjiang — and analyze all three diaspora responses in comparison to the Sikhs' response to the Golden Temple attack. This approach allows for a more explanatory and comparative look at how diasporas respond to traumatic events including ensuing mobilization in response to the event. The three events in question are the 1972 Bloody Sunday killings, the 1981 Irish hunger strike, and the 2009 Urumqi riots.

<u>Goals and Importance of Research:</u>

The aim of this research is to provide real-world, usable knowledge to government officials, policymakers, conflict resolution practitioners, and other specialists focused on ethnic conflict and political violence. Traumatic events are only one of many kinds of potential motivators that can connect violent ethnic groups with their diaspora supporters. However, the link between controversial episodes in the homeland and ethnic supporters in the diaspora has been embedded in several recent political conflicts, a point this research intends to illustrate.

The findings of this project could prove useful to specialists and practitioners working in regions of the world characterized by insurgency or ethnic conflict. They may have implications for policymakers attempting to curb, mitigate, reduce or otherwise resolve the problem of ethnic insurgencies in their state. Diasporas traditionally have been seen as a major and potent source of strength for ongoing ethnic insurgency movements (Byman *et al.* 2001). By helping to clarify how traumatic events in the homeland influence diasporas, this study could serve as a resource for those seeking to contain insurgency. This research should prove useful to government officials interested in understanding how to avoid alienating distant yet influential diaspora populations concerned for their co-ethnics. So far as it can be asserted that traumatic events do incite greater levels of support for armed aggression and/or separatism, this research can point to strategies designed to avoid adding fuel to the fire.

In terms of theoretical contributions, this research attempts to serve several of the main purposes of case studies including the testing of a specific theory, identifying and testing an important antecedent condition, and explaining cases of intrinsic importance (Van Evera 1997). More specifically, it contributes in three spheres. First, it seeks to contribute to our scholarly understanding of ethnic identity. In recent years, research has increasingly focused on ethnic nationalism outside the traditional prism of the relationship between ethnic groups and nation-states. This research can add to the literature in several important arenas, including the study of diasporas, ethnic groups, ethnic conflict, group behavior, mobilization, and civil wars.

Second, this research could boost our theoretical understanding about the causal mechanisms involving ethnic identity. Whether ethnic behavior is an elite-driven process, a byproduct of modernization, a response to economic forces, a product of culture, or if it derives from dynamics of the social community, these considerations all reflect broader and fundamental debates involving the makeup of ethnic identity. Findings in support of one or more of these propositions could point to specific ways of understanding ethnic identity.

Third, this research attempts to help clarify our scholarly understanding of the relative importance of ethnic identity as a determinant of group violence. Recent studies (Fearon and Latin 2003, Collier and Hoeffler 2000; Kalyvas 2006) have attempted to refute the "conventional belief," (Collier and Hoeffler 2000), that the occurrence of some kind of grievance serves as the most important predictor of political conflict. Their studies emphasize that violence is determined by rationalism and opportunity-seekers. Their research points to the contention that environmental conditions (such as a weak central government, poverty and political instability, or the presence of natural resources), shape the goals that self-interested actors and that these factors are the most important civil war determinants.[1] However, this important literature has not sufficiently taken into account the role of ethnic diasporas. If the current research project can establish a demonstrable role played by diasporas in violent conflict waged in the homeland, it

---

[1] For example, Weinstein (2006) proposes that insurgents become more predatory if the country has rich natural resources (Tarrow 2007). Kalyvas (2006) argues that civil wars develop their own internal logic among participants that does not nominally include ethnicity as a consideration; instead, self-interested citizens caught in civil wars cooperate with political actors to ensure their survival.

could join a body of scholarship reasserting the importance of ethnic identity as a primary causal factor.

A MODEL FOR PERCEPTION CREATION AND MOBILIZATION: MAJOR CONCEPTS AND HYPOTHESES

The purpose of this research is to develop a clearer understanding of how a single violent event can have a grave impact on diaspora views of a homeland ethnic separatist movement, and perhaps even more importantly, can reshape diaspora perceptions of the treatment of homeland co-ethnics by homeland governments. The basic notion underscoring this line of thought, of course, is that events matter: a single incident has the capacity to alter views about what is important, who is responsible, who is a victim, who is to blame. One might take for granted that events — particularly traumatic ones — can dramatically change or shape opinions. Yet, not *all* events herald such an impact. As shall be seen, in some cases, violent, widely publicized episodes of violence against homeland co-ethnics have failed to mobilize significant diaspora action in support of the objectives of the separatist movement as compared to other events. What matters then? This research seeks greater understanding of which event factors — as well as influences beyond the event — are most influential in determining perception shifts which then affects the likelihood that some diaspora members will decide to support separatist groups.

Physical and Symbolic Forms of Violence:

A traumatic event as I will define it is inherently violent, and in this research I have theorized that the level of violence involved in the event is a major determinant of a diaspora's response. However, violence can be interpreted in different ways. If violence were simply determined by the number of people injured or killed, it would be quite easy to predict when a traumatic event would generate diaspora mobilization. As we shall see, this is not the case.

In this research, acts of violence are interpreted according to two dimensions: the physical severity of the act itself as well as crucial details associated with the act resonating with the ethnic group's cultural heritage or shared understanding of their ethnic identity. I have labeled these two dimensions <u>physical violence</u> and <u>symbolic violence</u>. Violence is perceived not only in terms of its physical toll but also symbolically; this research project will assess the influence of both dimensions of violence on diaspora perceptions.

<u>Mobilization:</u>

Since my focus is on political behavior and the prospect for events to lead to action, I adopt a model for analyzing traumatic events based on the literature on social and political mobilization. There is general agreement among scholars of "contentious politics," also known as social movements, that three sets of factors drive groups to engage in collective action: mobilizing structures, framing processes, and political opportunities. <u>Mobilizing structures</u> are the organizational resources available to the group. <u>Political opportunities</u> refer to the external environment in which the movement operates. And <u>framing processes</u> are attempts to influence the worldviews of group members, establish sets of common grievances, and provide justifications for action (Tarrow 2011, Wayland 2004, Tsutsui 2004). It is within the prism of this last category that my research explores the impact of traumatic events on diaspora populations. As a framing process, a traumatic event can provide a crucial opportunity for ethnic entrepreneurs — members of the community who are responsible for reinforcing identity — to set or reset perceptions of the conflict, attract attention to its cause, and win new supporters to its side. It can result in diaspora members taking actions in support of the cause, including participating in public demonstrations, political advocacy, making donations to, or joining movement organizations, including in some cases, groups that are violent. I have labeled this process event galvanization, which I define as a process where a specific political episode that distresses the ethnic community effectively mobilizes an ethnic community.

A model depicting the overall relationship between these variables is shown below, and I will explain it in greater detail in chapter 3. It reflects that in addition to collective action frames, mobilizing structures and political opportunities also impacts mobilization.

Figure 1.1 Conceptualization of relationship between traumatic events and diaspora mobilization

Traumatic event in homeland	→	*Collective action frames*	→	*Diaspora perceptions*	→	*Ethnic mobilization*
X						(protests/ demonstrations)
Physical violence						(lobbying)
X						(forming new organizations)
Symbolic violence						(fundraising)
						X
						Mobilizing Structures
						X
						Political Opportunities

For clarity's sake, the relationship absent the condition variables is diagrammed below. This is the root model adopted by the hypotheses laid out next.

Figure 1.2 Simplified relationship between traumatic events and diaspora mobilization

<table>
<tr><td>*Traumatic event in homeland*</td><td>→</td><td>*Collective action frames*</td><td>→</td><td>*Diaspora perceptions*</td><td>→</td><td>*Ethnic mobilization*</td></tr>
</table>

<u>Hypotheses:</u>

To test the theoretical underpinnings of my argument that physically and symbolically violent events will galvanize the diaspora to increase support for separatism, I have developed hypotheses that will guide my analysis of data and allow me to assess the research model's consistency and accuracy. My prime hypothesis is the following:[2]

> **Hypothesis** – A traumatic event in the homeland impacts ethnic members symbolically and emotionally and directly influences perceptions in the diaspora in favor of the separatist movement. It will motivate some diaspora members to aid or support co-ethnic separatist groups.

This hypothesis assumes that movement entrepreneurs are capable of utilizing a traumatic event as a framing mechanism to provide a new symbolic and emotional pivot around which to rally support. The effect of this is to attract new supporters and turn fence-sitters against the government. In terms of measurement, violence can be thought of as ordinal and thus generally

---

[2] Van Evera (1997: 11-12) defines the prime hypothesis as "the overarching hypothesis that frames the relationship between a theory's independent and dependent variables," as opposed to explanatory hypotheses, "the intermediate hypotheses that constitute a theory's explanation."

measurable in terms of degree; it is not likely that traumatic events will be judged in the diaspora simply as "violent" or "not violent." Violence, however, has to be specified.

For physical violence, the number of deaths or injuries associated with the traumatic event, or alternatively the dollar amount of property damage that was committed, serves as the relevant measure. For symbolic violence, I attempt to assess how acts of violence are predisposed to significant cultural meaning, such as violence committed against sacred spaces, on important dates, against cherished cultural markers, or against members partaking in such activities. The relationship between these variables is shown below:

Figure 1.3 Impact of physical and symbolic violence on relationship between traumatic events and diaspora mobilization

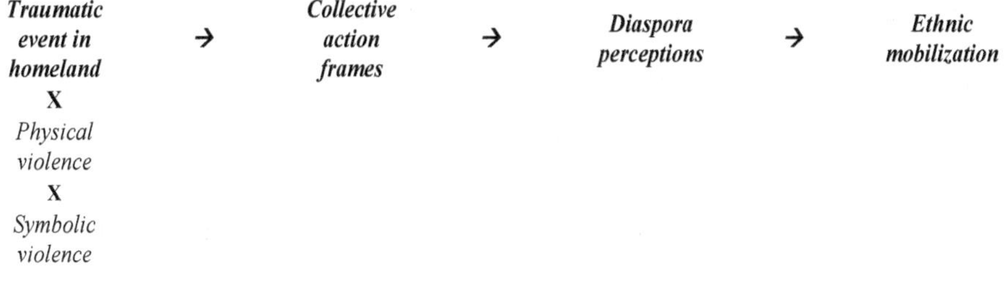

To assess the explanatory strength of each dimension above, I "unfold" the prime hypothesis into a series of smaller, sequential statements, which can then be evaluated:

H1a (physical violence): As the relative level of violent aggression or bloodshed involved in a traumatic event increases, separatist movements will attract new followers and persuade fence-sitters.

H1b (symbolic violence): When crucial details of a traumatic event gain symbolic significance or underscore specific and preexisting separatist frames from the conflict, separatist movements will attract new followers and persuade fence-sitters.

For these hypotheses to be supported, data must point to a relationship between a traumatic event and its core details on the one hand, and a detectable shift in diaspora perceptions on the other. The hypothesis can be refuted if ethnic members do not experience feelings of fear or resentment, if a "disconnect" with their affected co-ethnics is felt, or if they did experience those emotions but it can be shown that these emotions did not lead to any change in action. If the research cannot show the ethnic group's emotional response to details of the traumatic event to be relatively unified (i.e. if there are not widespread feelings of "fear" "rage" or "resentment"), this finding would also weaken the claim.

Lastly, I attempt to assess the relationship between changed perceptions in favor of the separatist movement, and the occurrence of activity in support of the separatist cause, completing the process of event galvanization:

H1c (event galvanization): As perceptions of the separatist movement improve and attract new followers, the likelihood of diaspora members providing greater levels of support to separatist groups in the homeland increases.

For this hypothesis to be supported, a relationship must be shown to exist between diaspora perceptions and decisions by some diaspora members to begin supporting, or to increase support for separatist groups operating in the homeland. The hypothesis can be refuted if there is no noticeable increase in active support for separatist groups despite any perception shifts in the diaspora.

Indicators – Indicators for physical violence include number of deaths or casualties and cost of physical damage. Indicators for symbolic violence include culturally meaningful features of the traumatic event — violence committed against sacred spaces or revered structures, violence taking place on cherished dates or days, or the involvement of other cultural markers. Indicators for "noticeable upticks in active support for separatist objectives" include evidence of increased political activism in the diaspora such as fundraising, protesting, lobbying, and raising public awareness. Although support for specific separatist groups is not specified in my hypotheses, this research will rely on structured interviewing in chapter 6, and increased or decreased membership and fundraising activity with suspected separatist groups in chapters 7 and 8, to offer a partial approximation for the level of support for separatist groups before and following a traumatic event.

METHODS AND DATA COLLECTION

As I have previously stated, this research entails both a single case study and multi-case approach to analyze diaspora perceptions and ensuing forms of mobilization in response to a traumatic event. These two research designs have required slightly different sets of data, and I therefore employ a different analytic technique and methodological approach to data collection for each part.

<u>First Research Design: Structured Interviewing with Sikhs in America:</u>

First, I carry out an intensive single-case study of a diaspora response to a traumatic event. The purpose of this part of the research is to provide a more detailed and nuanced picture of a single ethnic diaspora responding to a traumatic event, and to conduct a close examination of perception creation and ensuing mobilization. Here, my goal is to utilize a methods approach known as <u>process tracing</u>, a technique that analyzes the chain of events by which initial conditions are translated into outcomes. The researcher analyzes the data by "unwrapping," or breaking down, the cause-effect linkages connecting explanatory variables and outcomes, and then looking for observable evidence for each step.[3] To achieve the level of detail and observation needed to implement this approach effectively, my primary data collection technique is structured interviewing, which works especially well with process tracing techniques.[4]

In this part of my research I focus on the response of American Sikhs of Punjabi-Indian descent to a controversial military operation in India called Operation Blue Star. Between November 2011 and August 2012, I conducted structured interviews with Sikhs living in three different geographic areas in the United States. Fifteen of these interviews were conducted with

---

[3] Van Evera (1997: 64) uses the following example: "if 'asteroid impacts cause mass extinctions,' we should find evidence of an asteroid-caused mass killing mechanism in the sedimentary record of mass extinctions that coincide with asteroid impacts. Perhaps an impact would kill by spraying the world with molten rock, igniting global forest fires that blacken the skies in smoke, shutting out sunlight and freezing the earth. If so, the sedimentary record of mass extinctions should contain the remains of a vast continental or global molten rock shower, a layer of soot, and evidence of an abrupt mass dying of species—evidence of each step of the killing process."

[4] Interview data works well with process tracing because the researcher deduces the testimony of the actors involved to evaluate if there is evidence that a given stimulus causes a response. If multiple sources of evidence provided by several interviews all suggest the same (or different) cause-effect links or structure of events, this offers a strong test of that hypothesis under examination, although the investigator may still be less sure about what antecedent conditions the theory requires to operate. This strategy also proves most useful when data collected refers to specific examples and episodes (Van Evera 1997).

Sikhs living in the area of Yuba City, California; seven in the Washington DC metropolitan area; and four in the Boston metropolitan area. These discussions generally focus on two dynamics: 1) the perceptual impact of Operation Blue Star on the local Sikh community, and 2) any known actions taken by diaspora members to support or increase support for separatist groups in response to this event.

Second Research Design: Comparative Case Studies of the Sikh, Irish and Uyghur Diasporas:

In the second part of this research project, I examine the responses of two other diasporas to traumatic events, and then conduct a cross-national analysis of these cases and the Sikh response to Operation Blue Star. Comparison across cases is particularly helpful in yielding a clearer assessment of the relative strength of mobilization for each case, and the analytic approach used for this part of the research is known as controlled comparisons. This method allows the researcher to determine if values on paired observations of two or more case studies are congruent or incongruent with what theory predicts: "For example, if values on the independent variable (IV) are higher in case A than case B, values on the dependent variable (DV) should also be higher in case A than B" (Van Evera 1997: 57). This strategy is tailored for comparison across cases, during which the researcher essentially is checking for congruence between expectation and observation.

This research examines three cases of protracted ethnic conflict in which a traumatic event can be said to have taken place and then compares to Operation Blue Star: the response of the Irish-American diaspora to the 1972 Bloody Sunday killings, the same diaspora's response to the 1981 Irish hunger strike, and the response of the Chinese Uyghur diaspora to 2009 riots in Urumqi. To gauge the responses of each diaspora to traumatic events, I utilize prior scholarly work on each of the specific conflicts as well as news and media sources published within a three-year time frame of the event. I have also run newspaper database searches for key words associated with the diaspora community and traumatic event in question and have also consulted diaspora-affiliated newsletters and web sites when available.

Obviously these cases differ in many ways. The Sikh and Uyghur diasporas originated from developing countries in South and East Asia, while the Irish came from Western Europe. The homelands of the Irish and Sikh populations reside in democratic states, while the Uyghur population lives in Communist China. The Irish and Sikh diasporas are concentrated in the West, while the greatest number of Uyghurs found outside of China reside in Central Asia. However, a characteristic that these cases all share in common is that the ethnic community in question feels mistreated and has responded to its perceived mistreatment by offering various types of support for separatist movements. In all cases, this led to protracted ethnic conflict in the homeland, where the government has also alleged diaspora involvement in homeland insurgency. Further, these particular cases were selected because: 1) they each involve ethnic groups that had made known some kind of ethnic claim or grievance against the national government in the homeland; and 2) each diaspora has a presence in the United States, thereby providing a basic if imperfect control on some host state influences that could vary across states. This is not meant to suggest a complete control on divergent influences, but to point out that some advantages exist in examining three diaspora communities residing in the same state.

CHAPTERS AND ORGANIZATION OF THE DISSERTATION

I have divided this research project into three parts. Part I introduces my theory on traumatic events, highlights the relevant literature and justifies the explanatory model guiding analysis in later chapters. Chapter 2 presents the relevant literature on ethnic conflict, ethnic identity and diasporas. The goal of this chapter is to provide the groundwork for future discussion of ethnic responses to traumatic events and allow the reader to ascertain how this research project fits into the broader literature. Chapter 3 lays out my conceptual framework for analyzing traumatic events. In this chapter, I explain the theoretic model that serves as the overarching framework for my analyses in later chapters. I highlight hypotheses, variable relationships, and relevant terminology, and also briefly highlight the theoretical implications of this research.

Part II adopts the model outlined in chapter 3 to begin formally analyzing cases of protracted ethnic conflict involving a diaspora. These chapters focus on the Sikh diaspora and evaluate the response of Sikh diaspora communities in the United States to Operation Blue Star. Chapter 4 provides background on Sikhism, the separatist movement and the Sikh diaspora. Chapter 5 examines and analyzes the entire episode of Operation Blue Star, analyzes the impact of the attack on the conflict between Sikhs and the Indian government, and qualifies this episode as a traumatic event. Chapter 6 utilizes structured interviews I conducted with diaspora Sikhs to analyze their perceptions and response to Operation Blue Star. Together, these three chapters allow for a comprehensive study of the Sikh diaspora response to Operation Blue Star, which I assess galvanized the Sikh diaspora to offer a dramatic increase of support for the separatist cause. This offers a useful illustration of how a traumatic event can act as a catalyst for diaspora mobilization, but the section also highlights some of the limitations of my research model.

Part III attempts to develop a more explicitly comparative framework for analyzing traumatic events by introducing new cases and comparing these to the Sikhs. Chapter 7 focuses on two traumatic events in Northern Ireland — the 1972 Bloody Sunday killings and the 1981 Irish hunger strike — and assesses the impact of each event on the Irish diaspora living in the

United States. Although both events had galvanizing effects on the diaspora, this chapter finds that the hunger strike ultimately surpassed Bloody Sunday by leading to a stronger mobilization that attracted new followers to the Irish republican cause. Chapter 8 examines the response of the Chinese Uyghur diaspora to the Urumqi riots of 2009, arguing that the riots led only to a modest mobilization in part because the event failed to gain much cultural or religious symbolism. Chapter 9 is a comparative analysis of all four cases examined in this research. Through testing of each of the hypotheses, it assesses that the Sikh response to Operation Blue Star constituted the most intense form of event galvanization among the four cases, followed by the Irish hunger strike, Bloody Sunday, and the Urumqi riots. The chapter reaches the conclusion that symbolically powerful events such as Operation Blue Star or the Irish hunger strike, and to a lesser degree Bloody Sunday or the Urumqi riots, create a fertile environment for elites and movement entrepreneurs to increase levels of support for the movement. Chapter 10 concludes the research by considering policy and theoretical implications in light of the findings of this research, and identifying questions for future research.

2

ETHNICITY, ETHNIC CONFLICT, AND DIASPORAS

What is ethnicity? How is ethnic identity determined? What motivates those who participate in ethnic conflict? Why does someone choose to join an ethnic movement? These are important questions to answer because they go straight to the heart of explaining how traumatic events in the homeland affect the identity of ethnic members and how ethnically aligned separatist campaigns are capable of mobilizing supporters. The purpose of this chapter is to recount the academic literature and scholarly debates concerning three relevant fields of study: ethnicity, ethnic conflict, and diasporas. The first section discusses differing viewpoints on ethnicity and its relationship to nationalism. The second section considers several interpretations about ethnic conflict and its causes. The third section assesses the growing global role of diasporas, and their potential to support homeland separatist or insurgent groups.

ETHNICITY AND NATIONALISM

How ethnic identity is understood has changed over time, as scholars have sought to sharpen analytic terms and increase usefulness by making their field more applicable to events. Ethnicity is popularly understood to refer to specific racial or linguistic groups. However, scholars in the past half-century have broadened the definition to include groups that self-identify based on ascriptive traits — language, religion, race, tribe, kinship, caste, and culture are but a few of the most frequent examples (Horowitz 2000; Varshney 2003; Calhoun 1993). Since ascription activates certain markers to signal group membership, it enables ethnic groups to impose criteria for membership that in turn developed boundaries between groups.[5]

Scholars also sought to articulate the specific dynamics and features of the ethnic group, from which the group derives particular strength. For example, Anthony Smith (1993: 49) defined the *ethnie* or ethnic community as "a named human population with a myth of common ancestry, shared memories and cultural elements, a link with an historical territory or homeland and a measure of solidarity."[6] Indeed, one of the most profound elements of ethnicity is that its strength and intractability traces back to an intangible, emotional quality (Horowitz 2000; Connor 1994; Petersen 2002). According to Rex (1995), ethnic members derive emotional satisfaction from their ethnic identity, including positive feelings of "warmth." What provides the ethnic group its overpowering quality and intrinsic appeal to its members, Rex continues, are the emotional bonds that tie its members together, their shared belief in the group's myth of origin, and an almost transcendental belief in the "sacredness" of their social relations, of which they are a part, and which includes not only the living but also the dead.

In discussing ethnicity and nationalism or "ethnonationalism,"[7] it is important to acknowledge differing traditions. These differing traditions have characterized many of the academic debates and different understandings of ethnicity over the last thirty years. First,

---

[5] Ethnic solidarity refers to "the conscious identification with a given ethnic population and includes maintenance of strong ethnic interaction networks and institutions that socialize new members and reinforce social ties" (Olzak 1983: 356-7).

[6] Smith contended that six "properties"—recognition, common ancestry, historical memories, cultural markers, attachment to territory, and feelings of common solidarity—provide outward evidence of the psychological bonds that tie together members of the ethnic group.

[7] Connor argues that when used properly, "ethnicity" and "nation" both refer to groups sharing a psychological bond and assumptions about shared heredity; but since nationalism is frequently confused with patriotism, a new term is needed to ensure analytic clarity. For Connor, the new term is ethnonationalism.

primordialists emphasize the familial and kinship nature of nationalism. Some primordialists argue that over the course of history, natural selection favored those relying on strong kinship ties for survival, leading to clans or other familial groups and a kind of Darwinian survival of the kind cited in Barreto (2009: 12): "Fidelity to one's family was not just a positive social trait; ultimately, it was a quality necessary for human survival." (Shils 1957; Geertz 1973; Ridley 1996). Others acknowledge the presence of multiple genetic strains in virtually every ethnic group, but argue that the psychological essence of ethnicity is what makes its identity primordial. These scholars posit that ethnicity is primarily based on psychology and emotional connection among members of a group, allowing members subconsciously to believe in their own uniqueness, myth of ancestry and history of being even when they consciously know otherwise, allowing for powerful and protective ties among the ethnic clan to form (Connor 1994; Varshney 2002, 2003). However, primordialism when it has gone astray has treated ethnic groupings as fixed and exclusive categories, whereas the makeup and boundaries of the ethnic nation can be quite fluid.

The second major tradition of ethnic and nationalism studies is constructivism. Proponents of this approach argue that ethnic and nationalist groups socially construct their identity and that ethnic identity is the product of historical forces as well as the exchange of ideas. One of the most influential scholarly works in the constructivist tradition argues that all nations in fact are "imagined communities" or acts of the imagination, encouraged and facilitated by modern advances like print media or capitalism (Anderson 1983). Constructivism has become a dominant paradigm in the nationalism literature, although some point out that its influence is basically limited to academic circles (Motyl 2009).

A third approach is instrumentalism. This approach, which has proven popular in the United States in part to its embrace of rational choice theory, assumes that political elites are influential, self-interested actors, capable of strategically manipulating ethnicity for the sake of power. Ethnicity is an instrument of the elite, and that political and group leaders gain power by shaping and manipulating identity to suit their own interests. The instrumentalist approach contends that elites gain power by mobilizing ethnic groups into action – even if the elite does not "buy in" to the group's primordial belief of shared blood or common ancestry (Hechter 1995; Hardin 1995). Critics of the perspective argue that instrumentalist theories tend to exaggerate the influence of elites while ignoring or failing to concentrate on the potency and appeal of ethnicity (Varshney 2002).

In studying ethnicity, it is also essential to understand its linkages to nationalism, or movements by nations to achieve self-determination — the term "ethnic," originates from the Greek word *ethnos,* meaning "nation" (Connor 1994). Where they differentiate is that nationalism makes specific political demands on the state such as autonomy, separation, irredentism, whereas ethnicity does not (Eriksen 2002). There is considerable debate about when and how "nationalism" came into vogue,[8] but by 1815 nationalism had become the most dominant theory for political legitimacy (Calhoun 1993). Throughout the twentieth century, and especially after World War II, nationalist movements gained clout and legitimacy, much to the chagrin of Marxists and modernists who both had predicted its demise (Connor 1994).[9] Three

---

[8] According to Calhoun (1993: 212), "It is variously argued to have originated in the seventeenth century British rebellion against monarchy… the eighteenth century struggles of New World elites against Iberian colonialism…the French Revolution of 1789… and the German reaction to that revolution and to German disunity." Calhoun lists his sources for each origin point, also on p. 212.

[9] Olzak (1983: 364-5) argues that increased legitimacy for national self-determination movements can be party explained "in terms of increasing world pressure for geographical units to organize themselves as states," since only states can take such actions as making claims or formal protests in

ideal propositions had emerged by 1960: 1) humanity divides into nations, 2) these nations are known by certain characteristics, and 3) the only legitimate type of government is self-government (Calhoun 1993). However, the exact role played by ethnicity as an organizing principle for self-determination movements is intensely debated. Scholars such as Eric Hobsbawm and Terrence Ranger (1983) argue that nations are inherently modern; they intimated that since many traditions of ethno-nationalism are "invented," the associated identities are less real and therefore less valid (Calhoun 1993). In contrast, Anthony Smith (1986) has argued that while not primordial, ethnic origins are older than most scholars have been willing to accept. Certain myths and symbols carry over from one generation to the next. These symbols change over time, but the transition is slow enough that the process over centuries forms certain "molds"; and since ethnicity is very slow to change, the existence of a "genealogy of nations" is possible (Calhoun 1993).

Connor (1994: 194) employs a different rationale altogether; he contends that denying the descent or cultural bona fides of a nation "ignores the dictum that it is not *what* but *what is perceived as is* which influences attitudes and behavior." Connor stipulates that a psychological bond between members as well as subconscious belief in the group's uniqueness constitutes a nation's essence. Calhoun adds to this, disputing Hobsbawm and Ranger specifically. Since all traditions are "invented," Calhoun contends, there can be no more or less "real" tradition than any other. All traditions may be internally contested and continually reshaped, but these disputes

---

international forums. Modernization theories argued that non-state forms of identity would eventually fade as part of the nation-state building process. Marxism classified ethnicity as one of several identity forms that the working classes would eventually discard as a means of their subjugation by the ruling classes.

can be productive for the ethnic group rather than detrimental, facilitating new or reproducing prior ethnic understandings.[10]

The translation of ethnicity into nationalism requires the conversion of cultural traditions into more specific historical claims, which can then legitimize the claims of contemporary ethnic movements (Calhoun 1993). This requires interpretation and the exchange of ideas. It is for this reason that Gellner (1983) prescribed a literate "high culture" for nationalism to take place. Similarly, Anderson (1983) argued that nationalism only took effect through the development of print capitalism. Nationalists through the development of print media were able to record and circulate a certain version of events wrapped in nationalist mythology, thereby constructing the bonds of a nation that existed in the nationalist imagination, shared by members who yet remained unknown to one another.

Ethnic symbolism also helps facilitate the conversion of cultural tradition to ethnic claims. Ethnic symbolism typically refers to traditional language, religion, kinship systems, or folklore practices, which scholars consider vital to reinforcing identity and maintaining the ethnic ties of a group during times of social change (Eriksen 2002; Sanders 2002). Symbols are able to resonate with and touch the core psychology of an ethnic community because they signal to its members, in the words of Eriksen (2002: 68; qtd. in Grün 2009), "an unchanging stable core of a continuity with the past," providing a crucial source of self-esteem and authenticity in an age of modernity where the world is often perceived as in flux and make-believe. Symbols act as "markers" of "a virtually symbolic world" consecrated by the ethnic group's shared interpretation of its own reality (Srubar 2007: 540; qtd. in Grün 2009). They generate entire

---

[10] Calhoun (1993: 235) notes that "The relationship between nationalism and ethnicity is complex... while it is impossible to dissociate nationalism entirely from ethnicity, it is equally impossible to explain it simply as a continuation of ethnicity."

ethnic mythologies, or entire systems of symbolic meaning, that can sustain the group during times of hardship. Symbolism leads to the creation of a myth-symbol complex that enables a form of symbolic politics where "the critical causes of extreme ethnic violence are group myths that justify hostility, fears of group extinction and a symbolic politics of chauvinist mobilization" (Demmers 2012: 31). Of course states can attempt to harness the power of symbols, as when Malaysia and Pakistan made prolific use of Islamic symbols to increase the state's authority and shore up its legitimacy (Nasr 2001), but such policies can backfire.

The historical record for nationalism suggests that it has proven more attractive for nations to claim to be linked ethnically, rather than economically or ideologically (Connor 1994). The reason is that ethnicity confers the nation with an essence that is ancient and immutable. The claim "naturalizes" nationhood, allowing nationalists to see the nation as a product of "a long narrative of historical development that historically locates the proto-nation in primordial times," and leaving third parties "with the choice between recognizing a 'natural' human identity or denying it and possibly even condoning its 'genocide'" (Calhoun 1993: 221). What's important sociologically, Calhoun continues, is that the claim of continuity has a marked effect on certain orientations to social action. "Ethnicity or cultural traditions are bases for nationalism when they effectively constitute historical memory, when they inculcate it as habitus, or as 'prejudice'… not when (or because) the historical origins they claim are accurate" (222).

Apart from interpretations that see nationalism as a natural extension of ethnicity, it should be noted that there exists another, historically more dominant understanding that envisions nationalism as the achievement of convergence between nation and the modern state. This state-centered approach possessed a narrower view of nationalism's limits, contending that nations must include administrative reach over its territory—modern day states, in other words.

Modernization theory emphasizes state-centered nationalism while discouraging other forms, including ethnic nationalism. In its various forms, modernization theory suggests that non-state nationalism would eventually recede or moderate into patriotism (Talmon 1952, 1960; Parson 1960; see discussion in Calhoun 1993: 217-18). Nationalism therefore varies between statist forms that claim to have superseded traditional identities, and ethnicity-based forms linking sovereignty demands that are rooted in ancient ethnicity (Calhoun 1993). According to Calhoun, the modernization view clarified some elements of nationalism but obscured others, and failed to explain "why national identity can stir the passions it does," while encouraging analysts "either to ignore ethnic and other identities that do not coincide with states or to treat them as somehow naturally given" (219). Nonetheless, acknowledging the state-based view helps explain how claims made separately by competing non-state nationalist groups can lead to confrontation.

ETHNIC CONFLICT

Ethnic conflict is the often-violent confrontation that takes place between ethnic groups, where a pronounced element of strife, struggle or enduring collision distinguish it from other forms of ethnic competition (Horowitz 2000; Taras and Ganguly 2010). In these contests, ethnic groups are pitted against one another or against the state. And since ethnic groups self-identify based on ascription, it allows group members, as well as outsiders, to distinguish between members and non-members. It is this quality that encourages groups to bifurcate humanity into *Us* and *Them* categories, and it is one reason that ethnicity supplies such a potent source for conflict — by mandating the creation of potential rivals:

> We all have a need to form description of the world as a way to try and figure out
>
> what is going on. This is our 'cognitive imperative': the human need to impose

order on the world by mental processes. As such, we form categories of description: both physically and socially. We can make distinctions between tables and chairs, apples and pears, rivers and oceans, but we also classify people by means of certain prototypes: 'child,' 'adult,' 'male,' 'female.' (Demmers 2012: 38-9).

However, social categories are not only cognitive concepts but also evaluative and emotional: "As soon as people identify with a group, that group becomes the basis for thinking, feeling and acting" (Ibid.: 39). According to Haidt (2012: 318), it is at the point when differing group mentalities collide that the prospect of violence escalates: "We are deeply intuitive creatures whose gut feelings drive our strategic reasoning," argues Haidt, who clarifies that this makes it "difficult — but not impossible — to connect with those who live in other matrices 'built' on different configurations of the available moral foundations." However, ethnic conflict does not merely reflect the existence of two distinct groups, but reflects a more dynamic interaction between the two. Intergroup ethnic violence becomes likely when a group feels it can only feel positive about its own identity by degrading an out-group or if it feels that "the other" threatens its secure identity (Demmers 2012). It is important to acknowledge a distinction in the literature between ethnic conflict and ethnic violence, of which the latter explicitly refers to violence perpetrated across ethnic lines. Although violence is often conceptualized as a degree of conflict, scholars lack evidence suggesting higher levels of conflict lead to higher levels of violence (Demmers 2012). Instead, violence is a *form* of conflict, and while all ethnic violence can be said to constitute a form of ethnic conflict, not all episodes of ethnic conflict result in violence. For example, ethnic conflict occurrences can also play out politically without collapsing into violence. However, the level of strife associated with ethnic conflict frequently increases the odds for violence to occur. In both conflict and violence, at least one of the parties is not a state; and in both cases, conflict is seen or "coded" as integral rather than incidental (Brubaker and Laitin 1998).

Studies in ethnic conflict grew in prominence during the 1980s and '90s, as a host of ethno-nationalist struggles signified the failure in several states of state-based nation-building. The end of the Cold War did not mean the end of history as some scholars predicted, but rather shifted attention to ethnic conflicts in a number of states that had been either roiling or brewing for years or in some cases decades: Afghanistan, Bosnia, China, Georgia, India, Indonesia, Iraq, Lebanon, Northern Ireland, Pakistan, Rwanda, Sri Lanka, and Sudan, to name a few (Brown 2010). Since then, prevailing interpretive frames have favored conflict defined in ethnic rather than ideological terms. The decline of the Soviet Union may have left capitalism as the dominant ideology, but it also ruptured the balance of power between it and the United States that arguably had kept many conflicts at bay. Democratization also had the side effect of aggravating dormant ethnic rivalries and resentment or even manufacturing new ones (Ciepley 2013). Brubaker and Laitin (1998) argue a decline in state capacity, combined with increasing incentives to frame conflict in terms of ethnicity, has led groups to struggle over interpretations of violent acts — "conflicts over the nature of conflict." Ethnic wars have in turn impacted the strategic interests and moral calculations of the outside world, forcing governments to pay close attention to the realities and causes of ethnic conflict (Brown 2010).

Scholars and academics have encountered numerous obstacles in developing theories to explain the occurrence of ethnic conflict, not least of which can be attributed to the fundamental disagreements about the origins of ethno-nationalism. There are at least two other challenges. The first is the rampant confusion and disagreement about its critical terms (Connor 1994). This uncertainty, which Connor refers to as "terminological chaos," includes confusion between the words "state" and "nation," between "nationalism" and "patriotism," and the erroneous tendency by scholars and commentators alike to refer to countries with more than one ethnic group as a "nation-state." Until the terms used by scholars are brought into conformity and used correctly, it will remain difficult to constitute a uniform theory explaining ethnic conflict.

The second challenge is more fundamental — the inherent difficulty of studying emotional ties. According to Horowitz (2000), ethnic conflict occurs when an ethnic group not only enjoys an emotional attachment to each other, but also feels collectively insecure about its place in society — fearing for its political or literal survival. Explanation of ethnic conflict therefore requires theories that link elite to mass concerns and explain how and why ethnic followers choose to follow:

> The role of apprehension and group psychology needs specification, as does the importance of symbolic controversies in ethnic conflict. The sheer passion expended in pursuing ethnic conflict calls out for an explanation that does justice to the realm of the feelings. It is necessary to account, not merely for ambition, but for antipathy. A bloody phenomenon cannot be explained by a bloodless theory. (Horowitz 2000: 140).

The study of emotional qualities does not always lend itself easily to scholarship because it can be difficult to generalize. However, it is not impossible: examples include attempts to locate emotions such as "fear" and "rage" in the causal relationships leading to ethnic conflict, as well as more recent scholarship arguing that nationalist actors desire social and communal rewards as opposed to more "tangible" interests (Petersen 2002; Barreto 2009).

To what extent can policies be developed that aim to prevent, resolve, or at least manage conflict? The scholarship on ethnic conflict resolution and reduction strategies is richly diverse, if not always in complete agreement. Donald Horowitz and Arend Lijphart represent two differing schools of thought as it relates to institutional designs that can help to mitigate conflict — Lijphart (1968, 1977, 1999) favors power-sharing consociational mechanisms that facilitate consensus, encourage compromise, represent a greater proportion of citizens, and are more likely to protect minority rights, while Horowitz (2000) embraces federal structures and local empowerment meant to manage conflict rather than seek to extinguish it. Both strategies have certain merits and the question of which one to use may rely as much on the case being examined as it does the inherent rightness of either approach.[11] However, governments need not only consider new institutional schemes in order to decrease the chances of ethnic violence. Ashutosh Varshney's work (2003) examining the relationship between ethnic conflict and civic ties attests to the capacity for interethnic civic groups and organizations to play a valuable role in preventing, containing or resolving conflict. Governments interested in adopting policies that seek to mitigate ethnic conflict therefore may be just as interested in finding some way to promote or support inter-communal organizations and civic ties, especially in diverse urban population areas, as they are in settling on an appropriate institutional design for governance.

Ethnic Mobilization, Values, and Rationality:

We now return to the questions posed at the onset of this chapter. What motivates those who participate in ethnic conflict? Why does someone choose to join an ethnic movement? These

---

[11] Take Northern Ireland as an example: consociational measures have enjoyed some degree of recent success. However, the difficulty and length of time it took to establish peace in Northern Ireland, as well as the communal tensions that still exist and result in occasional flare-ups in ethnic violence, underscores Horowitz's point that conflict requires management as opposed to resolution.

questions go straight to the heart of explanations addressing how ethnically aligned separatist campaigns are capable of mobilizing supporters.[12]

There are two different comparative perspectives that explain ethnic mobilizations; these two approaches have dominated academic analyses of ethnic conflict and violence. The first is the rationalist perspective. Rationalists argue that individuals join ethnic social movements because it serves their self-interests. According to this perspective, ethnic violence is rational, and best explained through the prism of goal-seeking actors (Hechter 1995). Political actors perform cost-benefit analyses to determine which of several options is most advantageous. The perspective frequently assumes that leaders are strategic and capable of manipulating ethnicity for the sake of power. Rationalists rule out competing causal variables such as emotions or irrationality, and are also skeptical that individual action can be rooted in group interests. There are various strands of rationalist study on ethnic conflict and violence, including approaches that utilize game theory, rational action theory, and traditional international relations approaches (Brubaker and Laitin 1998).

More recently, a vibrant new literature on civil wars has emerged within this tradition, questioning the "conventional belief" that ethnic grievances lead to conflict, and instead point to self-interested opportunity incentives. In recent years, a new tradition of scholarship, focused on the causes of civil wars and relying primarily on large-N data, has questioned the role of ethnicity as a causal variable of conflict. Collier and Hoeffler (2000), for example, contend that the critical determinants of civil wars are "opportunities" as opposed to "grievances." Fearon and Laitin (2003: 88) argued that the key societal condition favoring insurgency is the occurrence of

---

[12] Ethnic mobilization is defined as the process by which groups organize around some feature of ethnic identity in pursuit of collective ends. It is collective action that uses ethnic markers as a principal criterion for membership (Olzak 1983).

a weak central government as indicated by poverty and political instability. These conditions, they contend, "are better predictors of which countries are at risk for civil war than are indicators of ethnic and religious diversity or measures of grievances..." Other studies have sought to explain variation in violence levels occurring in civil wars and insurgencies. Weinstein (2006) proposes that environments rich in natural resources lead insurgents to become more predatory (Tarrow, 2007). And Kalyvas (2006) argues that civil wars develop their own internal logic among participants that does not nominally include ethnicity as a consideration; instead, self-interested citizens caught in civil wars cooperate with political actors to ensure their survival. Taken together, these studies have pushed back against the "conventional belief," as Collier and Hoeffler put it, that ethnic or political grievances is the most important predictor of conflict. These studies and others raise important questions about the relative influence of ethnicity on group violence and conflict, forcing many scholars and practitioners to reassess their assumptions. However, some of these studies may also exaggerate the role of instrumental rationality in determining ethnic behavior, as the ensuing discussion on value and instrumental forms of rationality will underscore.

Although rationalism has made many contributions to the study of nationalism, it has been criticized for its failure to explain the strength of ethnic mobilizations, particularly when the cost of participation is high. Instrumentalists fail to explain why ethnic leaders appeal to national identity in the first place, as opposed to economic or ideological beliefs. And since it would be rational for individuals to "free ride" — not joining the ethnic movement but benefiting from its successes — how can a rational theory of ethnic mobilization explain the decision of those who do join?[13] Barreto (2009) account for this disconnect by taking into account the pursuit among rational actors of more than one kind of reward. He argues that in addition to material objects, nationalists also engage in collective action out of their desire for emotional satisfaction as well as the emotive individual benefits deriving from an achieved sense of social belonging. Barreto's argument is an example of an untraditional and expansive interpretation of rational choice. Most accounts, however, attempt explanation of ethnic violence only after ethnic preferences are in place and prospects for the success of mobilization have improved (Varshney 2003).

The second perspective is the culturalist approach. Rather than self-interest, a culturalist argues that norms and values are deeply embedded in our psychology. These analyses characterize ethnic violence as culturally constructed, imbued with actions that are meaningful and symbolic. According to Brubaker and Laitin (1998: 441), "culturalists claim that (ethnic) violence makes sense not in instrumental terms but in terms of its meaningful relation to or resonance with other elements of the culturally defined context." That "context" is constructed in a number of ways. Both in historical and psychological terms, culturalists focus attention on the cultural construction of fear, or "the rhetorical processes, symbolic resources, and representational forms through which a demonized, dehumanized, or otherwise threatening ethnically defined 'other' has been constructed" (Ibid.: 442). Dignity—the quest for dignity—is another cultural construction that falls under the auspices of culturalism. Varshney (2002: 92) argues that pursuits for dignity propelled nationalist movements right as traditional social hierarchies broke down and decayed: "As a result, for the first time in history a new individual motivation [had] arisen: a self-awareness of dignity. One does not take one's 'station' as inevitable" (92).

---

[13] Varshney (2002: 87-90) details the best attempts by rationalists to account for this discrepancy, though he argues that these theories still fall short.

To shed light on how these emotions are constructed, cultural analyses focus attention on myths, legends, rituals, even songs and poems. Using these methods, culturalists typically have found that the nation, paradoxically, is considered both alive and eternal. It comes to be seen as having person-like "traits" – it has talents and deficiencies, is capable of taking action, and can experience abuse (Calhoun 1993). The nation can come to be considered a martyr-nation, and yet is considered eternal. In the ethnic imagination, the nation can united prior and current generations, and the living with the dead (Anderson 1983).[14] All of which helps to explain how the nation can demand such extraordinary sacrifices from its members.

On the subject of ethnic mobilization, culturalism offers to rationalism a rejoinder. The reason that ethnic movements attract participants, even when the cost of participation is high, is because the individual is linked to the group emotionally and psychologically. Should the individual not participate as an ethnic member, she would suffer a "reduced mode of being," unable to respect herself for failing to participate (Varshney 2002). According to Varshney, when an ethnic mobilization takes place, value rationality overcomes the principal difficulty faced by a purely instrumental explanation. A critical mass of individuals is all that is required to explain the origins of an ethnic movement. Even in cases where all ethnic members do not share a strong identity, the mobilization can become identity-forming, as state hegemony gives way to self-respect.

Critics of cultural analyses argue that culture is too broad to employ as a unit of analysis. One criticism is that there can never be certainty about evidence because conceptions of culture

---

[14] According to Calhoun (1993: 232), "Not only does the nation locate individuals temporally in relation to past and future generations, and in the global context as members of one among many nations, the nation also locates each individual's biography and quotidian narrative as one among the many comparable biographies of the members of the specific nation."

inherently are vague: "It is difficult to know whether, when, where, to what extent, and in what manner the posited beliefs and fears were actually held" (Brubaker and Laitin 1998: 442). Culture is not easily recognizable since it is not a social or political organization nor does it contain readily identifiable boundaries (Ross 1997b: 61). Others argue it is impossible to distinguish culture from other related concepts such as social organization or political behavior (Ibid.). One scholar even describes cultural studies as "a black box" into all leftover unexplained variables can be poured. As a result of this nebulousness and imprecision, critics argue that cultural accounts explain too much and tend to over-predict ethnic violence. Cultural analyses also risk the loss of *leverage* — the ability of a study to explain social phenomena across different settings (King, Keohane and Verba 1994) — because so many of these studies favor "thick description" over multiple case comparisons.

In Pursuit of a "Thick" Research Program:

This discussion has thus far highlighted some of the strengths and criticisms of the two main approaches to understanding ethnic collective action that are commonly cited in the contemporary literature. However, the purpose of highlighting both traditions has not been to ultimately embrace one as the winner over the other, competing approach. While the various approaches have provided a battleground for many scholars to fight out the differences, little has been gained from the ensuing struggle. What is centrally important is that the researcher is conscious of the strengths and weaknesses of all three approaches when deciding her study. If that were all that could be accomplished, we would stop here.

However, comparativist scholars such as Lichbach and Zuckerman (1997) have refused to settle for the "messy center" of comparative politics, and have instead embraced the prospect of "creative confrontations" between multiple approaches. These academics have shepherded a call for synthesis — "crossover" scholarship drawing heavily from one perspective and yet integrating key insights from the others, which researchers describe as "thick" versions of their research programs. "Thin" research programs stick closely to their traditional cores, and their exclusivity slights the complex empirical world and produce unsatisfactory results. Thick research programs, by contrast, add elements from other approaches in such a way that reduces inherent theoretical weakness and strengthens the relevance of its findings. Scholarly works in comparative politics should attempt to engage in strong theoretical reflection and should embrace the creative confrontations that interactions between these different perspectives might produce. With the goal of achieving "greater theoretical dialogue," Lichbach and Zuckerman (1997) stipulate the need for researchers to adopt theoretical designs that synthesize between two or more of the research traditions. This "thick" research design involves adopting a primary comparative approach but also utilizing one of the other schools to address inherent weaknesses therein. If the scalpel is wielded with enough precision, the researcher will strengthen the analytic and explanatory power of his/her research.

There are at least two scholarly works on ethno-national collective action that fit the bill that Lichbach and Zuckerman describe. In attempting to explain why rational actors continue to engage in collective action despite being aware of "free riders," Barreto (2009) argues that nationalists engage in collective action out of their desire for emotional satisfaction and a sense of belonging as well as the traditional rational goal of material gain. "We do not participate in the collective struggles of every group — only those for which we have a strong emotive attachment," Barreto points out (2009: 6), and this framework allows the author to examine emotion-driven psychological components such as pride, personal satisfaction and the pursuit of immortalization as rational goals.

Varshney (2003) also utilizes a theoretical model for understanding ethnic mobilization that collaborates between different traditions. He argues that the best means of understanding ethnic conflict requires a comprehension of instrumental and value-laden forms of rationality, the latter of which he refers to as "behavior produced by conscious, ethical, aesthetic, religious or other belief." It is important to note, however, that Varshney frames his argument as a broad critique of the instrumentalist-rationalist perspective and the increasing number of scholars who employ it in isolation to examine the origins of ethnic conflict. Varshney argues that instrumental rationality fails to account for the origin of mobilization, but can help explain ethnic behavior once mobilization has reached a critical point. By contrast, value rationality helps to explain the origins of ethnic mobilization but fails to explain how the movement sustains over the long term (Varshney 2003). Although Varshney clearly aspires to elevate his cultural-based perspective to an equal footing with the rational choice approaches embraced by American political scientists, Varsheny's final embrace is that ethnic mobilization cannot proceed on either type of rationality alone, but requires a fusion between each approach to explain the full process of ethnic group-based collective action. In Varshney's words:

> The pure case of value rationality may account for the origins of ethnic mobilization but not for its sustenance; the pure case of instrumental rationality cannot explain why ethnic mobilization commences, although it may begin to explain behavior once mobilization has reached a critical point; and the combination of value and instrumental rationality can explain both why ethnic mobilization begins and how it is sustained (Varshney 2003: 95).

In other words, for ethnicity to be used instrumentally, it must first exist as a valued good. As a movement advances, however, the movement will evolve to the point that it becomes more politically sophisticated. It will then consider the best means to achieve its ethnic ends — even if that means is violence.

The studies cited above, as well as others, raise important questions about the relative influence of ethnicity on group violence and conflict, forcing many scholars and practitioners to reassess their assumptions. If further analyses can provide greater understanding of what motivates participants in violent conflict, they would contribute significantly to the scholarly debate.

DIASPORAS: THEIR IDENTITY AND HOMELAND ATTACHMENTS

We now turn to the role the diaspora plays in homeland ethnic conflicts. I first introduce a basic framework for understanding diaspora behavior and explain how our conceptualization of diaspora identity has evolved over time. I then discuss the profile of the diaspora's psychological attachment to the ethnic homeland, and assess the means by which a diaspora can support homeland insurgencies or violent separatist movements.

A diaspora is a segment of people outside the homeland that has migrated to one or more new countries, where it continues to operate as a unified social or political entity (Sheffer 1986; Connor 1986). Frequently members of the diaspora share other characteristics: 1) they retain "a collective memory, vision or myth" about the homeland, 2) they believe that they will encounter difficulties integrating into the new society and therefore feel alienated, 3) they regard the ancient homeland as their "true" home and believe their descendants should return there, 4) they believe that the diaspora should remain committed to the maintenance and restoration of the homeland, and 5) they continue to relate personally, emotionally and vicariously to the homeland, a view that is shared within the diaspora that raises ethnic solidarity (Safran 1991; Connor 1986). However, a crucial element to the diaspora traits that are described above is the extent to which a diaspora continues to emphasize its ethno-national solidarity. Cultural mechanisms reinforce group-supportive behaviors and shared interpretations of the world (Ross 1997a). Groups that maintain firm ethnic boundaries — patterns of interaction that promote the group's identity — are more likely to reinforce these attitudes while also confirming to outsiders that these perceptions are what makes the group distinct (Eriksen 2002; Sanders 2002).

A diaspora for an ethnic group is a potent resource: they can provide sources of funding and additional channels to foreign governments. Dynamic new leaders can come from the diaspora, and as a consequence may have freedoms of speech and movement that ethnic leaders in the homeland do not enjoy. Nevertheless, diasporas, like the ethnic groups from with they derive, vary in their shape, sizes, customs, leadership, and strength of commitment to their co-ethnics in the homeland (Danforth 1995). It is not assured that every diaspora can be mobilized to support ethnic groups back home, nor is it always clear what events can propel the diaspora toward such an outcome.

Interest in ethnic diaspora studies grew significantly during the 1990s as scholars worked to expound theories of ethno-nationalism taking place in a single global space (Danforth 1995; see also Cohen 1997; King and Melvin 1999/2000; Sheffer 1986; Weiner 1993). According to the old view, immigrants in pursuit of a "fresh beginning" left behind their old country completely. It was untenable that migrants would settle permanently in the old country but maintain ties to the old world. It was instead reasoned that populations would assimilate as part of the inevitable process of nation-state building, in which technological advancement, wealth and modernity would all pave the way for ethnic cleavages to dissipate (Schiller, Basch & Blanc 1995; see also Gellner 1983; Hobsbawm 1990). Suffice it to say that this view did not always mirror reality in the late-nineteenth and twentieth centuries. Multiple populations maintained their "Old World" networks and interconnections. European emigrant groups such as the Irish, Czechs, Slovaks and Hungarians contributed to nationalist movements in Europe from their bases in the United States (Schiller, Basch & Blanc 1995). More recently, scholars have begun to argue that "transmigrant" immigrant groups can maintain ties to the homeland even while becoming rooted and established in the new state.

In the second half of the twentieth century, transmigration, technology and other forces of globalization forced scholars to advance new models of nationalism for a globalized world.[15] A prime example of this is Danforth (1995), who argues that ethnic groups by enabling its members to reconstruct or reinvent their traditions outside the homeland now function as "transnational national communities." Others have argued that technology has facilitated rather than caused these shifts. The reluctance of ethnic communities to assimilate derives from their inability to reach full social acceptance, a problem exacerbated by a global economy that makes it more difficult for migrant populations to find full incorporation in the countries within which they have resettled (Schiller, Basch & Blanc 1995: 52). It has been argued that ethnic movements as a whole have morphed into "transnational national communities" and increasingly conduct their struggles on the *global* stage (Danforth 1995). Meanwhile, immigration scholars have taken to classifying diaspora groups as "transnational migrants" or "transmigrants," meant to connote

---

[15] More broadly, Schiller and her co-authors argue that the forces of globalization have restructured and reconfigured global capital with significant consequences both for international migration and nation-state building: "The new circuits of capital provide the context in which migrants and the descendants of migrants, often fully incorporated in the countries of settlement such as the U.S., maintain or construct anew transnational interconnections that differ in their intensity and significance from the home ties maintained by past migrations" (Schiller, Basch & Blanc 1995: 52).

how immigrants increasingly maintain their ties to the homeland (Schiller, Basch & Blanc 1995).[16]

These processes have allowed new models of nationalism to form, allowing diasporas to continue, reconstruct, or reinvent their traditions outside the homeland. Given the distance, space, and time separating them from their co-ethnics, diasporas retain flexibility to shape their identity. They are constituted, in the words of Cohen (1996: 516), as "acts of the imagination," because "in the age of cyberspace, a diaspora can, to some degree, be held together or re-created through the mind, through cultural artifacts and through a shared imagination." Yet, the essence of the diaspora remains unaltered by virtue of a group's history, folklore, folkways, or homeland, all which remains unchanged. Other definitions and typologies exist as there is "considerable debate" about what constitutes a diaspora (Wayland 2004: 408);[17] yet these essential traits and characteristics allow us to understand and study diasporas conceptually and comparatively.

---

[16] Transnationality and Transmigration represent a significant departure from the traditional view that immigrants must leave behind their homeland country completely in favor of full assimilation and incorporation into a new society and culture (Schiller, Basch & Blanc 1995). According to the old view, it was untenable that migrants would settle permanently in the old country but maintain ties to the old world.

[17] The definition used by Wayland (2004: 408) and inspired by Safran's discussion (1991) emphasizes the forced or involuntary dispersal of the ethnic group from the homeland, which would appear to exclude ethnic members that leave the homeland for migrant work opportunities or the lure of economic promise. Cohen (1996) suggests two notions of a diaspora: "diasporas of active colonization," and "victim diasporas," of which classic examples include the Irish (famine), Armenian (dispossessed by Turks), Jewish (holocaust) and Arab Palestinians (post-1948 history). Sheffer (1986) divides diasporas into two types – stateless and state-based. Relevant to this research, Sheffer also notes that in cases where the homeland is especially weak or recently established, an ethnic diaspora can prove to be especially strong.

Nature of the Diaspora's Psychological Attachments to the Homeland:

Of particular significance is the diaspora's cherished memory of the homeland. Among diaspora groups living afar, the homeland assumes a sacred and "soteriological" (i.e. the doctrine of salvation) quality (Cohen 1997: 105). Among the most common features of the diaspora is the "idealization of the putative ancestral home and a collective commitment to its maintenance, restoration, safety and prosperity, even to its creation"; as well as "a collective memory and myth about the homeland, including its location, history and achievements" (Ibid.: 26). Often the homeland takes on maternal and paternal attributes: "Motherland" is perceived as warm, nurturing, a provider of nourishment; while "Fatherland" visualizes the homeland as indomitable, protective, even sacrificial (Connor 1986; Cohen 1997).

The diaspora's attachment to the homeland derives from the emotional connection of ethnic members to the group as a whole. Aside from this emotional core, other scholars emphasize that the idea of homeland is largely "imagined" (Anderson 1983; Danforth 1995). Despite faulty premises used by the ethnic group, the actions of elites in promulgating the homeland narrative, or questionable interpretations of history, ethnic members nevertheless perceive these links as facts and that is where the homeland attachment derives its value (Connor 1986).

Diasporic Forms of Support for Insurgent Campaigns:

Diasporas have a history of supporting insurgencies in their homelands; examples from the second half of the twentieth century include Algeria, Azerbaijan, Egypt, India (Punjab and Kashmir), Indonesia, Ireland, Israel, Lebanon, Russia, Rwanda, Sri Lanka, Turkey, Northern Ireland and Kosovo (Byman *et al.* 2001; Wayland 2004). Diaspora support is especially crucial if the insurgency cannot secure backing from a state sponsor and can therefore help prolong if not win an insurgent campaign (Ibid.).[18] That the collapse of the Soviet Union caused a number of Moscow-backed insurgencies to fold during the 1990s only underscores how influential diasporas have become since the end of the Cold War (Byman *et al.* 2001). Unlike states that choose to sponsor insurgencies for strategic reasons, diasporas genuinely desire to support their ethnic group's national ambitions. In some cases, diaspora members feel genuine sympathy for the nationalist struggle being waged in the homeland. At other times, members may feel a sense of guilt because they enjoy relative safety and security while their co-ethnics suffer (Byman *et al.* 2001). The end result is that diasporas often seek an "active role" in conflicts in the homeland. While the terms of their support need not always involve arming and abetting an insurgency, diasporas are ideally suited to provide this assistance.

Diasporas can support insurgencies and violent separatist movements in a number of ways. Activities that directly aid an insurgent movement can include recruitment, training, financing, propaganda, supplying arms and weapons, and providing intelligence (Sheffer 1994; Shain and Barth 2003; Forest 2010). There are two main resources that diaspora communities provide to homeland insurgencies. One is outreach. In a new state, diasporas can organize and fund sympathetic front groups ranging from charities to friendly media organizations to disseminate propaganda and integrate political support for the national movement. From the political activism of Canadian Tamils in support of the Tamil cause, to the support received by Islamic militants in India's Kashmiri state, to the much flaunted Irish-American embrace of

---

[18] The overall prospects for most insurgency campaigns remain a complex puzzle. While it is true that most insurgencies fail, unconventional wars more than conventional wars have resulted in significant political change within the nation, and insurgency remains the only type of war that has recently defeated a superpower, as the Soviet adventure in Afghanistan and American experiences in Vietnam and Somalia can attest. See Hammes (2007), Connable and Libicki (2010).

Northern Ireland republicanism, diaspora groups associated with a wide variety of ideologies and political aspirations have become associated with insurgencies and separatist campaigns in the homeland. The second is fundraising. Diaspora members can fund insurgent movements directly, or siphon funds in a variety of ways, including redirecting donations made to nonprofits or charities into the coffers of violent separatist or insurgent organizations. Such was the case with the Tamil paramilitary organization Liberation Tigers of Tamil Eelam, which employed fundraisers abroad who made monthly and in some cases weekly solicitations for donations (Wayland 2004). Diaspora elements can also use the financial instruments and domestic banks in their new countries to help launder or invest money, and the LTTE has been able to set up a number of successful business enterprises in Canada where the Tigers covered initial capital costs and then split the profits with the company's ostensible owner (Byman *et al.* 2001).

Diasporas can also aid the insurgent or separatist cause without directly condoning the insurgency itself. One way to do this is to demonstrate moral support for the goals of the movement, perhaps by demonstrating or holding mass rallies in the countries where the diaspora resides, allowing diaspora members to make a show of support for their homeland co-ethnics and to protest the conduct of the homeland government or some other perceived oppressor. The presence of diaspora members at public functions such as commemorations or parades, helps to legitimate the separatists' cause even without overt approval of the insurgent groups, their tactics, or ambitions. Such was the case of Tamils living in Toronto who attended Heroes Day celebrations or marches on the Canadian legislature, forms of participation that helped legitimize the causes of the insurgent group Liberation Tigers of Tamil Eelam (LTTE) (Wayland 2004). They might also seek to influence the foreign policy stances of their new states by lobbying the national government or attempting to lure public opinion to its side. The involvement of the

Jewish diaspora in the pro-Israel lobby, which has attracted considerable public attention in recent years, is one such example (Mearsheimer and Walt 2007).

SUMMARY AND CONCLUSION

This chapter has provided a brief survey of the relevant literature on ethnic identity, conflict, and diasporas. Although ethnicity is popularly understood to refer to racial or linguistic groups, scholars have broadened the definition to include groups that self-identify based on ascriptive traits – language, religion, race, tribe, kinship, caste, and culture. Increased scholarly attention to the national aspirations of ethnic group has also led to differing traditions of study over the essential nature of ethno-national identity; these schools include primordialism, constructivism, and instrumentalism. Ethnic conflict is the often-violent confrontation that takes place between these ethnic groups, and these conflicts frequently pit ethnic groups against one another or the state.

Broadly speaking, there are also dueling approaches for understanding and explaining ethnic mobilization; that have dominated academic analyses of ethnic conflict and violence. The rationalist perspective argues that individuals join ethnic social movements because it serves their self-interests. According to this perspective, ethnic violence is rational, and best explained through the prism of goal-seeking actors (Hechter 1995). The culturalist perspective argues that that norms and values are deeply embedded in our psychology. These analyses characterize ethnic violence as culturally constructed, imbued with actions that are meaningful and symbolic. Bearing in mind Lichbach and Zuckerman's (1997) argument in favor of a "thick" research design or synthesis of multiple approaches, this research has embraced the outlook of both

Barreto (2009) and Varshney (2003) to develop an appropriate synthesis for the study of ethnic mobilization.

The mass migration in the twentieth century of ethnic communal groups to new countries, combined with the advent of new technologies and communication capabilities, has allowed diaspora populations the chance to resuscitate but also reinvent their traditions outside the homeland. This has created new models for understanding nationalism, one in which the ethnic group is increasingly transnational. At the same time, the diaspora's cherished memory of the homeland deriving from an emotional connection to the group and its own sense of history continues to remain central to diasporic identity. Both these elements of the modern day diaspora are essential for understanding the process through which diaspora members elect to support separatist movements in the homeland. The ways in which diaspora communities can lend their support to violent separatist groups and insurgencies are myriad. They can provide direct aid through fundraising, recruitment and training, arms-dealing, or propaganda, as well as indirect forms of support. They can also support the insurgent or separatist cause without directly condoning the insurgency itself by lobbying the governments where they reside to adopt foreign policy positions that challenge the homeland government, or create international pressure for human rights reform through the work of international organizations and NGOs.

Having reviewed some of the various debates, arguments, and approaches that make up the growing literature on ethnic conflict studies and civil wars will facilitate in future chapters a discussion of ethnic responses to traumatic events that is more cogent and aligned with previous research. Awareness of these works will also allow the reader to judge if this research project has enhanced our understanding of ethnic nationalism, diaspora behavior, the causal mechanisms involved in ethnic mobilization, or the role of identity in determining intergroup violence. The next chapter focuses on development of my own theory on ethnic groups and their responses to traumatic events and will outline the explanatory model that will guide the remainder of this research project.

3

TRAUMATIC EVENTS

A traumatic event is an episode of a political nature that members of an ethnic group view as physically or symbolically threatening to their ethnic group's survival. They can be acts of government oppression, military coups, or an invasion by another country. Assassinations, rioting, terrorist attacks, or other outbreaks of violence all can constitute a traumatic event. They are shocking and controversial, a dramatic departure from the norm, a jarring shake to the status quo. They frequently lead to worsening political tensions between groups, can result in separatist violence, and can even spark civil war. Horowitz (2000) finds that ethnic anxiety over the group's station in relation to other ethnic groups constitutes one of the most recurrent reasons why ethnic groups — especially "backward" groups in developing regions — aspire to secede; a traumatic event can allow the separatists to exploit these tensions among the general population. They attract high levels of public and media attention, and afterward can remain the subject of intense scrutiny for months.

Traumatic events inherently are violent: it is the rapid absorption of casualties or loss of life that functions as a "scar" on the collective ethnic mind and memory. Violence is key because it signifies the threat to the group's status while exploiting its insecurities. The relative threat of violence involved in a traumatic event trumps the risk of every-day political dealings, distinguishing these events from other political episodes. However, the violence of these events threatens symbolically as well, frequently by invoking religious and cultural symbols that represent the ethnic group's unchanging continuity with its past. Violence directed against sacred spaces or at religious sites therefore possesses an extra quality steeped in symbolic overtones, intensifying the emotional and psychological impact of the threat to the ethnic population in question. Religion in particular historically has proven a constant precursor of violence because it equips society with such fundamental assertions as a common moral fabric, a developed sense of identity, an origin story, and belief in an afterlife. As Pinker (2011: 671) notes.: "The scriptures present a God who delights in genocide, rape, slavery, and the execution of nonconformists, and for millennia those writings were used to rationalize the massacre of infidels..." These aspects of one's being are non-negotiable and thus can portend conflict between members of different religious beliefs. According to Haidt (2012), it is not that religious groups are not capable of being altruistic, but people tends to aim their altruism primarily at members of their own groups. Religion is key because it has historically operated as a binding mechanism for groups to form and to help them create communities with a shared reality.

There are both recent and historic examples that can help illustrate the concept. In Iraq, the 2006 bombing of the Golden Mosque in Samarra, destroying one of the most revered shrines in all of Shi'a Islam, "[set] off a day of almost unparalleled sectarian fury in cities and towns across Iraq" (Worth 2006). The attack provided justification for Shi'as to intensify their opposition to cooperation with the Sunni minority, and in its aftermath protesting mobs took to the streets, chanted for revenge, and set fire to dozens of Sunni mosques. The bombing of the Golden Mosque was quickly labeled the onset of a new phase of sectarian violence in Iraq, perilously close to civil war. Likewise, the decision by the Pakistani government in 2007 to storm the Red Mosque, which was seen by the government to have become a hotbed for radicalism, was also perceived as a turn for the worst, souring the already frayed relationship between the central government and different tribal groups. The assault, which killed more than 150 people, prompted pro-Taliban militants along the Afghan border to scrap an existing peace agreement with the government, and led to an upsurge of violence concentrated in Northern Waziristan (BBC News 2007). In 2011, the Islamist sect Boko Haram carried out a series of Christmas day bombings that roiled Nigeria. Here again was an event, steeped in symbolism, that observers and citizens alike came to perceive as a point of worsening tensions between two ethnic groups. The Christmas day bombings were called "a new, religion-tinged front, a tactic that threatened to exploit the already frayed relations between Nigeria's nearly evenly split populations of Christians and Muslims" (Nossiter 2011).

These recent episodes invoke fundamentalist interpretations of Islam, but the pernicious and lingering effects of a traumatic event are not limited to the Muslim world. Take the Rwandan Genocide for example: for both Hutus and Tutsis, the majority religion in both groups is Christian, and religion has not been seen as a significant factor in explaining the rift between the groups, though cultural differences are a different matter. The Genocide itself was a response to a separate traumatic event — the assassination of the Rwandan President, which led Rwanda's Hutu miliitias to immediately suspect Rwanda's Tutsi prime minister as having a hand in his death (Burkhalter 1994/95; Amstutz 2006).[19] Of course the Holocaust, both in its severity and the mobilizing effect on its survivors, serves as the archetypal traumatic event, laying the groundwork for the creation of the state of Israel. The 1983 "Black July" rioting in Sri Lanka that killed thousands of Tamils coincided with the creation of the Liberation Tigers of Tamil Eelam

---

[19] Following the Genocide, the rebel Tutsi group Rwandan Patriotic Front (RPF) launched a new military offensive that overwhelmed its Hutu rivals, eventually leading to the removal of the Hutu government.

(LTTE). And according to America's own origin story, the perceived brutality of the Boston Massacre, depicted in Paul Revere's illustration of the violence and further spun by Samuel Adams and a host of pro-independence publications, mortified thousands and swayed public opinion against British rule, serving as a pivotal turning point in the run-up to the American Revolution (Behdad 2005).

Other examples of traumatic events include the 1984 Indian government's attack on militants who sought refuge inside the Golden Temple of Amritsar; the 2009 rioting and violence between Uyghurs and Hans that erupted in the capital of the western province of Xinjiang in China, claiming the lives of almost 200; and in Northern Ireland, both the 1972 "Bloody Sunday" killings and the Irish Hunger Strikes of 1981. This research treats each of these as case studies and examines them in greater detail in later chapters.

There are several ways that traumatic events are politically significant. First, they are frequently viewed as "turning points" on the roadmap of navigating contentious ethnic relations because of the consequences they engender. A traumatic event can unleash a darker, more violent period in the history of a conflict. Such was the case when Sunnis destroyed the Golden Mosque, signifying a violent shift in the trajectory of ethnic relations inside the country. Second, a traumatic event can curb, disrupt, or completely destroy ongoing efforts to resolve ethnic tensions and contentious issues without escalation. Second, the occurrence of violence during a traumatic event, and the way in which it transpires, cripples the appeal made by advocates for cooperation; while buttressing the arguments of activists calling for radical, more confrontational measures. In Northern Ireland, for example, the Bloody Sunday killings undermined the efforts of civil rights and political leaders attempting to resolve the conflict peacefully, while dramatically increasing the hardliner appeal of the Irish Republican Army. Third, the event can become a symbol of the intolerance practiced by a governing regime or another ethnic rival. The effects of this symbolism can linger for months or even years after the occurrence, disrupting further attempts at resolution while the aggrieved ethnic group remains angry at its occurrence and distrustful of its rival. Fourth, a traumatic event taps into — to some extent, crystallizes — the innermost fears and insecurities of the ethnic group and their place in the state's overall power structure. It reinforces the constant dread among ethnic members that rival ethnic groups aim to control or overwhelm them, or that the government is unable (or unwilling) to protect them.

Figure 3.1 Political Significance of a Traumatic Event

<table>
<tr><td>Political Significance of a Traumatic Event</td></tr>
<tr><td>

1. Can constitute a "turning point" in the conflict, politically and emotionally
2. Can curb, disrupt, or destroy ongoing efforts to resolve ethnic tensions peacefully
3. Can become a symbol of intolerance by the governing regime or other ethnic rival
4. Can impact ethnic members on an emotional and psychological level, tapping into their innermost fears

</td></tr>
</table>

<u>Symbolism, Ethnic Entrepreneurism, and Emotions Surrounding a Traumatic Event:</u>

Symbolism can be expected to play a major role in shaping diaspora perceptions in the case of a traumatic event. Recall from chapter 2 that symbols resonate with the ethnic community because they signal continuity with the past, which provides a crucial source of self-esteem and authenticity in a constantly changing world. Symbols act as "markers" of "a virtually symbolic world" consecrated by the ethnic group's shared interpretation of its own reality (Srubar 2007: 540; qtd. in Grün 2009). When these symbols come under attack during a traumatic event, ethnic community members feel threatened because these symbols serve as an extension of the group itself.

Traumatic events are crucial symbolic events because of their emotional impact on ethnic members, leading to a circular process where ethnic members make subjective interpretations, which helps crystallize the group's understanding of its own community identity, which shapes and inspires further interpretations. Sydney Tarrow argues that "emotion work" helps to maintain solidarity among activists and transform claims into action. According to Tarrow (2011),[20] "high points of contention may produce emotional pivots around which the future direction of a movement turns." This is where the role of subjective interpretations comes in. Through symbolic interpretation, a historic event can become the nationalist community's "direct and sublime expression of the nation's will" at which point the interpretation becomes "part and parcel" of the event itself (Sewell 1996: 861). This was the case with the taking of the Bastille in 1789, which was hardly a significant military achievement but through the event's interpretation came to be seen as the founding action of the French Revolution (Ibid.).

Traumatic events provide fertile ground for "ethnic entrepreneurs" — members of the community who are responsible for reinforcing an identity, uniting co-ethnics and excluding outsiders, and who exploit customs, beliefs, and cultural elements to further define group boundaries, "forg[ing] an artificial sense of kinship by objectifying symbols and shared sense of cultural characteristics" (Barreto 2009: 27). Ethnic entrepreneurs use historical events to their

---

[20] This passage was cited in an electronic version without page numbers. The passage can be found in ch. 7, section 4, subsection 2, para. 3.

advantage by employing them in the central narratives of the ethnic group's "story," which is shared with ethnic group members to demonstrate how "we were great" but also that "we have suffered." How these apparent mythmakers weave — or omit — these events from their narrative is key; in some cases ethnic entrepreneurs can even discard details of or entire events when they no longer fit with the favored narrative of the conflict (Behdad 2005). We see this frequently to be the case when events are labeled "massacres" when in fact relatively few people were killed, such as the Boston Massacre which is treated as a deeply violent and malicious attack in American mythology but in reality killed only five people.

Emotion is a powerful element of the ethnic group's reaction to a traumatic eventand must therefore be taken into account to understand the responses of ethnic populations; as Horowitz (2000: 140) suggests, "A bloody phenomenon cannot be explained by a bloodless theory." In his analysis of the relationship between emotion and ethnic conflict, Petersen (2002), who analyzes ethnic violence occurrences in Eastern Europe, finds that emotion helps explain why individuals engage in violent acts even when they are likely to later regret their behavior, and argues that emotions such as fear, hatred, rage, and resentment are predictive of ethnic violence with varying levels of accuracy (Petersen 2002).[21] Resentment is especially powerful, Petersen argues, because of the imbalanced power relationship — or at least the perception thereof — it reflects: if an individual identities with group A, and group B surpasses me either because B has risen or A has fallen, it leaves the individual feeling vulnerable. This connects the individual with the collective. In this respect, a traumatic event, which by definition is emotionally and psychologically perceived, directly impacts ethnic members by increasing solidarity and the potential for action.

---

[21] Petersen ultimately concludes that Resentment, in response to structural changes, is the most accurate predictor of the four emotions.

This leads to another interesting factor regarding the impact of traumatic events: most ethnic members do not experience the event directly, but learn about it from other ethnic members, through local or national media sources, or from global bodies and international organizations. Owing in part to the way in which the news is portrayed, culturally resonant forms, such as myths, poems, songs, stories, and legends, can be expected to develop, in part to explain the group's interpretation of what happened to other members and outsiders, and in part to express the psychological impact on its collective psyche. In these tellings, new characters will be created, fresh heroes and villains to add to the group canon. Interpretation of the deeper meaning of the event will also become culturally imbued, colored by the member's personal beliefs, sense of community, and ethnic identity. The myths, anecdotes, stories, and other interpretations surrounding and emerging from the event lays the groundwork for ethnic members to subjectively interpret the event as a symbol of how the ethnic group is treated in the homeland and if the ethnic group feels threatened. For those previously uninvolved or who harbor strong doubts about ongoing resistance movements or campaigns for greater self-determination, the emotional resonance of a traumatic event, and genuine concern that the event engenders, can help to overcome — or ignore — whatever reservations had existed.

In sum, nationalists consciously invent and imagine the ethnic group's national story (Motyl 1999); traumatic events lay a specific groundwork and serve as a crucial building block for this process to take place. However, this process is not purely transactional. These interpretations will fail to kick in on the recipient's side unless the emotional content embedded in the ethnic group's identity is evident. The most alienating details of the event allow ethnic entrepreneurs to tap into their followers' most volatile emotions, such as fear, hatred, or resentment, but these details must tie in to the group's ethnic identity and sense of peril.

But how exactly does this process of mobilization work?

<u>"Event Galvanization"</u>:

Since this research focuses on political behavior and the prospect for events to lead to action, I have adopted a model for analyzing traumatic events based on the literature on "contentious politics," or social movements. To help frame the relationships between variables that this research assesses, I should make clear a number of associated assumptions. There is general agreement among scholars of "contentious politics," or social movements, that three sets of factors drive groups to engage in collective action: mobilizing structures, framing processes, and political opportunities. <u>Mobilizing structures</u> are the organizational resources available to the group. <u>Political opportunities</u> refer to the external environment in which the movement operates. And <u>framing processes</u> are attempts to influence group members' worldview, establish sets of common grievances, and provide justifications for action. (Tarrow 1998, 2011; McAdam, Tarrow, and Tilley 2001; Wayland 2004; Tsutsui 2004).

It is within the prism of this last category that this research explores the impact of traumatic events. As a framing process, a traumatic event can provide a crucial opportunity for a separatist movement to set or reset perceptions of the conflict, attract attention to its cause, win new supporters to its side, and increase overall involvement in the cause by some members of the ethnic group. Framing is an "interpretive scheme," responsible for simplifying and condensing "the world out there." Collective action frames can help illustrate, underscore, or embellish the "seriousness" or "injustice" of a social condition, helping to "redefine as unjust and immoral what was previously seen as unfortunate but perhaps tolerable" (Snow and Benford 1992, p. 137; qtd. in Tarrow 2011). Social movements can become especially committed to framing specific grievances as a means to dignifying their claims or helping to produce or reinforce a collective identity (Tarrow 2011). This is where traumatic events come in. Provided the right timing and necessary political skills, movement entrepreneurs can use a traumatic event — which by definition is illustrative of some threat posed to the ethnic group — to attract new followers to the cause, or persuade fence-sitters of the insensitivity or viciousness of the opposition. This is a process that I refer to as <u>event galvanization</u> — where a specific political episode distresses and effectively mobilizes an ethnic community to respond with some form of political action.

A traumatic event can therefore help pave the way for ethnic members to mobilize either in support of separatist groups or in support of the goals of the separatist movement. These actions can take shape in a number of forms. Ethnic members may be persuaded to join separatist organizations, including groups that espouse violence to achieve its objectives. They can participate in public demonstrations, engage in political advocacy, or fundraise on behalf of homeland separatist movements, the last of which has been demonstrated to be crucial to the success or failure of an ethnic insurgency (Collier and Hoeffler 2000; Fearon and Laitin 2003). In some cases, traumatic events may convince ethnic members to empower groups willing to employ violence by supplying them with funds, weapons, equipment, or in the most extreme case, enlisting as foot soldiers with a violent group.

Figure 3.2 Terms and definitions for understanding traumatic events and mobilization

Term	*Definition*	*Relevance to mobilization*
Traumatic event	Episode of a political nature that ethnic members view as physically or symbolically threatening to their ethnic group's survival	Has the capacity to act as a catalyst for mobilization and collective action among members of the ethnic group
Event galvanization	Process where a political episode that distresses the ethnic community to the point of mobilization	Can lead ethnic members to engage in political activity such as participation in public demonstrations, political advocacy, or making donation to, or joining movement organizations
Ethnic Symbolism	Resonate with ethnic community because they signal continuity with the past, which provides a crucial source of self-esteem and authenticity in a constantly changing world	When symbols come under attack during a traumatic event, it helps crystallize the inner-most fears and insecurities of the ethnic community and their place in the state's overall power structure because these symbols serve as an extension of the group itself
Collective action frame	Attempts to influence group members' worldview, establish sets of common grievances, and provide justifications for action	Can lead to mobilization by helping to illustrate, underscore, or embellish the "seriousness" or "injustice" of a social condition

This research therefore assumes that traumatic events can act as event galvanizers by reshaping collective action frames being used by separatists to influence perceptions, leading to increased mobilization as described above. The relationships between these variables are shown below:

Figure 3.3 Event Galvanization

Traumatic event in homeland	→	*Collective action frames*	→	*Diaspora perceptions*	→	*Ethnic mobilization*
				(Event Galvanization)		*X*
						Mobilizing structures
						X
						Political opportunities

Some caveats are in order. This is not meant to suggest that separatists can easily manipulate a traumatic event to produce a desired effect that works to the political advantage of the separatist movement. Although separatists can and will do their utmost to exploit a traumatic event, by examining what makes a traumatic event so inherently powerful this research aims to sheds light on the difficulty of trying to control and manipulate an event. There is also no doubt that an individual's decision to support separatist groups will have been subject to a variety of causes and influences beyond one's environment, including (but not limited to) personality, family background, and the manner in which the individual and organization interact (Forest 2010). The process is dynamic and complex. Nonetheless, an actor's environment matters, notwithstanding the recent advances in neuroscience that have led some scientists to argue that the brain enables the mind; as Gazzaniga (2011) argues, human nature is never so easily broken down into such distinct choices, but individuals are subject to all their life experiences that impacts the interaction between our brain and our mind. A traumatic event can therefore become a special kind of environmental influence. It can act as an environmental trigger — a specific action, policy or event that enhances community perceptions of a need to take action. According to Forest (2010: 36), these "are very dynamic and time-relevant, and seized upon by the propagandists of terrorist organizations in their attempts to enhance the resonance of their ideology." The passage is in reference to terrorist groups, but the same can be said of insurgency organizations seeking new supporters.

In discussing the motivation to provide aid to insurgents or participate in acts of terrorism, one might view as misplaced focusing on communities as the appropriate level of analysis, rather than individuals. The decision to engage in illegal, violent, or terrorist activity is, after all, a matter of personal and individual choice. However, individuals and their perceptions are also influenced by interactions with organizations and their environment. Family, peers and role models all affect perceptions of a given individual seeking to understand his or her environment, events, and conditions (Forest 2010). One can only understand mobilizing processes completely by taking into account the context of a particular environment.

TRAUMATIC EVENTS AND DISASPORAS

Thus far the case has been made that traumatic events can significantly influence an ethnic population by transforming perceptions, and that this process increases the chance for mobilization. However, the focus of this research is more explicit. It examines the impact of traumatic events in the diaspora. Diasporas would seem an unlikely candidate for mobilization given their distance in time and space from the homeland. However, some have argued that diaspora members by their very nature continue to harbor and emphasize their collective ethnic identity (Sheffer 1986; Connor 1986). If diasporas do feel the emotional burden of a traumatic event despite this distance, it would possibly speak to the emotional bonds shared between ethnic members as well as the continuing strength of one's ethnic identity.

However, there are features of a diaspora community that might even increase the likelihood that a traumatic event could lead to an energized and widespread community galvanization. First, movement entrepreneurs may face fewer structural challenges in telling and publicizing their version of events than they would in the homeland. At minimum, a homeland government would not be able to counteract as effectively the ethnic group's prevailing interpretation of events, or take the steps it perceives are necessary to prevent "disinformation." The "myth-making" following a traumatic event could evolve at a faster rate given the comparative freedom of speech a diaspora might enjoy. Outside the homeland, movement entrepreneurs will have greater reign to shape perceptions as they see fit. Second, the diaspora's ability to operate with relative impunity from the actions of the homeland government may not only give it more capacity, but also could result in the greater willingness of diaspora members to defy homeland government authorities and insist on or pursue a separatist agenda.

A final reason has to do with the diaspora's emotional and psychological attachment to the homeland, by far the most crucial factor in determining the diaspora's response to homeland trauma. According to Connor (1986), Safran (1991), and Shain (2002), the homeland frequently defines or shapes the diaspora's strength of identity, collective psychology, and understanding of history. When the homeland is threatened, it can cause a sense of "diasporic peril" that can be either definite or psychological (Shain 2002: 125). A threat to the homeland can harm diaspora members because of continuing economic linkages or danger posed to homeland kin, or it can deliver a psychological blow to the prestige of the ethnic group or shake a member's confidence of the group's ability to survive. For "victim diasporas," the homeland is especially significant both as a representation of what has been lost and as a political goal of what the group must regain (Cohen 1996).

While not universally applicable, many diaspora members will envision the homeland as their one true home; others will believe in the right and duty of their descendants to eventually return. Diaspora members who identify with the aspirations and struggles of their co-ethnic homeland members may feel compelled to seek out an active role in either resolving or escalating conflict. The diaspora's remembrance of the homeland in its ideal state — as it *was* rather than as it *is* — will also predispose some diaspora members to rise to its defense (Cohen 1996). Especially in cases where despair, exhaustion or cynicism has set in among members of the homeland ethnic population, separatist movements can also benefit from the romanticized memories amongst diaspora members of a homeland "frozen in time." Even among those who have lost all interest in returning to their "home" countries — perhaps due to political persecution or instability — they would likely view the condition of their homeland as a tragedy and sympathize with those ethnic members who are unable to escape the homeland's fate.

One therefore does not have to use much imagination to predict how a traumatic event might upset diaspora members and transform collective perceptions. In the eyes of the diaspora, any traumatic political event that is seen as sufficiently significant, sudden, and threatening, will come to be perceived not as an act committed against a finite number of co-ethnics, but as an attack upon the notion of the homeland and the ethnic group's claim to the land. If a sufficient scale is reached, a traumatic event in the homeland will even make a permanent etching in the collective psyche of the ethnic group. Consider Robin Cohen's following rumination on "victim diasporas":

> The scarring historical event—for the Jews 'Babylon', for the Africans slavery, for the Irish the famine, for the Armenians the genocide and for the Palestinians the formation of the state of Israel—lends a particular colouring to each of these five diasporas. They are, above all, victim diasporas. This does not mean that they do not share several characteristics of other sorts of diasporas… merely that their inauspicious histories are either self-affirmed or accepted by outside observers as determining their *essential* characters (Cohen 1996: 513).

In Cohen's telling, not only has the traumatic event served its role in alienating the diaspora group, but the pivotal events listed above shape the diaspora's identity. At minimum, a traumatic event has the capacity to mobilize members of the diaspora to political action; in some cases, it can come to shape, define, or recreate new formations of ethnic identity. According to Cohen, the homeland, in the imagination of the diaspora, assumes a sacred, soteriological quality. It is idealized to the point of myth-making. As the diaspora community increasingly relies on story-telling to explain its origins and history, the homeland — so frequently the setting, political prize, or source of honor in these tales — gains increased symbolic and emotional resonance. Along with traditions passed down, the homeland becomes the one constant, its possession connecting prior and future generations.

The political ramifications of increased sympathy in the diaspora for an ethnic movement or insurgency are profound. Increased awareness could profit violent separatist organizations in ways that are unexpected or unintended. It could allow diaspora organizations to divert ostensibly charitable donations to violent groups instead, unbeknownst to the original donor. Increased diaspora awareness and sympathy for the plight of their homeland co-ethnics could also strengthen the hand of certain movement leaders, including those willing to use violence, by encouraging them to adopt harder line tactics in light of increasing international support from overseas.

In examining the effect of traumatic events on diasporas, it is important to clarify what is *not* being contended: that a diaspora in its entirety will support armed violence or even separatist objectives. It is certainly possible that some ethnic members will become directly involved with violent groups fighting for the cause. Their involvement could come in several respects: joining diaspora organizations with paramilitary links, making donations from their new country to organizations known to espouse violence, or in the most extreme case, enlisting as a foot soldier with a violent group operating in the homeland. These effects are important and should be analyzed, but this behavior by the group as a whole is not expected to be unified or monolithic.

In sum, this chapter thus far has theorized that movement entrepreneurs in the diaspora can use traumatic events as frames for collective action that can significantly increase support or sympathy for the movement, though this does not necessarily mean the outright endorsement of violence or violent groups. For many reasons, diasporas present a particularly compelling case for understanding the relationship between traumatic events and perceptions. Depending also on the mobilizing structures and political opportunities available to it, a diaspora community could mobilize greater levels of support for the ethnic cause. And for a minority of its members, this could mean becoming directly involved with violent separatist organizations.

TRAUMATIC EVENTS AND THE VALUE-RATIONALITY DEBATE

In making the fundamental argument that a traumatic event in the homeland impacts ethnic members symbolically and emotionally to the point of galvanizing diaspora members into action, this research reflects a core argument posited by Varshney (2003) in chapter 2 — that one must comprehend the role of values as well as rational choice to understand how ethnic mobilization begins and is sustained.

If a traumatic event has a transformative effect on diaspora members' perceptions, or if members are driven to political action in response to these events, this would suggest that emotions and cultural beliefs are at least partly responsible for trends in ethnic behavior — what Varshney refers to as value-rationality. According to the value rationalist, the overall resonance of the ethnic community's response will be organic, not manipulated; the product of the subconscious ethno-national bond, not instrumental desire. Upon learning of the traumatic event, the diaspora member's response will be emotional, for the event will have tapped into her subconscious understanding of her own identity, as opposed to any self-interested pursuits individually and consciously sought. And in terms of tangible action, should the ethnic member elect to ignore her feelings or minimize her emotional reaction, she will risk the "reduced mode of being" that Varshney (2003) earlier described — she would come to feel less than whole. This is not to say that instrumental rationality has no role to play in the process of mobilization. Earlier in this chapter I described how ethnic and movement entrepreneurs affect, but do not control, the formation of identity and perceptions of events. Elites and rational actors also exert their direct influence on the mobilization process once the mobilization has reached a crescendo, at which point it is up to leaders to provide strategy and direct the movement toward its core objectives. However, this comes later in the mobilization process, whereas value rationality helps to explain where the ethnic group's mobilization response derives its value and meaning in the first place — prior to the moment instrumental actors provide direction.

A traumatic event thus constitutes a tipping point, transforming perceptions against the new government or rival ethnic group. It is only after this point is reached that actors can possibly begin to harness, craft, or manipulate the community toward some desired end. This speaks to a much broader debate in the study of ethnic conflict and suggests that understanding ethnic behavior does require a full and nuanced appreciation of the symbolic and cultural currency embedded in ethnic relations.

HYPOTHESES

At this point it is useful to return to the hypotheses meant to allow for assessment of the theories and concepts this chapter has described. As stated in chapter 1, this research design will test the following prime hypothesis:[22]

---

[22] Van Evera (1997: 11-12) defines the prime hypothesis as "the overarching hypothesis that frames the relationship between a theory's independent and dependent variables," as opposed to explanatory hypotheses, "the intermediate hypotheses that constitute a theory's explanation."

Hypothesis – A traumatic event in the homeland impacts ethnic members symbolically and emotionally and directly influences perceptions in the diaspora in favor of the separatist movement. It will motivate some diaspora members to aid or support co-ethnic separatist groups.

This hypothesis reflects my assumption that a traumatic event plays a significant role in influencing diaspora mobilization. It assumes that movement entrepreneurs are capable of utilizing a traumatic event as a framing mechanism to provide a new symbolic/emotional pivot around which to rally support. The effect of this is to attract new supporters and turn fence-sitters against the government.

In terms of measurement, perceptions of violence can be thought of as ordinal and thus generally measurable in terms of degree. Acts of violence are interpreted according to two dimensions: perceptions of the physical severity of the act itself as well as perceived details associated with the act resonating with the ethnic group's cultural heritage or shared understanding of its ethnic identity. In the first dimension (intensity of <u>physical violence</u>), the number of deaths or injuries associated with the traumatic event, or alternatively the dollar amount of property damage that was committed, serves as the relevant measure. For the second dimension (intensity of <u>symbolic violence</u>), I attempt to assess how certain acts of violence are predisposed to significant cultural meaning, such as violence committed against sacred spaces, on important dates, against cherished cultural markers, or against members partaking in such activities. The relationship between these variables is shown below:

Figure 3.4 The effect of physical and symbolic violence on event galvanization

Traumatic event in homeland	→	*Collective action frames*	→	*Diaspora perceptions*	→	*Ethnic mobilization*
X						*X*
Physical violence				*Event Galvanization*		*Mobilizing structures*
X						*X*
Symbolic violence						*Political opportunities*

To assess the explanatory strength of each dimension above, I "unfold" the prime hypothesis into a series of smaller, sequential statements, which can then be evaluated:

H1a (physical violence): As the relative level of violent aggression or bloodshed involved in a traumatic event increases, separatist movements will attract new followers and persuade fence-sitters.

H1b (symbolic violence): When crucial details of a traumatic event gain symbolic significance or underscore specific and preexisting separatist frames from the conflict, separatist movements will attract new followers and persuade fence-sitters.

For these hypotheses to be supported, data must point to a relationship between a traumatic event and its core details on the one hand, and a detectable shift in diaspora perceptions on the other. The hypothesis can be refuted if ethnic members do not experience feelings of fear or resentment, if a "disconnect" with their affected co-ethnics is felt, or if they did experience those emotions but it can be shown that these were not a relatively strong determinant in the diaspora's collective response. If the ethnic group's emotional response to details of the traumatic event cannot be shown to be relatively unified (i.e. widespread feelings of "fear," "rage," or "resentment"), this finding would also weaken the claim.

Lastly, I attempt to assess the relationship between changed perceptions favorable to the separatist cause, and the occurrence of activity in support of the separatist movement, completing the process of event galvanization:

H1c (event galvanization): As perceptions of the separatist movement improve and attract new followers, the likelihood of diaspora members providing greater levels of support to separatist objectives in the homeland increases.

For this hypothesis to be supported, a relationship must be shown to exist between diaspora perceptions and decisions by some diaspora members to begin supporting, or to increase support for separatist groups operating in the homeland. The hypothesis can be refuted if there is no noticeable uptick in active support for separatist groups despite any perception shifts in the diaspora.

CONCLUSION

This chapter has sought to outline a conceptual framework for analyzing traumatic events and the impact they have on ethnic diaspora groups. It has been argued that a traumatic event, acting as an event galvanizer, serves as an especially poignant collective action frame that can be used to mobilize members of the diaspora. This affords separatist movements a crucial opportunity to set or reset perceptions of the conflict, attract attention to its cause, and win new supporters to its side. Having laid out this framework and explained some of the conceptual fundamentals and inner-workings, the next chapter will begin to test its explanatory value — by analyzing as a case study the Punjabi Sikh diaspora and its response to the 1984 attack on the Golden Temple of Amritsar.

PART II

THE SIKH DIASPORA AND GOLDEN TEMPLE ATTACK

4

BACKGROUND OF SIKHISM, SIKH IDENTITY AND THE SEPARATIST MOVEMENT

I now turn to the case of the Sikh diaspora and its response to Operation Blue Star, which I examine as a comprehensive case study. While the next two chapters will explicitly analyze the perceptions and response of diaspora Sikhs to this controversial military operation, full comprehension of the significance of this attack depends on a fuller understanding of Sikhism, its history, the roots of Punjab's inter-communal tensions between Sikhs and Hindus and the evolution of Sikh nationalism throughout the twentieth century. These forces in the 1980s coincided to pave the way for a violent separatist insurgency to take place, engulfing the Punjab and constituting the worst threat to India's territorial integrity since partition; it became known as the "Punjab Crisis" (Chima 2010; Fair 2005). The Sikh case offers a strong example of an ethnic movement that evolved into a nationalist campaign through increasing political demands and which received support and inspiration from the ethnic diaspora community (Eriksen 2002). This case also demonstrates how ethnic violence can originate from the growing insecurity of an ethnic community. As shall be seen, violence did not ensue only a result of Sikh political demands, which had existed in some version or the other since the creation of the Indian state, but came about when these demands merged with the growing conviction among Sikhs that their identity and way of life had become threatened by "the other" (Horowitz 2000; Demmers 2012).

The demands of the insurgents varied between greater autonomy, increased religious rights, and complete independence. Many Sikhs fought for the creation of a new Sikh state called "Khalistan." The idea of a Sikh state based in Punjab, which Sikhs viewed as their ancestral homeland, had been around at least since the early twentieth century; in fact, the idea of partition and accompanying notion that each major faith would have its own country — particularly Jinnah's conception of an independent state reserved for the subcontinent's Muslim population — had fueled the notion of Khalistan before Sikhs found it in their favor to instead cast their lot with the new Hindu governing majority in India. However, the violence that erupted as a result of these demands took the country by surprise since India had been relatively tranquil throughout most of India's existence. The campaign that Sikhs waged against the Indian government and security forces forty years later included instigating sectarian violence, economic sabotage, targeted assassination, and armed confrontation with the police. These forces combined to destabilize the region and occasionally send the Indian polity into crisis, such as when the militancy or its allies assassinated high-profile leaders, including Prime Minister Indira Gandhi. Between 21,000 and 40,000 people were killed during this conflict, more than the number killed during all of India's wars with Pakistan combined (Chima 2010; Fair 2005).

This chapter seeks to provide an outline of the history of the Sikhs as well as the trajectory of the insurgency in the run-up to Blue Star. First, it discusses the background of the Sikhs including the genesis of Sikhism and development of Sikh identity. The Sikhs' early history, their participation in the independence movement, and the status of the Sikh community in post-colonial India are all considered. Second, the chapter examines the history and background of the Sikh diaspora, including its history of migration since the nineteenth century. It also accounts for the diaspora's participation in the Sikh separatist campaign that engulfed

Punjab during the 1980s — exploring the support diaspora members provided the separatist movement from overseas. Third, the chapter accounts for the roots of the Punjab Crisis and events leading up to Operation Blue Star.

BACKGROUND, IDENTITY AND HISTORY OF THE SIKHS

Sikhism is a relatively new religion. It first emerged during the 15th and 16th centuries, when Guru Nanak Dev (1469-1539), born in the Punjab region near Lahore, founded a new spiritual community rooted in religious mysticism — especially the mystics of the Sufi Islamic tradition — and "the search for the heart of religion" (Tully and Jacob 1985: 17). Sikhism stressed the belief in a single God and the equality of mankind. Nanak's philosophy borrowed from many elements of Hinduism and Islam — Nanak for example adopted the Hindu doctrines of reincarnation and karma, and drew inspiration from Islam's monotheistic beliefs and emphasis on brotherhood (Ibid.). However, Nanak abandoned certain traditions deemed morally objectionable, such as caste and worshiping of idols, and "Historians generally agree that Nanak was influenced by the *bhakti* (devotion) movement in north [I]ndia that criticized the religious leadership and many of the beliefs of both Hinduism and Islam of the contemporary times" (Chima 2010: 22; see also Cohen 1997; Tatla 1999).

Over the next two centuries, Nanak's followers established Sikhism as major religion and distinct from Hinduism and Islam. The development of its own important attributes and institutions, such as a religious script called Gurmukhi, a sacred "living" text called the Guru Granth Sahib, communal temples known as "gurdwaras," and the emergence of unique rituals and traditions further differentiated the Sikhs from other religious communities (Chima 2010). The Sikh identity, meanwhile, became strongly and singularly rooted in the distinct religious tradition of the "Khalsa," meaning pure one (Tatla 1999). Beginning in 1699, Sikhs baptized into the Order of the Khalsa adopted social markers distinguishing them from non-Sikhs, which helped to affirm a greater sense of community and uniqueness. To this day, many Sikhs abide by "the five Ks" of the Khalsa as a testimony to their faith and identity, which allows outsiders to tell them apart: (1) the *kes* meaning unkempt hair, (2) the *kasha* or an iron bracelet worn on the right wrist, (3) the *kirpon* or a ceremonial sword that Sikhs are to wear wherever they go, (4) the *kacha,* a distinctive form of breeches, and (5) the *kangha,* a wooden comb (Cohen 1997). All these adoptions serve as powerful symbols of the faith and help to preserve a separate identity for the Sikh community (Chima 2010; Tully and Jacob 1985). The Sikhs have also maintained a distinct language and religion, a high degree of political and social cohesion, and self-awareness of its own "peoplehood" (Chima 2010).

These were important developments for the Sikh community's evolution as a nation because they created specific objective boundary markers clearly designating members of the Sikh community, bringing the Sikhs as a whole a step closer to the realization of a discernably different national community (Eriksen 2002; Sanders 2002). Sikhism is also animated by the "constant fear… of being reabsorbed into Hinduism," which has led ethnic entrepreneurs to bolster boundary definition and boundary maintenance (Chima 2010: 27). However, it has been argued that certain Sikh customs and traits have at times operated paradoxically (Ibid.). Even through the nineteenth century, the boundaries between Sikhism and Hinduism could become blurred due to various factors, including that Sikhism grew partially out of Hinduism, intermarriage between Sikhs and Hindus was common through the 1880s, and Hindu families often brought up their firstborn son as a Sikh. "Thus, boundaries between the two religious 'communities' were quite permeable and, in fact, often overlapped" (Chima 2010: 27). That many Sikhs identify as both Indian and Punjabi has also complicated Sikh identity.

Today, there are four categories of religious commitment within Sikhism, each moving further away from the core ideal of Sikh identity (Chima 2010). The top category is the *Amritdhari* Khalsa, those who have taken the *amrit* baptism and abide by the 5 Ks. Next are *Kheshdhari* Sikhs, who have not taken the *amrit,* but keep unshorn hair. By one estimate, this grouping accounts for somewhere between two-thirds and three-quarters of the population. The third category includes Sahajdhari Sikhs ("those who take the slow path") — referring to Sikhs who identify exclusively with the faith but do not keep unshorn hair. At bottom are a variety of Hindu-Sikh and reformist sects such as the Nirankaris, Radha Swamis, or Nanakpanthis, whose beliefs and customs are considered by orthodox Sikhs to be incongruous with Sikhism.

Sikhs also claim Punjab as their ancestral homeland, which they stake on the Sikhs' historical roots in the region, the presence of several significant Sikh shrines dotting the Punjabi countryside, and Punjab's image as the "cradle" of the Punjab language spoken by most Sikhs (Tatla 1999). Recent studies have argued that the Sikhs claim on Punjab is a recent formulation and that for the majority of Sikh history the territory was not a substantial element of Sikh self-description (Oberoi 1988; Fair 2005). Oberoi (1988) traces the origin of these claims to the 1930s and '40s, when ethnic elites sought to imitate the ongoing political quests of the Hindus and Muslims for their own separate countries and mobilized a narrative of Punjab as the ancient homeland of the Sikhs. Although this argument makes an important point about the way that ethnic communities imagine their own ancestral histories, it is perhaps too dismissive of the emotive connection ethnic members feel about the homeland and ignores the collective mythology and aura that surrounds that terrain. No matter the origin of the myth, Sikhs came to perceive the plains of Punjab as emblematic of the greatness of the Sikh people and the territory that nourished the Punjabi language, Sikh religion and culture. In the words of Tatla (1999: 33): "Punjab commands a mysterious bond; its many songs narrate the region's beauty and its many tragedies."

Sikhs are ordained to follow the teachings of ten "gurus" — historical figures who successively served as leaders of the faith and are primarily responsible for its evolution. Guru Nanak rejected the caste system and instituted the important Sikh tradition of taking *langar*, or communal meals in which people of all backgrounds eat together (Tully and Jacob 1985). Later gurus would also fundamentally shape the Sikh faith. The fifth guru, Arjun Dev (1563-1606), was the first to begin compiling Sikhism's book of sacred scriptures, known then as the Adi Granth and today as the Guru Granth Sahib. Arjun placed the holy texts at the Golden Temple, thus anointing the Amritsar shrine the most sacred in all Sikhism. When the Mogul Emperor Jehangir imprisoned Arjun in Lahore and tortured him to death, he became the first of Sikhism's celebrated martyrs, conferring Sikhism with its militaristic streak. The sixth guru, Hargobind, added to the Golden Temple complex by building the Akal Takht (meaning "immortal throne") adjacent to the Harmandir Sahib, thereby centralizing religious authority in Amritsar. Hargobind also contributed the symbolically resonant image of two swords — one standing for religious authority and the other for temporal power — that has become strongly associated with Sikhism and can be found in most gurdwaras today (Tatla 1999). The tenth guru, Gobind Singh (1666-1708), was especially influential in shaping the Sikhs' modern identity. Gobind ruled not only at a time when the region's Muslim rulers had become openly hostile toward the Sikhs, but also when Sikhs concurrently confronted the threat of reabsorption into Hinduism (Tully and Jacob 1985). Gobind Singh therefore initiated the Order of the Khalsa at Anandpur in 1699, a cadre of followers who strenuously observed the aforementioned "5 Ks," adopted the surname "Singh," meaning *lion* (Women meanwhile took the surname "Kaur" meaning *lioness* or *princess*, and acted as protectors of the faith. Gobind through such actions started many of Sikhism's martial traditions that exist to the present day (Chima 2010). As Tully and Jacob (1985: 21) note, "When Guru Gobind Singh was assassinated in 1708, he left behind him the legend of a poet, preacher and guide, skilled in warfare, courageous, defiant and unbowed, to fire the imagination of future generations of Sikhs."

HISTORY OF THE SIKHS

The next several sections highlight the history of the Sikh population in India and trace the origins of Sikh nationalism and the ethnic separatist movement.

Rise and Fall of the Sikh Golden Era: 1699-1902:

The epoch of Sikh history between 1699 and 1849 fundamentally shaped and inspired later Sikh movements. During these years, the Sikhs became increasingly militarized, fought valiantly against Moghul and Afghan occupiers and expanded their territorial holdings, all which simultaneously nurtured a militant mentality and gave later generations of Sikhs a sense of a golden age. It is to this era that most Sikh nationalists point when they assert that the Sikhs once stood as an independent nation, and this shared belief in their own history also conferred the Sikh people with the sense of destiny and common ties that characterizes so many ethno-nationalist movements (Connor 1994; Varshney 2002, 2003).

During era of Mughal rule of India, successive emperors oppressed and frequently humiliated Sikhs and Hindus alike; the Sikhs under Gobind Singh responded in 1699 by creating the Khalsa and militarizing the community to counter the growing threat. When Gobind was assassinated in 1708, Banda Singh Bahadur, a rising military commander, assumed nominal leadership of the Sikhs. He would become one of Sikhism's revered heroes and martyrs, remembered for leading the struggle against the Moguls and even sacking the Mogul provincial capital of Sirhind in 1710. However, he too was eventually captured and executed.[23] For most of the next century, the Khalsa fought valiantly but were unable to defeat the Mogul armies, and the two sides remained basically deadlocked. By the middle of the eighteenth century, the declining Mogul Empire ceded Punjab to the Afghan ruler Ahmad Shal Abdali. This was the beginning of a difficult and threatening period for the Sikh community. Badali pursued the Sikhs and engaged their armies in two major battles, killing 5,000 in 1746 and nearly wiping out the entire Sikh force in 1762; these two battles are now remembered by the Sikhs as *ghallugharas* or "holocausts" (Tatla 1999; 15). However, few events would haunt the imaginations of Sikhs as the destruction by Abdali's forces of the Golden Temple, in the nineteenth century — in response to the Sikhs attacking his troops and baggage trains — which "[filled] the holy pool with the carcasses of slaughtered cattle" (Tully and Jacob 1985: 21).[24] Later generations of Sikhs would often invoke this traumatic attack when discussing perceived threats to the Sikh community, and it afforded an obvious comparison to the attack on the Golden Temple.

As horrific as these setbacks were to the Sikh community, it made it all the more remarkable — and added to the lore of Sikh mythology — when a one-eyed, illiterate, 21-year

---

[23] Interestingly, the ruling Mogul governors sensed a moment of weakness and sought to deal a fatal blow to the Sikhs, going so far as to demand that their armies bring back their unshaven heads (Tatla 1999). The Khalsa thwarted these efforts, proving to be "adept in the use of arms and trained in the methods of guerrilla warfare" (Kohli 1921-2; qtd. in Jacob and Tully 1985: 21).

[24] The Sikhs did benefit from at least one promising development during that period: Sikh chiefs began meeting annually at Amritsar to resolve differences and set collective tasks, allowing the Sikhs to consolidate as a community and build a more collective identity, and paved the way for Ranjit Singh to expand the Punjab empire (Tatla 1999).

old Sikh soldier named Ranjit Singh in 1799 welded together the various tribes of the Punjab region, defeat the Moguls, and created a Sikh empire stretching from Kashmir and the borders of China in the northeast to the Khyber Pass and frontiers of Sindh in the southwest. Under this Empire of Punjab, over which Ranjit presided as Maharaja, the Sikhs rebuilt and refurbished the Punjabi city of Lahore, which served as the Empire's capital. Amritsar grew into a flourishing center of trade, and Ranjit made his mark on Sikh tradition by rebuilding the Golden Temple complex and encasing the central shrine in gold, providing the temple its namesake (Tully and Jacob 1985). Overall Sikh influence achieved unprecedented reach during this era, and Sikhs today celebrate it not only because the Sikhs established self-rule in Punjab, but also because the empire attested to Sikh might (Cohen 1997). Although the regime eventually collapsed, memories of a sovereign Punjab would live on and become a part of Sikh folklore, and Maharaja Ranjit Singh's nineteenth century kingdom provided modern Sikh leaders with "a particularly salient pool of historical ethnic symbols from which to draw, including the notion of Sikhs being an exceptionally courageous fighting force that once controlled a vast empire in north India" (Chima 2010: 27).

After Ranjit Singh's death in 1839, a brutal succession struggle ensued, creating a disastrous power gap that the British were able to exploit. In 1845, the British invaded Punjab, and by 1849, after many battles and skirmishes, they had defeated the Sikhs and Punjab was formally annexed (Cohen 1997). However, rather than risk further alienation, the British sought to gain favor with the region's Sikh population. The British policy of favoring and recruiting local minorities – part and parcel of "divide and rule" — also ensured that minorities such as the Sikhs of India were presumed more loyal to the European metropole than the colonial unit where they were born. British administrators came to respect the Sikhs and value their soldierly skills, and so it played to the British advantage to encourage Sikhs to preserve their identity. In fact, British army regulations not only permitted Sikhs to wear their beards and turbans, but also would not permit Sikh soldiers from *discontinuing* these practices (Tully and Jacob 1985). As a result, Sikhs spread out across the subcontinent and the world in service of the British Empire, and sided with the British during the Sepoy Mutiny of 1857 (Cohen 1997).[25] The British awarded the Sikhs with pensions, wages, favorable assignments in employment and the army, higher incomes and preferential land policies (Tatla 1999). Over time the Raj developed "a special concern for Punjab's rural peasants, a client-patron relationship whose interests were jealously protected" (Tatla 1999: 16). They allowed the Sikhs to retain partial control of their affairs and instituted development reforms that improved the region's economic fortunes.

In spite of the comparatively generous sponsorship of the British, Sikh identity underwent a crisis during the second half of the nineteenth century due to the perceived dual threats of proselytizing by Christian missionaries and the growing prominence of Hindu groups such as the Aryan Samaj.[26] Sikhs responded to these threats by forming modern organizations such as Singh "Sabhas" (congregations) to educate Sikhs and make them more aware of their religion and cultural heritage (Tully and Jacob 1985; Telford 1992). In 1902, Sikhs started the first explicitly political Sikh organization, Chief Khalsa Diwan, which served as an umbrella for

---

[25] The Sepoy Mutiny began in May 1857 when Indian soldiers rose up against the East Indian Company as a result of various grievances, including the British directive to soldiers to bite off of the tips of their paper cartridges that were greased in animal fat. The Mutiny grew into a series of mutinies and rebellions that would last two years, and led the British in 1858 to formally dissolve the East Indian Company and instituted the British Raj. For a complete accounting of the Mutiny, see Nayar (2007).

[26] The Aryan Samaj believed Punjabi Muslims and Sikhs in an earlier life had been Hindus and thus sought to convert them back to their "true" faith.

Singh Sabhas.[27] By the end of the nineteenth century, Sikhs had largely succeeded in their efforts

to protect their identity, and the establishment of new print media at Amritsar and Lahore further

allowed Sikh reformists to promote a new group consciousness based around the Sikhs' religious

identity and the community's embrace of the Punjabi language and Gurumukhi script (Tatla

1999). The Sikh religious texts are written in Gurmukhi, making the script, according to Chima

(2010: 28), an "especially salient symbol for the Sikhs" – one that has been repeatedly used in

modern day campaigns for Sikh causes. These deeply meaningful symbols provide a substantive

supply of symbolic content that has been used effectively by elites for mobilization.

<u>Political Sikhism and India's Push for Independence:</u>

In the early parts of the twentieth century, Sikh, Hindu, and Muslim political groups began to

embrace the same ideals of nation-ness that were then sweeping across most of Europe's colonial

holdings in Africa and Asia, part of the final phase of nationalism's evolution made possible by

the advent of new technologies (Anderson 1983). In addition, the Sikh community's increasing

national aspirations were due to a confluence of factors. The emergence of Hindu organizations

engaged in "re-purification" campaigns — aimed at persuading Sikhs to "throw away" their Sikh

adornments and "rejoin the Hindu faith" — had also motivated Sikhs to embrace political

activism and reassert the uniqueness of their ethnic identity (Chima 2010). Sikh leaders were

therefore able to create new groups and organizations such as Chief Khalsa Diwan that were

committed to maintaining the Sikh faith; these proved invaluable for mobilizing Sikhs in pursuit

of political goals. At the same time, a number of domestic factors helped weaken the Sikhs'

---

[27] According to Chima (2010), Chief Khalsa Diwan had three functions: 1) to promote the Khalsa identity, primarily through schools and publications, 2) to counteract the proselytizing efforts of Christian missionaries and Hindu organizations taking place, and 3) to represent Sikh interests to the British Crown.

fidelity to the British. From 1914 to 1918, Sikhs returning from the battlegrounds of World War I were forced to cope with many devastating realities, including the state's ruthless suppression of the revolutionary and Bolshevik-aligned Ghadrite movement; the failure of a summer monsoon; the imposition of new taxes; and a deadly strain of influenza that wiped out 100,000 people (Cohen 1997). Deteriorating social and economic conditions were not the only cause for unrest. Racism abounded throughout the British Empire and even in the armed forces. Sikh soldiers were not paid the same as white soldiers during World War I, and privates would refuse to salute higher-ranking Sikh officers (Cohen 1997; Tatla 1999).

The emergence of the Akali movement in the early 1920s for control of Sikhism's most historic shrines animated the Sikh movement and led the ethnic group further down the road toward nationalism.[28] During the standoff, the Akali Dal was founded to coordinate teams of Khalsa volunteers to forcibly capture the disputed shrines. The Shiromani Gurdwara Parbandhak Committee (SGPC) was also founded at this time, and its responsibility was to work in tandem with the Akalis and manage the temples following their acquisition. These two organizations would grow into two of Sikhism's most powerful modern political bodies. The Akali Dal grew into the main political party representing Sikh interests in India's secular democratic system, while the SGPC evolved into a sort of "mini-parliament of the Sikhs," with jurisdiction over gurdwaras in Punjab and other states in northern India (Chima 2010).

---

[28] These gurdwaras had come under the de facto ownership of Hindu merchants and custodians, many of whom failed to upkeep the temples or preserve their sanctity; in the case of the Golden Temple, Sikhs alleged that within its walls idols were being worshipped, pornographic material was freely sold, and visitors were congregating with neighboring brothels (Tully and Jacob 1985). During the Sikhs' campaign, which became known as the Akali Movement, the British initially upheld the legal right of the merchant classes to control the shrines, alienating Sikh activists (Chima 2010). The Sikhs and British eventually came to terms on the status of Sikh shrines via the Gurdwara Act of 1925, which placed control of places of Sikh worship with a government-appointed board made up of Sikhs.

Around the same time, India's Sikh, Hindu, and Muslim communities were beginning to mobilize against British rule, and in 1919 violence erupted in Punjab that would lead to deep unrest in the region, further fraying the relationship between Sikhs and the British. In April 1919, The Akali Dal would evolve into the main political party representing Sikh interests in India's secular democratic system. a British soldier opened fire during a protest in Amritsar, killing 6 people and injuring 30. When news of the casualties spread, mobs formed against British banks and Christian clergy. At least five European civilians were killed in retaliation, and a missionary was also assaulted (Cohen 1997).

What transpired afterward shook the Indian nation and alienated thousands if not millions against British rule. Learning that an illegal meeting was taking place, British troops advanced to its location in a courtyard near the Golden Temple, opening fire on a large, unarmed crowd. When the smoke had cleared, the assault had killed 379 civilians and injured over 2,000 people. The Jallianwala Bagh Massacre had a pronounced effect on how Sikhs viewed self-rule and the homeland. Weeks of severe martial law followed the incident, leading to further Sikh participation in Gandhi and Nehru's campaigns (and actually helped to spark the Akali movement). According to Cohen, the massacre reawakened the Sikh sense of political activism and religious exuberance and energized the Sikh desire for an independent homeland:

The rage of the Sikhs was augmented by the horror felt all over India at this attack on unarmed civilians. An all-India nationalist, rather than sectarian, consciousness was the primary reaction to Amritsar, but the event also marked the reawakening of Sikh political activism and religious enthusiasm. The old litany *raj karey ga Khalsa* (The Khalsa shall rule) was loudly proclaimed again. As it became evident that the British would have to go, Sikhs reasserted their historic 'right' to rule the Punjab, even though they constituted a minority within the area

(Cohen 1997: 111)

Despite these calls for a Sikh state, the Sikhs eventually cast their lot with the Hindu Congress Party in the anti-colonial struggle against British control. Although the Akalis, like the Muslim League, feared they would be overrun in a majority Hindu state, Sikhs still retained their aversion to Indian Muslims, "brought up as they were on stories of the Mughal persecution of the Gurus" (Tully and Jacob 1985: 33). At the dawn of India's independence, Sikhs had therefore positioned themselves as an influential minority in the new Indian state.

Unfortunately, more tragedy awaited the Sikhs before they could take stock of their status in India. Following the British decision in 1947 to offer independence to the subcontinent, the British Raj enlisted the services of a government barrister named Sir Cyril Radcliffe to determine how best to partition Punjab between the newly founded states of India and Pakistan. The challenge at the time of partition was that Punjab under the British Raj was an extremely heterogeneous province with large numbers of Muslims, Sikhs and Hindus. Partition wrought chaos and hardship on all populations living in Punjab, and over half a million people died as a result of the unprecedented level of lawlessness, severe ethnic rioting, and campaigns of ethnic cleansing waged by the various communities. Twelve millions Sikhs, Hindus and Muslims are estimated to have relocated across the border; Hindus and Sikhs rushed to join India, while Muslims flocked westward to Pakistan. Partition forced 40% of all Sikhs to vacate thousands of acres of farming land in Pakistan that had been in the possession of their families for centuries and flee to India. The survival of as many as 140 sacred Sikh shrines and Gurdwaras also serves as a lasting reminder of the flight of the Sikhs (Tully and Jacob 1985; Tatla 1999).

Notwithstanding the immeasurable amount of suffering wrought by partition, there was reason for Sikh leaders to be proud and optimistic as it set out to help chart India's new course. As stated by Tatla (1999: 20): "Through interethnic elite competition, they had clearly demarcated themselves as a separate community, with historic shrines controlled by a representative body, and rituals and ceremonies sharply distinguished from their parent society of Hindus." Ironically, partition had also left the Sikhs geographically more concentrated than before and even forming majorities in some districts. Before independence, Punjab had been 61% Muslim, 26% Hindu, and 13% Sikh; afterward, Punjab had become 61% Hindu and 35% Sikh (Chima 2010). A larger concentration of Sikhs made it easier to unite politically and protect their culture and language. It also transformed the Sikhs' vision of a Punjab homeland into a realistic project (Tatla 1999). However, the Sikhs had also cast their lot with the Hindus, whose reassurance that a secular India would allow Sikhism to thrive had probably enabled the Sikhs to deliver Punjab to India. The Sikh community also demonstrated their commitment to the new Indian state through its continuing tradition of military service. Sikhs as of 1962 constituted almost 40% of the Indian Army's brigadiers and over 45% of its major generals despite comprising fewer than 3% of India's population (Kundu 1994). As India charted its new course, it counted the Sikhs as a loyal and valuable element, despite the fierce independence for which the group had become known.

For those skeptical of a "secular" India (or thought it code for a Hindu majority state), the political party Akali Dal promoted itself as the most capable steward of Sikh interests in the emerging polity. Following independence, the Sikhs had to cope with some new realities. No longer did they benefit from built-in advantages enjoyed under the Raj, such as legislative seat quotas or separate communal electorates. As Chima (2010: 29) notes, "[s]uch arrangements had been instrumental in reaffirming Sikh ethnic identity and providing Sikhs with significant group power in the political process during the British Raj," but within the new and secular Indian state, Sikhs would have to fend for themselves. Thus Akali leaders set out to negotiate significant minority rights and increased autonomy for the Sikhs.

The Akali Dal adopted a dual strategy of trying to negotiate the maximum amount of protections and benefits for the Sikh community, while coordinating agitation campaigns designed to achieve a Sikh majority state. The party achieved relative success in fulfilling the first task.[29] However, the goal of achieving a Sikh majority state within India proved more elusive, in part due to the organization of India's states according to linguistic identity. Following partition, the Sikhs had been coupled with Punjabi-speaking Hindus and formed only a third of Punjab's population. The Sikhs' statewide minority status made it very difficult to influence the center or win elections. During early state elections, the Akali Dal struggled to win seats, gaining only 13 of 126 seats in the state assembly in 1952 and 19 seats in 1962 (Chima 2010). Electoral failure reinforced the need for a Sikh state. The Akalis launched new campaigns for a Punjabi *Suba* ("State") in 1955 and 1961, but their demands were both times portrayed as separatist campaigns and dismissed (Tatla 1999). The party therefore launched a series of *morchas*, or agitations, meant to secure the creation of a Punjabi-speaking state with a large Sikh population.[30]

---

[29] During the initial period of independence from 1947 to 1951, the central government was persuaded to: (1) provide an undisclosed proportion of government positions to Sikhs, (2) guarantee an equal number of seats to Sikhs and Hindus in Punjab's state ministry, and (3) divide Punjab into Punjabi and Hindi-speaking areas, in which the dominant language was used as the medium taught in local schools (Chima 2010).

[30] For example, during one campaign they enlisted tens of thousands of supporters to court arrest (Chima 2010). In 1965, the Akali Dal's unveiled its latest proposal for a Punjabi *Suba* that adopted language calling Punjab the homeland of the Sikhs but proclaiming India as its "motherland," which blunted portrayals of the Sikhs' demands as separatist. The new proposal also portrayed the demand for a

Yet, it was the Indo-Pak War of September 1965, when Sikhs rallied to the support of the state, which finally emboldened the center to consider granting the Sikh community's request. When the war broke out, the Akali Dal suspended its *Suba* campaign to focus its full attention on supporting the war effort; in the battlefield, of course, Sikhs fought valiantly against India's rival. The enthusiastic role that the Akalis assumed helped reaffirm their nationalist credentials and demonstrated their loyalty to India (Chima 2010). After the war, the center endorsed plans to bifurcate Punjab into two smaller states, one of which would be a smaller Punjab where the majority language was Punjabi and that was 60% Sikh and 37% Hindu (Ibid.).

<u>Glimpses of Power and Seeds of Separatism: 1965-1978</u>:

More than fifteen years into India's existence, the Sikhs had reached their goal of a majority state, which not only led to communal pride but also newfound electoral success.[31] Rather than completely resolve tensions between Sikhs and the center, however, the agreement bred new tensions and complaints based on a number of related decisions taken by the center, among them the government's decision to assume control of certain river dam projects and to classify the city of Chandigarh as a Union territory rather than Punjab's capital. The government also resisted Sikh demands to incorporate a number of Punjabi-speaking areas into the new state. These actions infuriated the Akali Dal, which issued new demands and publicized their grievances (Chima 2010; Tatla 1999). At the same time, the Akalis in the post-Punjabi Suba era continued

reorganized Punjab state according to linguistic, rather than religious criteria, thereby conforming to the method that India had used to set up its federal system (Tatla 1999).

[31] The Akali Dal won 24 seats to Congress' 48 in the next round of elections, preventing Congress from a state majority for the first time. In 1967, the Akalis for the first time joined a coalition government controlling the state ministry, while Congress found itself in the opposition. The Akali Dal and Congress would trade places the next two elections, and throughout the decade they continued to butt heads over state-center issues as well as other disagreements. These included control of gurdwaras in Delhi and Congress's attempt to amend parts of the 1925 Sikh Gurdwara Act (Chima 2010).

using a largely secular strategy to increase its appeal to non-Sikh Punjabis, whose votes the party needed in order to stay in power, despite the risk of alienating staunch Sikh nationalists (Telford 1992). These tensions lingered for the next decade, eventually evolving into demands for autonomy.

In 1973, the Akali Dal approved a list of political demands known as the Anandpur Sahib Resolution. A widely encompassing Sikh manifesto, the Anandpur Sahib Resolution reasserts that the Akali Dal is responsible for the "sovereignty" of the Sikhs. It makes a number of specific demands for greater autonomy, including control of Chandigarh and Punjabi-speaking areas outside of Punjab, control of various dam projects, and a redistricting of river waters flowing through the state. The resolution does not call for independence, but demands that the center devolve significant power to the Sikhs to control their own affairs (Chima 2010: 47). The resolution was not initially successful, but in future years the document would serve as a primary point of reference for Sikh demands.

It was also during this time that a former finance minister of the Punjab government, Dr. Jagjit Singh Chohan, first publicly articulated the need for an independent Sikh homeland. In October 1971, he took out a half-page advertisement in the New York Times, declaring that the Congress Party had misled Sikhs at the time of independence. However, his efforts mostly concentrated on persuading members of the Sikh diaspora in Britain, Canada, the United States and Pakistan (Cohen 1997). Most Sikhs, who still felt great affection for India at this point, deemed his activity to be anti-Indian (Tatla 1999: 103).

In the mid-1970s, events would unfold that would foreshadow the coming tensions between Sikhs and the center that would eventually help underscore the threat that Sikhs increasingly felt as an ethnic community at the hands of the Hindu majority. In 1975, Prime

Minister Indira Gandhi responded to a corruption conviction by declaring a national emergency across the whole India, allowing her essentially to rule by decree. Like most of the political opposition, the Akalis saw the move as a blatant and unprecedented power grab, but when the Akalis, skilled as they were in the *morcha,* launched a "Save Democracy" campaign, it became "the nation's only sustained, large-scale agitation against the Emergency" (Chima 2010: 33). Hundreds of Akali activists were arrested and imprisoned.

When new elections were called, voters dealt Congress a historic loss and relegated it to the national minority for the first time. A new coalition government led by the Hindu nationalist Bharatiya Janata Party (BJP) assumed control of India, and the BJP soon invited the Akalis to help form a coalition government, the first time that the Akali Dal would have a governing role nationally (Chima 2010). Heading into 1978, Sikh political prospects appeared to be promising.

SIKH SEPARATISM AND THE DEVELOPING INSURGENCY: 1978-1983

The insurgency engulfing Punjab in the 1980s became an unprecedented crisis in India's history, no less shocking because the insurgency took place in a part of India that had remained relatively tranquil ever since partition. Prior to the escalating violence, Punjab was most widely reputed as the "granary of India" before and during the Green Revolution. The Sikhs, meanwhile, had been considered "well-integrated into the 'national mainstream'" before the conflict began, and the fact that thousands were enlisted in the Indian army and had fought valiantly against Pakistan only increased their prestige (Chima 2010: 3). Yet, the Sikhs had maintained their communal identity and distinctiveness from Hindus ever since the founding of the Indian state. However, it was only after Sikhs became convinced that the Indian government had badly mismanaged Sikh political and religious demands that they began to take up arms (Fair 2008).

Although it goes beyond the focus of this research to theorize what caused the crisis, it is useful to note the varying interpretations that have emerged in the scholarly literature. Scholars have sought to explain the crisis according to many dynamics, including regional and socio-economic factors, Marxist interpretations, evolving divisions in India's center-local relationship, outside conspiracies, and intensifying Sikh nationalism leading to increased perceptions of discrimination by the Indian state (Chima 2010; Tatla 1999).[32] The insurgency's relative decline after 1987 has received comparatively less attention, but scholars have explained it according to at least four interpretations: (1) India's improvement in implementing effective counter-terror measures, (2) references to Punjab's social structure — for example, that *Jat* Sikh political culture, which stresses personal power and honor, was hardly ideal to sustain a "corporatist" separatist struggle, (3) the Indian government's "managed disorder" of the insurgency, in which the center was able to loosely and cynically control affiliated insurgent groups, and discarded them when they no longer proved useful, and (4) patterns of political leadership that saw elements of the insurgency relatively united (and the opposition divided) during the movement's rise, and internally divided and fragmented in later years allowing the state to regain the upper hand (Chima 2010: 6-7). It is also important to note that the increasing resonance and public support of the Sikh insurgency among the Sikh community coincided with the decline of moderating influences such as the Akali Dal. A lack of constraining forces is something that is often seen in the developmental story of an extremist movement.

The beginning of Sikh extremism in Punjab can be traced to a series of skirmishes that took place between the Sikh and Nirankari communities in 1978. The Nirankaris are a sect of

---

[32] A number of scholarly works and commentaries exemplify these various explanatory perspectives on the explosion of Sikh nationalism during the 1980s. See for example Kapur 1987; Singh 1987; Koehn 1991; Telford 1992; Chima 1994; Singh 1996; Crossette 2004; Singh 2007; and Bakke 2010.

Sikhism whose faith in a living guru conflicts with Sikhism's monotheistic beliefs and opposition to idol worship. Sikhs and Nirankaris had clashed periodically at least since the 1950s, but tensions would dramatically escalate on April 13, 1978 in Amritsar, when a procession of Sikhs confronted Nirankari members attending the latter group's convention. During the confrontation, bodyguards for the Nirankari guru shot and killed 13 of the Sikhs, four of whom were affiliated with an orthodox Sikh organization called Damdami Taksal and the remainder to the Khalsa group Akhand Kirtani Jatha (Chima 2010). As a result of the incident, tensions between the two communities escalated rapidly, and the Sikhs staged massive demonstrations in Amritsar, leading to more unrest. The situation deteriorated further when the Sikh *jathedar*, a priest that controls the highest seat of religious authority in Sikhism (the Akal Takht), issued an especially volatile religious edict called a *hukamnama*.[33] Although the *jathedar* later clarified that the edict was not meant to imply violence, militant Sikh groups such as the Babbar Khalsa interpreted it as an authorization to use violence to protect the faith and avenge the deaths of the 13 killed at the Nirankari clash (Chima 2010).[34] The Sikhs focused their anger at the central government, which it felt had acted too slowly to punish the Nirankaris involved in the incident.

Importantly, these events also denoted the rise of a charismatic Sikh priest named Sant Jarnail Singh Bhindranwale, a stirring orator who was the head of Damdami Taksal. As the head

---

[33] Describing Nirankaris as "enemies of dharma (religion) and Sikhism" the *hukamnama* urged Sikhs to use "all appropriate means" to prevent the sect from flourishing.

[34] The Babbar Khalsa was an especially violent and orthodox group that first grew in 1981 and drew its membership from ex-servicemen, policemen, and various Sikh organizations. Though it operated against the Indian government, the Babbar Khalsa actually opposed other Sikh militant leaders such as Sant Jarnail Singh Bhindranwale, and deviated from him strategically and ideologically. It was less committed to idea of establishing an independent Khalistani state, but was willing to use violence to enforce its orthodox version of Sikh law (Fair 2008).

of a Sikh teaching institution that traced its history to the tenth guru, Bhindranwale enjoyed a significant degree of instant credibility as a Sikh religious and political leader (Fair 2008). Bhindranwale counted among his most ardent followers the Sikh farmers of the agricultural *Jat* class, as well as young men affiliated with the All India Sikh Students Federation; both of whom were "concerned with the protection of Sikh culture and religion and the plight of small forms in Punjab's modernizing economy" (Bakke 2010: 237). Ironically, it was the desires of Indira Gandhi and Congress to sow division in the Akali ranks and solidify support among Hindus in northern India that fueled Bhindranwale's rise (Tatla 1999). In an effort to illuminate the Akalis' timidity and moderation, Indira's son Sanjay and Congress politician and future Indian President Giani Zail Singh propped up the militant Bhindranwale, which proved a tremendous miscalculation as it allowed Bhindranwale and his brand of militancy to gain extraordinary popularity among certain sections of the Sikh population (Telford 1992; Fair 2008).[35]

From 1979 to 1981, Bhindranwale, Babbar Khalsa, Dal Khalsa, and the Panth Khalsa all competed against each other with the more moderate Akali Dal for political influence and the loyalty of Punjabi Sikhs. Though the radicals lost badly when they contested SGPC elections against Akali candidates in 1979, support for "Bhindranwale's candidates" continued to grow. Meanwhile, Akali infighting and leadership rivalries devastated the Akali Dal's fragile alliance

---

[35] Bhindranwale was not the only recipient of support from elements of the out-of-power Congress Party. As communal unrest took place in Punjab, elements of Congress, including Sanjay Gandhi, and former Punjab Chief Minister (and later Indian President) Giani Zail Singh, saw several opportunities to sow discord in the ranks of their rivals the Akalis. Thus, elements in Congress provided start-up funds to several Sikh extremist groups as part of a cynical ploy to destabilize the Akali Dal and improve the Punjab electoral prospects of Congress (Chima 2010). One such group was Dal Khalsa, formed in 1978 to "liberate" Sikhs from Hindu control. It is important to note, however, that its activities were primarily non-violent and mainly consisted of raising awareness through seminars and conferences. A second group was the Panth Khalsa, which championed the idea of a Sikh independent state. The most hazardous move by far, however, was the dalliance between Congress and Bhindranwale.

with Janata. Right as Sikh extremist elements were gaining strength, the Sikhs' primary political party and source of moderation was experiencing a crisis of leadership (Chima 2010).

Eventually, Akali political paralysis proved self-destructive. In 1980, elections returned Congress to power in Punjab as well as at the center. Indira Gandhi was once again prime minister, and Congress once again controlled the political fortunes of Punjab. In the aftermath of its defeat, the Akali Dal split into factions, and over the next few years these ruptured groups managed to accomplish little but ethnically "outbid" each other via demand-making and political agitation against the central government. The net effect of the Akalis' incompetence and disunity was to increase the overall appeal of Sikh radicals and extremists, which gained increasing momentum by filling the power vacuum left by the quarrelling Akalis.

The actions of the militants soon grew bolder and indicated they were growing more hardline. In 1979, the Shiromani Gurdwara Prabandhak Committee (SGPC), without the required approval from Delhi, allowed a group run by Dr. Jagjit Singh Chohan, the former government minister committed to creating a separate Sikh state, to install a radio transmitter at the Golden Temple to broadcast the *gurbani* (Sikh scriptures and religious hymns) and *kirtan* (devotional hymns). The messages only carried a few hundred yards, but the fact that the SGPC had defied the central government signaled the militancy's growing influence. The following year, Chohan's group openly called for independence and changed its name to the National Council of Khalistan. In 1981, Dal Khalsa activists distributed new passports, stamps, and currency; at a march later that year, they raised pro-Khalistan flags for the first time (Chima 2010).[36] The separatist movement was gaining political strength and wider support across Punjab.

---

[36] Both events received widespread media attention, leading to speculation that Congress ministers had facilitated coverage of these events to put even greater pressure on the Akalis.

<u>Escalation of Militant Violence:</u>

Over the next several years, sectarian violence in Punjab became more pronounced, leading to the highest level of communal tensions between Sikhs and Hindus since independence. This outbreak underscores the role security in determining ethnic violence (Horowitz 2000; Demmers 2012). As the Sikh population felt increasingly threatened by the Hindu majority partly as a result of the Indian government's failure to take action against the Nirankaris and partly due to India's own increasing nationalism, Sikhs felt increasingly vulnerable and made more demands to ensure their security. These demands were hardly uniform; while some sought to establish a new Sikh state, others favored greater autonomy within India and a return to religious orthodoxy. For his part, Sant Jarnail Singh Bhindranwale did not explicitly support independence; however, his exact thoughts on the subject could be extremely opaque. His standard reply was, "I am neither for independence nor against it, but if I am offered it I will not refuse it" (Tully and Jacob 1985: 129). In a speech to supporters, Bhindranwale framed the issue this way:

> Brothers, I don't oppose it nor do I support it. We are silent. However, one thing is definite, if this time the Queen of India [Indira Gandhi] does give it to us, we shall certainly take it. We won't reject it. We shall not repeat the mistake of 1947. As yet we do not ask for it… [W]e like to live in India. Indira should tell us whether she wants to keep us or not. (Chima 2010: 91)

Notwithstanding this mixed bag of demands from the various elements, the ambition and capability of the combined Sikh militancy increased dramatically during this period, and its portfolio of tactics — which grew to include sabotage, political assassination, plane hijackings and the desecration of religious symbols — also served to highlight the Akali Dal's political inefficacy and the central government's loss of control.

A common thread between several of the attacks appeared to be the involvement of Bhindranwale, who had grown into the spiritual and nominal figurehead of the Sikh militancy.[37] In April 1980, Sikh militants committed their highest profile attack to that point, assassinating the Nirankari guru, Baba Gurbachan Singh, in New Delhi. Followers of Bhindranwale were suspected of carrying out the hit, but Bhindranwale managed to avoid arrest. A year later, Bhindranwale organized a massive march in Amritsar attended by an estimated 20,000 people, many carrying Khalistan flags. The Sikh procession confronted a Hindu march and chaos ensued, leading to the first significant communal violence between Hindus and Sikhs since the Punjabi Suba movement (Chima 2010).[38] In September 1981, Bhindranwale was again implicated in the assassination of a high profile figure, this time newspaper editor Lala Jagat Narain, recognized as an important Hindu leader and outspoken critic of the Akali Dal. The police issued a warrant for Bhindranwale's arrest, but by the they sought him out at his Chando Kalan location in the neighboring state of Haryana, he had escaped to his gurdwara in Mehta Chowk, located outside Amritsar.[39] The next month, Bhindranwale turned himself into police, but not before delivering a fiery speech to 75,000 followers assembled outside his gurdwara. His supporters then clashed with the police, leading to the death of eighteen protestors.

In the remaining weeks of October, Sikh extremists hijacked an Indian Airlines plane, derailed a goods train traveling through Punjab, and set off a series of bomb blasts (Chima 2010).

---

[37] Since 1978, Bhindranwale had managed to cultivate many allies, including various Sikh religious and political leaders, personnel within the SGPC and the All India Sikh Students Foundation (AISSF) (Fair 2008).

[38] Bhindranwale's protest was intended to buttress Sikh demands to ban tobacco sale in Amritsar, which Hindus had adamantly opposed – since tobacco is taboo to Sikhs, the tobacco ban adversely affected Hindu shopkeepers and merchants.

[39] It has been speculated that at this point Bhindranwale turned on his Congress handlers, after learning that the police in Chando Kalan had roughed up his followers and burned copies of the Granth Sahib and texts of his sermons (Chima 2010).

For its part, the Akali Dal attempted to show solidarity with the increasingly popular Bhindranwale, threatening to wage a campaign of civil disobedience unless Bhindranwale was released. Under extraordinary pressure, the government released Bhindranwale in October 1981. By this point, his defiance had essentially made him "a household name" in Punjab (Chima 2010: 65). Many Sikhs took pride in one of their own standing up to the Indian government, demanding justice for those whom the Nirankaris killed and increased religious rights that would more ably protect Sikhism. Bhindranwale despite his likely stewardship of some of the militant violence had also assumed a spiritual leadership role, espousing his orthodox Sikh views in lengthy sermons and advising Punjabi Sikhs to abandon tobacco, alcohol and other vices and return to the true Sikh faith. The mythology that would surround Bhindranwale at the end of his life and connect him in the minds of his followers to Sikhism's historic leaders was beginning to take shape.

The only chance for avoiding further escalation now rested with the possibility of a political settlement between the Akali Dal and the central government. The Akalis entered into several rounds of talks with Indira Gandhi's government, entering negotiations with a revised list of 15 religious and political demands revolving around "the distribution of river waters, the status of Chandigarh, and the inclusion of Punjabi-speaking areas into Punjab" (Chima 2010: 66-7). All these issues proved contentious. The Akalis and Congress could reach no compromise, and by April 1982, with the talks hopelessly broken down, the Akali Dal announced it would resume its agitation activity.

Throughout the remainder of that year, the militant groups intensified their campaigns and increasingly sought confrontation with the Indian government, hijacking two more Indian Airlines flights and attempting to assassinate the Chief Minister of Punjab, Darbara Singh

(Chima 2010). Following the arrest of AISSF president and close ally Bhai Amrik Singh in connection with an attack on a Nirankari leader, Bhindranwale launched his own *morcha* calling for Amrik Singh's release, which attracted impressive support from peasants and farmers in the Sikh community. Attempting to piggy-back on the effort, the Akali Dal launched its own agitation, endorsed by Bhindranwale, called the *Dharam Yudh morcha*, meaning religious war or war of righteousness. As part of the campaign, party activists courted arrest every day trying to overflow Punjab's jails (Chima 2010). Meanwhile, symbolic acts of defiance led still to more atrocities, and certain sectarian Hindu groups adopted more extremist tactics. Dal Khalsa activists placed the heads of two severed cows outside a Hindu temple to protest government policies; in retaliation, Hindu communalists raided several gurdwaras and desecrated their sacred texts. Volumes of the Guru Granth Sahib were found partially burned, and Hindus placed cigarettes in the Akal Takht and a number of gurdwaras in Delhi, sparking huge protests and more communal violence.

During the summer of 1982, police allegedly began torturing detainees and were reputed to have adopted "faked encounter" tactics, where security forces eliminated suspects in custody but claimed that they had been killed during armed standoffs. Also that summer, Bhindranwale's militants initiated a new campaign of targeted assassination against police officers. Their combined tactics transformed the Sikh agitation into a "bloody and brutal 'mini-war' between Bhindranwale's followers and the Punjab police, [involving] an escalating cycle of killing and counter-killings, [that] would continue unmitigated for the next several years" (Chima 2010: 68).

In July 1982, Sant Jarnail Singh Bhindranwale and his lieutenants, as well as a number of members of Babbar Khalsa, entered the Golden Temple complex and took refuge following the arrest of the Bhai Amrik Singh, the president of AISSF and one of Bhindranwale's close allies

(Chima 2010). Then on December 15, 1983, Bhindranwale abruptly abandoned the residential areas outside the temple and moved into rooms adjacent to the Akal Takht, deep within the complex (Ibid).[40] If the Indian government intended to arrest Bhindranwale, it would now have to order security forces deep into the Golden Temple complex, an act considered by most Sikhs to be sacrilege.[41]

Relations between Sikhs and Hindus became even more frayed following a number of political developments brought on by the Akalis' political shortcomings and the central government's failure to manage Sikh demands.[42] A year later, in October 1983, extremists hijacked a bus, singled out Hindu passengers, and shot six of them dead. This brutal attack shocked the entire country and caused thousands of Indians to seriously question the loyalty of Sikhs for the first time. It also led to dramatic action by Indira Gandhi, who promptly sacked the state government, declared Punjab a "disturbed area," imposed direct rule, and ordered the government to round up 4,000 suspected extremists for questioning. The Akali Dal condemned the attacks, but questioned the government's motive and heavy-handed tactics that followed. For

---

[40] Bhindranwale's move to the Akal Takht was actually motivated by a feud between his followers and Babbar Khalsa, which was angered that Bhindranwale's men were receiving credit for some of their attacks. Babbar Khalsa ordered Bhindranwale and his followers to vacate the premises, but rather than leave entirely Bhindranwale surprised the Golden Temple leadership and elected to move deeper into the complex, to the Akal Takht. See Chima (2010: 86-7)

[41] It should be noted that Bhindranwale and the militants were able to base themselves inside the Golden Temple only because key Sikh institutions such as the SGPC, the All India Sikh Students Foundation (AISSF), and some members of the Akali Dal sanctioned the move, either willingly or under threat of coercion (Fair: 2008).

[42] In October 1982, Indira Gandhi reneged on two agreements with the Akali Dal, deeply embarrassing the party and further strengthening the militancy over the moderates. The Akalis' response was to agitate in front of the Asian Games held that year in Delhi, but their efforts were thwarted by multiple checkpoints that profiled and discriminated against Sikhs en route to the games, a moment that Chima (2010: 73) cites as when Punjabi Sikhs "previously unsympathetic to both the Akali *morcha* [non-violent political agitation] and Bhindranwale began actively sympathizing with them... having experienced humiliation by the government first hand."

his part, Bhindranwale also condemned the massacre, but wondered why the killing of 200 Sikhs by Punjab police had not engendered a similar outcry (Chima 2010).

Following several rounds of failed talks in 1983, the central government and Akali Dal entered into "secret" talks in the early months of 1984; by February, these discussions appeared to be bearing fruit. Unfortunately, the eruption of more communal violence in Punjab and neighboring Haryana forced the parties to call off the negotiations, which never resumed. More rioting and attacks in Haryana that month resulted in the death of more than a dozen Sikhs as well as the torching of several gurdwaras, while Sikh militants targeted and killed Hindus suspected of belonging to sectarian organizations. During the last week of February 1983 alone, the death toll reached more than 60, making it the worst week of Hindu-Sikh violence in recent memory (Chima 2010).

CONCLUSION

This chapter has sought both to summarize the most salient issues leading to the development of Sikh separatism and to trace the growth of Sikh nationalism leading up to Operation Blue Star. In sketching an outline of Sikh history, from its early beginnings in the fifteenth century to the rise of the Sikh separatist movement that first emerged as a growing political force in the 1970s and morphed into insurgency in the early '80s, the aim of this chapter has been to provide much needed context to comprehend the political significance and symbolic weight of Operation Blue Star, described and analyzed in the next chapter.

OPERATION BLUE STAR

A defining moment in the history of the conflict took place in 1984, when the Indian government executed Operation Blue Star, a massive military operation ordered by Prime Minister Indira Gandhi to forcibly remove Sikh militants taking refuge in Sikhism's most revered shrine, the Golden Temple in Amritsar. The operation lasted for three days in the face of fierce resistance; when the smoke had finally cleared, the temple complex was badly damaged, and hundreds of civilians had been killed. The event horrified Sikh ethnic communities scattered across the world. Blue Star served as a major catalyst in turning Sikhs against the Indian state, and led to political crisis throughout the country, including the assassination of Prime Minister Indira Gandhi four months later. The communal rioting that ensued after Gandhi's death, in which Hindu mobs targeted and killed thousands of Sikhs, left the entire Sikh population around the world disillusioned with the Indian state. Sikhs would come to see the attack as an unforgiveable act of sacrilege by the Indian government, and it would lead to unprecedented levels of chaos in India. This chapter examines details and most salient features of Operation Blue Star. Using the framework developed in chapter 3, it qualifies the episode as a traumatic event and focuses particular attention on the relative levels of physical and symbolic violence. Finally, this chapter assesses the initial impact on the Sikh diaspora, a topic that the next chapter will investigate in much greater depth by relying on structured interviews with diaspora Sikhs.

EVOLUTION OF THE SIKH DIASPORA

It is important to preface discussion of the Sikh diaspora reaction to Operation Blue Star, and its response to events in Punjab more generally, by providing an overview of history and migration of the Sikh diaspora. A rough estimate of the total Sikh population in the world today, including India, provided by the CIA World Factbook (2013) is roughly 24.5 million people. Although the majority of Sikhs live in Punjab and adjacent northern Indian states, more than a million Sikhs reside outside of India, and of these approximately half reside in Britain (500,000), Canada (150,000), and the United States (125,000) (Tatla 1999; Fair 2008). To understand how the Sikhs came to found significant ethnic communities in Britain and North America, we must briefly expound on the history of Sikh migration, which took place in at least two phases: colonial emigration, and postcolonial emigration (Tatla 1999).[43]

This history of global Sikh migration got its start in 1849, when the British took control of Punjab and immediately looked to take advantage of the Sikhs' military and combat skills. In response to preferential British policies, which in turn was motivated by the reputation of the Sikhs as skilled warriors, thousands of Sikhs enlisted in the British Colonial Army and traveled throughout the world in service of the British Empire. From 1858 to the first World War, the British deployed thousands of Sikhs to the far reaches of its colonial holdings, including stations in the Far East, Mediterranean, British African colonies and protectorates, and in Europe (Tatla 1999; Cohen 1997). According to Tatla (1999), the romanticized adventures told by Sikh soldiers upon their return, combined with the fashionable residences they were able to afford on a

---

[43] A third wave of migration can be said to have taken place after 1984, when violence and instability forced thousands of Sikhs to flee Punjab and resettle abroad, frequently where diaspora communities were already established

soldier's salary, inspired future generations of Sikhs to embrace the same trailblazing spirit and to envision a future beyond the fields of Punjab for the first time.

In the 1860s, Sikhs began enlisting to work in the Far East as independent laborers; for the rest of the century, Sikhs would migrate all over the region in pursuit of economic opportunity such as in the sugar cane industry, or to join local police services.[44] Tatla (1999) has been able to document the Sikh population growth that followed a number of these journeys; for example, the migration of a hundred Sikhs to Hong Kong in 1867 to join the local police service founded a small Sikh presence of 700 in southern China that constitute a major segment of the Hong Kong police service by 1939. Likewise, a small contingent of Sikhs who went to Malaya in 1873 to defeat Chinese insurgents would establish enough of an overseas presence to allow later population waves of Sikhs to work in the tin mines. In fact, Malaya became an important staging point for thousands of Sikhs on the move further east — to Thailand, Australia, Fiji, and New Zealand. As the early Sikh diaspora communities grew, so too did the overall number of Sikhs migrating out of Punjab. For the entire period of 1865-1940, an estimated 30,000-45,000 Sikhs migrated to Malaysia and 25,000-30,000 to Singapore, and between 1890 and 1910, at least 5,000 Sikhs moved to Australia, 2,000 to New Zealand, and more than 1,200 to Fiji (Cohen 1997).[45]

---

[44] Tatla emphasizes that this early generation of Sikh independent laborers were ill suited for their work given the fierce independence and combativeness of the Sikh identity. For example, the British handlers of one group complained that these Punjabis were "unsuited" for the work as they were, according to one planter in the West Indies, "very objectionable... refused to work in the fields, and nearly all have been unruly and troublesome"; Another remarked with apparent surprise that "Sikhs were an unusual group in the India emigration: they were prepared to fight for their rights" (Tinker, 1976: 29; cited in Tatla, 1999: 47).

[45] Each estimate represents the bottom number of a provided range.

During the same era, a smaller but significant number of Sikh soldiers and laborers relocated to Britain's colonial holdings in eastern Africa. Thousands traveled to Kenya and Uganda to work as railroad laborers or in the local security forces, while a far smaller cohort enlisted into the East African Rifles unit based in Coast Province, helping to put down a mutiny by Sudanese troops in 1895. The establishment of small outposts for skilled workers in Nairobi and Mombasa laid the seed for the gradual growth of a Sikh population in Kenya, where the number of Sikhs increased from 324 in 1911, to approximately 1,600 in 1921, to 10,000 in 1948, and to more than 21,000 in 1960. Most Sikhs departed East Africa after the various colonies achieved independence from Britain in the mid-twentieth century, many relocating to the United Kingdom (Tatla 1999: 51).

By the turn of the twentieth century, Sikhs had spread throughout East Africa and the Pacific Rim, and had also established small settlements in the Middle East (Cohen 1997). North America was next. Sikhs in the early twentieth century succeeded in establishing small settlements in the frontiers of western Canada and the United States. The first known arrival of Sikhs in North America was in 1887, when a Sikh regiment visited British Columbia before returning to Punjab after a long deployment. Early Sikh communities in western Canada experienced solid growth: the number of Sikhs in British Columbia increased from 300 in 1903 to well over 5,000 in 1908. Unfortunately for the Sikhs, the early years of twentieth century frontier life coincided with an uptick in racial tensions, and Canada passed a series of discriminatory immigration laws that would last to the end of World War II. As a result, Sikhs were pressured to leave Canada, and thousands crossed into the United States, working primarily in the lumber industry, on the Pacific Railways, or as roaming farm laborers. Over the next two decades, Sikhs rapidly settled mostly in California — where the Sikh population grew from only a few hundred in 1904 to 10,000 by 1923 — but also in Washington and Oregon. However, the impact of America's own draconian immigration laws — including the US Supreme Court's decision in 1923 in *US v. Thind,* in which the Court ruled Indians although white in an anthropological sense were not in a popular sense, and therefore were ineligible for immigration and naturalization (Menon 1995) — dramatically downsized the migration of Sikhs to the US. By 1947, the number of Sikhs in the US had dwindled to about 3,000 (Tatla 1999).

Following the end of World War II, an unprecedented wave of Sikh migration to Britain and North America began that would last for two decades. The sudden burst of transmigration could be linked to several factors. First, the 1948 partitioning of Punjab dislocated many Sikhs from their ancestral homes, and the trauma of partition prompted many to emigrate outside of India, rather than resettle elsewhere in India. Second, after World War II the United States and Canada finally relaxed their respective standards for accepting immigrants, alluring thousands of Sikhs who already had family members residing there. Third, Britain — which also reformed its immigration laws during this time — absorbed most of the Sikh labor force that was relocating from recently independent African countries, where new governments were not as likely to adopt policies favoring the Sikhs. In fact, the number of Sikhs who migrated to London and other northern English cities assured Britain with the largest overseas population of Sikhs outside of India. These highly skilled migrants — who had departed post-colonial Africa out of fear that new nationalist governments would not treat their Sikh minorities as had the British — soon became the most affluent section of the Sikh Diaspora (Biswas 2004).

When the United States relaxed its own immigration standards with the passage of the Luce-Cellar bill in 1946 — thereby removing Asian Indians from its "Barred Zone" — thousands of Sikh migrants emigrated to the US. They settled in California where a sizable Sikh presence already existed, and went to work in the rural valley as farmers and laborers, and also in the East Coast's more emigrant-friendly urban corridor (Tatla 1999). Yuba City was a case in point. A peach-growing community with a climate and rural setting evoking the Punjabi countryside, this northern California town in the valley saw its Sikh population grow from 400 Sikhs in 1948 to 6,000 by 1981. Yuba has grown into one of the most widely recognizable locations in the Sikh diaspora, with annual parades and festivals that attract Sikhs worldwide. One of its most famous residents, a Sikh businessman named Didar Singh Bains, helped found the World Sikh Organization and would become its chief spokesperson.

More recently, Sikhs branched out beyond the California and New England regions, developing a significant presence in the Mid-Atlantic region and also making inroads in the South and Midwest (Tatla 1999). By 1980, the Sikh population had grown to 60,000; by 1990, it had increased to 180,000. As Sikhs have become more established in the United States, their upward mobility has also improved, bolstered in part by increased education and the absorption of Indian emigrants who were more highly skilled. The end result has been the ongoing transformation of American Sikhs from rural farmers and day laborers to urban professionals and skilled workers (Tatla 1999). However, to imply that Sikhs have reached a point of assimilation that it has divorced them from their social and cultural roots in Punjab would be false. Rather, diaspora Sikhs have sought to reproduce in their homes and social networks the norms and values of their culture. According to Tatla (1999: 63), overseas Sikhs have maintained "a complex web of exchanges with the Punjab in an ongoing process of mutual dependence." Cheaper air travel, improved communication, and the increasing availability of media have also enhanced connections between Sikhs and the homeland. Punjab has remained at the center of Sikh identity, even as Sikh dispersal has created "multiple centers of Sikh identity production that vie for legitimacy and authenticity" (Fair 2008: 131). As a result, Sikh cultural elements remain embedded in the diaspora's collective identity, while local and national influences also shape and formulate the experiences and environment of the diaspora Sikh.

A TRAUMATIC EVENT IN PUNJAB

The Golden Temple is a rectangular complex made up of fortified walls, surrounding a large pool of sacred water called a *sarowar*, and the Harmandir Sahib, which is the inner sanctum encased in gold that sits in the middle of that pool and serves as the namesake of the complex. The temple perimeter has four doors instead of one, constructed to symbolize Sikhism's openness to all four of the caste divisions of Hindu society (Tully and Jacob 1985). The Harmandir Sahib houses the sacred scripture Guru Granth Sahib, and serves as the inspiration for the name of the complex. A walkway called a *parikrama* surrounds the sacred pool and inner sanctum; by tradition, pilgrim worshipers walk along the *parikrama* around the Harmandir before lining up along a causeway to enter the shrine. Opposite the Harmandir Sahib, sitting at the other end of the *parikrama*, is the Akal Takht, meaning "timeless" or "immortal" throne. It serves as the highest seat of religious authority and symbolizes the endowment of divine powers on the Khalsa (Tatla 1999). The temple is located in a densely populated section of Amritsar, made up of a hostel complex, restaurants, bazaars, and buildings and temple-associated offices.

The objective of Operation Blue Star was to wrest control of the Golden Temple from Bhindranwale and the militants, who had taken refuge there in July 1982 and over the next two years fortified and consolidated their control over the temple complex. The Indian army was responsible for conducting the operation, with support from Punjab police and paramilitary services. On the night of June 3, 1984, the national army moved into Punjab and enforced a statewide curfew. Over 70,000 armed service personnel, seeking to cut Punjab off from the rest of the country, halted all transportation in and out of the state, expelled journalists, forbid foreign global media from entering, and shut down all phone communication (Fair 2008). The army encircled the Golden Temple right as the martyrdom anniversary of the 5th guru, Arjun Dev, was underway; as a result, thousands of Sikh pilgrims were effectively trapped inside (Chima 2010). On June 4, leaders of the Akalis engaged in a last-ditch effort to convince Bhindranwale to leave voluntarily. The army briefly lifted the curfew, allowing Akali leaders to reason with Bhindranwale a final time, but Bhindranwale again refused (Chima 2010).[46] The army then commenced military action meant to "soften up" the Golden Temple's fortifications, in preparation for a full nighttime raid.

The essence of the military's plan was to isolate the hostel complex from the Golden Temple complex, then to use commando operations to storm the Golden Temple (Tully and Jacob 1985). Tanks were only to be used as platforms for machine-gun fire. However, there was little preparation by the Indian government on how to be sensitive to the sacredness of the shrine, with the exception that the government generally stated its desire to avoid damage to the Harmandir Sahib if possible (Fair 2008: 46). Prior to the operation, the government ordered the army to use "the bare minimum of force" needed flush out the militants, and to "minimize casualties to both sides"; right before the attack started, the major general in charge of the operation instructed the army that no man was to fire at either the Harmandir Sahib or Akal Takht without direct orders. He also said that entering the Golden Temple was a "last resort," but that the action was necessary to "stop the country being held to ransom any longer" (Tully and Jacob 1985: 156-7).

---

[46] Chima (2010) speculates that at this point the Akali Dal probably authorized the army to move into the temple and arrest Bhindranwale.

At 10:30 p.m. on the night of June 5th, the army initiated the first phase of the operation, attempting to move into the temple complex first by overtaking the Akal Takht where the militants were headquartered (military forces also raided 37 gurdwaras across Punjab simultaneously, looking for extremists) (Fair 2008). What the army quite unexpectedly encountered inside the Golden Temple was a highly motivated militancy that was better equipped and trained than had been anticipated (Chima 2010). The resistance was fierce, and the army was unable to take the Akal Takht as the plan first called. Instead, the army withstood heavy fire from the militants, who were armed with automatic weapons and were relying on sophisticated fortifications, including "sandbag and brick gun emplacements in its windows and arches, and holes had been made in its sacred marble to provide firing positions." According to Tully and Jacob (1985: 161):

> Commandos from the 1st Battalion, the Parachute Regiment, wearing black denims, were ordered to run down the steps under the clock tower on to the *parikrama*, or pavement, turn right and move as quickly as they could round the edge of the sacred tank to the Akal Takht. But as the paratroopers entered the main gateway of the Temple they were mown down. Most of the casualties were caused by Sikhs with light machine-guns who were hiding on either side of the steps leading down to the *parikrama*. The few commandos who did get down the steps were driven back by a barrage of fire from the buildings on the south side of the sacred pool.

The battle raged all night as the two sides remained deadlocked and the Indian army proved unable to turn the corner of the *parikrama* and surround the Akal Takht despite repeated waves. During these attempts, the army suffered almost 20% casualties, turning the courtyard in front of the Akal Takht, in the words of the commanding general, into a "killing ground" (Tully and Jacob 1985: 162-3).

Eventually, the army made the decision to bring tanks into the complex and employ machine gun fire and, allegedly, explosive squash-head shells.[47] Still, the militants were able to resist, holding back the army's advances for several more hours. As tanks and armored personnel carriers moved into position inside the temple, they came under fire from armor-piercing, rocket-propelled grenade launchers. Previous intelligence reports had not suggested that the militants possessed such firepower. As daylight approached, the army was finally able to clear the Akal Takht of militants twelve hours after the battle had begun, much longer than the army had anticipated (Fair 2008). However, sporadic gunfire from overlooking buildings signaled the presence of militants elsewhere in the complex, and the army did not want to follow up the tank attack during daylight hours (Tully and Jacob 1985). It took two more days of military operations, including clearing operations from building to building, before the army declared with confidence that the rest of the complex had been wrested from the militants (Fair 2008).

Following the operation, damage to the complex was extensive. The Akal Takht had been nearly destroyed from heavy tank fire, and its entire front wall had almost completely crumbled. Over 300 bullet holes maligned the façade of the Hamandir Sahib, and the library, housing countless invaluable manuscripts including handwritten copies of the Guru Granth Sahib, had been burned.[48] Dead bodies littered the temple's sacred reservoir, and the various buildings and

---

[47] After the operation had ended, the army denied using the high-explosive squash heads, and that only one tank was employed to fire a machine gun. However, this was highly improbable given the extent of damage to the Akal Takht, including the complete destruction of its front wall. A highly decorated Lieutenant General in the Indian Army, Jagjit Singh Aurora, after studying the destruction, estimated that as many as eighty of these shells likely struck the shrine (Tully and Jacob 1985).

[48] The burning of the library proved to be a major point of contention, as many Sikhs came to believe the army intentionally set it on fire as a means of destroying the Sikhs' culture.

structures along the *parikrama* were badly damaged from tank movement (Fair 2008). During the assault, Bhindranwale, AISSF President Bhai Amrik Singh, Major General Shahbeg Singh, and hundreds of Bhindranwale's followers had been killed (Cohen 1997; Fair 2008; Chima 2010). According to some eyewitness accounts, Bhindranwale and thirty of his followers assembled in the main hall of the Akal Takht shortly after the tank barrage, then leapt out into the courtyard in an apparent bid for martyrdom. The militants were mowed down by a wave of gunfire from the army, and an Akal Takht priest said that Bhindranwale was shot in the thigh during the attempted escape, then carried back into the Akal Takht. No survivor saw Bhindranwale die; the government would later report that his body was found inside the basement of the Akal Takht (Tully and Jacob 1985).

As for the total number of casualties including civilian deaths, major disagreement exists. According to the government's official White Paper, 83 soldiers and 493 Sikhs were killed during the attack, while 249 soldiers and 86 Sikhs were injured. *India Today,* by contrast, calculated the death toll to be 1,000 Sikhs and more than 200 army personnel killed during the attack (Chima 2010: 99). Survivors and other eyewitness accounts also reported seeing Indian soldiers executing Sikh pilgrims and SGPC employees inside the complex, many with their hands bound.[49] There were also many reports of atrocities committed by the militants, including throwing grenades at civilians, torturing two junior commissioned officers, and skinning one alive before blowing him up (Tully and Jacob 1985).

During and after Blue Star, Sikh villagers who had learned about Blue Star attempted to reach Amritsar despite the army's curfew, but were intercepted "by Army personnel, tanks, and

---

[49] The government and army denied all reports of soldiers executing civilians. However, a senior officer confirmed to Tully and Jacob (1985: 190) that "the soldiers were in a very bad mood because of the casualties that Bhindranwale's followers had inflicted on them and it was very difficult to control soldiers in that sort of mood."

even helicopters," with hundreds dying during the resulting skirmishes (Chima 2010: 95). Over 2,000 Sikh soldiers mutinied, and they too dashed to Amritsar, where most were killed in skirmishes with the troops. Many prominent Sikhs resigned their positions from the government, Sikh officers deserted the army, and rioting and police clashes consumed the capital, killing dozens. In the weeks following, the army launched Operation Woodrose, a series of raids across Punjab that aimed to clear extremists from all temples (Fair 2008). The military arrested thousands of suspected extremists, while many youths crossed over into Pakistan to escape detention and abuse. Months of enmity and communal tensions followed. The government attempted to rebuild the Akal Takht in a bid to heal relations, but Amritsar Sikhs were in no mood to reconcile, and tore the building down (Tatla 1999).

In October 1984, months after the attack, Gandhi's two Sikh bodyguards assassinated her for revenge at her residence. Her assassination unleashed a bloody wave of Hindu rioting in Delhi and northern Indian cities, killing 4,000 Sikhs (Tatla 1999). The combination of Operation Blue Star, Gandhi's assassination, and the riots that followed transformed what had been a middling militancy with increasing political clout into a widespread Sikh insurgency against the Indian state that would last for the next decade (Cohen 1997).

<u>Events leading up to the Attack:</u>

A number of developments precipitated the event, including a severe clampdown by the Indian government, the declaration of emergency rule by Indira Gandhi, and stockpiling of arms by militants inside the Golden Temple complex (Cohen 1997). Sant Jarnail Singh Bhindranwale and his lieutenants had taken refuge in the Golden Temple in July 1982. A retired military general named Shahbeg Singh and other Sikh army officers joined Bhindranwale shortly thereafter and began arming and training the Sikh youths inside the complex. Thinking that the Indian government would be hesitant to enter the temple, Bhindranwale and his commanders over the next several months transformed the shrine into a stronghold — adding bunkers and observation posts to its interior and preparing "an elaborate network of fortifications inside the complex, including stockpiles of arms, ammunition, and rations" (Fair 2008: 40).[50]

There were other, symbolic advantages influencing the decision. According to Fair (2008), establishing a base of operations inside the Golden Temple allowed the militants to further portray themselves as holy warriors, and their dispute with the Indian government as a holy war. During the time they stationed themselves at the temple, movement leaders manipulated Sikh hagiography and were able to portray their cause as part of Sikhism's long martial tradition. For example, the militants showed pictures and illustrations of those killed during the conflict alongside traditional artistic renderings depicting Sikh saints being tormented, tortured, and executed in defense of their faith. Khalistan folk songs and dances celebrating the sacrifices of the militancy also became popular during this time. According to Fair (2008), the Golden Temple was strategically advantageous because it provided easy access to young

---

[50] According to Fair (2008), Bhindranwale actually violated a number of important temple rules upon which the Indian government could have capitalized. For example, the fact that the militants were tearing down sacred structures in order to fortify the temple could have been portrayed as violating the reverence of the shrine. Fair notes that there is some precedent for amassing and storing arms in the temple or using it as a resource for waging war, but that there is not much evidence that the militants attempted to portray their stay in this manner. Another transgression was that Bhindranwale slept in a level above the *Guru Granth Sahib*, whereas the custom is to sleep below it. A more visible infraction, according to Fair, was that Bhindranwale's men committed acts of murder inside the temple and disposed of the dead in gutters around or underneath the complex, all of which contravened the temple's rules and norms. Fair argues that this afforded the Indian government the chance to have turned public perceptions against the militants, but that decisions taken during the assault produced the opposite effect and wasted the opportunity. "Despite actions that clearly would undermine support from pious elements of the Sikh community, in the early years of the violence the Indian counterinsurgency forces (police, army, paramilitary) failed to develop a systematic information offensive to publicize these misdeeds and to counter the militants' claims to religious sanction" (Fair 2008; 45).

recruits, who would witness the impressive presence of the militants in the holiest of Sikh temples.

Following his release from police detention in 1981, Bhindranwale had become the most influential and powerful Akali leader in Punjab, having built up a "Robin Hood-type image" that especially endeared him to the peasant and farmer classes as well as amongst the Sikh youth (Chima 2010: 87). As Bhindranwale's fame and popularity had grown, Akali moderates sought ways to align with his platform without sharing his extremist views. But when Bhindranwale became more critical of the Akali Dal leadership as well, these moderates became increasingly alienated from Bhindranwale, and a divide started to grow. In April 1984, the feud turned deadly when an alleged Akali plot killed one of Bhindranwale's most trusted assassins. In response, Bhindranwale's men killed three Sikhs alleged to have been involved in the plot, then hung a notice on the wall of the Temple complex taunting the Akali leadership (Tully and Jacob 1985). When the Akalis then attempted to shore up their ranks, approximately 130 Akalis as well as 40 members of the SGPC publicly swore allegiance to Bhindranwale in front of the Akal Takht (Chima 2010). Although Bhindranwale, who had always considered his position to be non-political, ultimately dismissed his new followers, the episode was steeped in symbolic meaning — few could miss the symbolism of Bhindranwale standing at the foot of the Akal Takht consolidating his ranks and receiving new allies. It set off many alarms, not only inside the central government but also within the Akali Dal; Chima (2010: 91) notes that at this point, "Bhindranwale had apparently become the most powerful Sikh leader in Punjab, eclipsing even the traditional Akali leadership." The primary political party for the Sikhs now realized the need to reign Bhindranwale in, even if it meant cooperating with Indira Gandhi.

Pressure was also mounting for the central government to tame Bhindranwale's militancy. A new round of murder and assassination linked back to Bhindranwale had reinforced the need the government to take dramatic action, lest it lose control of the situation. In April 1984, Sikh motorcyclists shot a Hindu shopkeeper and commission agent, actions that appeared consistent with an injunction by Bhindranwale "to buy arms and motorcycles and attack the enemies of the Sikhs" (Tully and Jacob 1985: 130). On April 30, two Sikh militants assassinated the former Deputy Superintendent of Police Bachan Singh, along with his wife and daughter, in the streets of Amritsar. On May 12th, militants shot dead Romesh Chander, the son of Lala Jagat Narain, the newspaper editor whom Bhindranwale's men were alleged to have killed three years prior leading to Bhindranwale's arrest. Both men were known to be on Bhindranwale's "hit list," and the assassinations demonstrated in quick order that the government had lost control of Punjab and that Bhindranwale was operating above the law. The Gandhi government now feared that Bhindranwale had grown too powerful; if he eventually chose to endorse Sikh independence, his decision could compel thousands of Sikhs to join the insurgency overnight. Unfortunately, the government could not arrest Bhindranwale without some form of cooperation from the Sikh community; the repercussions of entering the Golden Temple without any form of Sikh endorsement would be too great. The Akalis' change-of-heart regarding Bhindranwale was therefore the missing piece of the puzzle, and final element that Indira Gandhi had needed to take the enormous risk of ordering military action against the Golden Temple.

In early May 1984, Congress released those Akali leaders that had been detained, and the Akalis began secret and limited cooperation with the government, the goal of which was to neutralize Bhindranwale. In late May, the Akal Dal and national government via a "carrot-and-stick approach" tried to convince Bhindranwale to abandon his Golden Temple fortifications and vacate the complex; Bhindranwale adamantly refused. On June 1, security forces and the militants engaged in a massive exchange of gunfire that lasted for six hours, a major development that pierced the normal placidity surrounding the temple walls (Chima 2010). The circumstances of that standoff were unclear; some guessed that the military was trying to frighten Bhindranwale into a last-minute surrender, while military experts theorized that the exercise was a deliberate attempt to draw out the militants' fire so that their weapons and positioning could be assessed (Tully and Jacob 1985). Whatever the motive, in retrospect the exchange certainly appears to have signaled that the militancy had finally exhausted the government's restraint. On the eve of June 1984, Bhindranwale's militants had allegedly killed 165 Hindus and Nirankaris as well as 39 Sikhs who opposed Bhindranwale since the Akali morcha had begun in September 1982, this according to the government's estimates (Tully and Jacob 1985).

Fallout from the Attack:

Operation Blue Star achieved its immediate objective of ridding the Golden Temple of militants, but did so at great cost to the overall status of Hindu-Sikh relations and the stability of Punjab. A number of operational and strategic failures stand out about the operation and have added to its notorious legacy amongst members of the Sikh community. Blue Star and Operation Woodrose were largely ineffectual and counter-productive in quelling the militancy. Chima (2010: 95) notes that "violence and sabotage continued" throughout the summer as "Sikh villagers and extremists engaged the Army and other government security forces in continued armed resistance, resulting in a daily death toll throughout the state." The failure of Blue Star allowed the nationalist movement over the next decade to escalate from an agitation for autonomy first into a driven secessionist movement enjoying popular support in the Sikh community, and then in 1987 into a spiraling insurgency campaign with a staggering level of violence that would last into the next decade (Telford 1992; Bakke 2010).

One problem was the Indian government's lack of imagination and failure to plan for or analyze the situation coherently. Several officers questioned why the operation's planners did not elect to "seize" the temple complex, cut off its food, water and electricity supply, and wait for the militants to come out or starve.[51] As will be seen in the case of the Uyghurs, critics of the Chinese government response to the Urumqi riots also questioned the preparation and strategy of Chinese security forces to resolve the 2009 Urumqi riots. Bad intelligence was another factor. In this case, the army was caught off guard by the militants' possession of anti-armor grenade launchers, which had not turned up in previous intelligence reports (Tully and Jacob 1985). Officers also reported afterward that they did not know the layout of the complex, which complicated their efforts to root out militants and avoid hidden gunfire. Under very different circumstances, faulty intelligence in the form of false bomb threat warnings also led British security forces to overreact during the Bloody Sunday violence of 1972. The role of bad intelligence in both cases should underscore the importance of receiving the right information to avoid or mitigate the effects of a traumatic event.

Not only did the government underestimate the costs of staging the operation, it also failed to recognize opportunities where they existed. For example, because of the media blackout, journalists who later saw the damage assumed that Indian forces had committed most of the damage, and as pictures of the destruction made their way out of Punjab, it was depicted as primarily the army's responsibility. Almost no effort was made to convey the truth: that the militants, in the process of fortifying the temple, had tore down and defaced much of the temple

---

[51] On this score, the government responded that Bhindranwale had imminent plans to launch a new wave of violence across Punjab, forcing the government's hand (Tully and Jacob 1985).

themselves. The Indian government offered no narrative or argument making this case, and as a result, the Indian government received most of the blame for carrying out a reckless and cruel operation against the Sikhs' most cherished sanctuary, a perception that went unmitigated by the militants' own transgressions, "despite the numerous photos of the numerous arms caches and preponderant evidence of the dissoluteness and sacrilegious conduct of Bhindranwale and his supporters" (Fair 2008: 50-1). Although it surely would not have silenced all criticism, an information campaign could have blunted some of this fallout by making the public aware of the militants' own mistreatment of the shrine. The failure to craft a coherent message after a traumatic event offers an important lesson to all governments dealing with strife.

The attack on the Golden Temple set into motion a transformation of Sikh perceptions with damaging repercussions for the Indian state. According to Chima (2010: 95), Operation Blue Star essentially created "the basis for an overtly separatist Sikh ethnonationalist movement of the creation of Khalistan." If the original purpose of the operation was to root out militants in hiding, the overall effect was that it alienated Sikhs around the world, and would lead to some of the worst ethnic violence that India had ever seen, including the assassination of Indian Prime Minister Indira Gandhi. Some separatist leaders based in North America were clearly buoyed after her death, remarking to the Canadian *Globe and Mail* that their movement was "halfway to Khalistan already" (Kashmeri 1984). Although it succeeded in eliminating Bhindranwale, the attack alienated large sections of the Sikh community in Punjab and throughout the world. For many Sikhs, "Bhindranwale became a 'martyr' overnight who died 'defending' the Sikh holiest shrine and the dignity of the Sikh Panth" (Ibid.). In other words, Operation Blue Star served as genesis of the independence campaign, and the government by killing Bhindranwale inside the

Golden Temple essentially reified Bhindranwale. A better awareness Sikhism's ethnic mythology might have avoided this.

ANALYSIS OF OPERATION BLUE STAR AS A TRAUMATIC EVENT

Operation Blue Star meets almost all of the criteria defining a traumatic event as outlined in chapter 3. Sikhs perceived the Indian army to have struck the Golden Temple with suddenness and ferocity. The episode was extremely violent, leading to the deaths of at least hundreds and possibly thousands, much of the carnage done in the space of just a few hours. Although violence had gradually risen and the various political episodes leading up to the attack were months in the making, Blue Star shocked Sikhs in Punjab and across the world; as will be seen in the next chapter, most Sikhs had never even entertained the thought of the Indian army storming the Golden Temple. Despite the media ban the Indian government hung over Punjab during and after the attack, the magnitude of India conducting a major military operation inside the holiest shrine of one of its ethnic minorities ensured that the attack remained the subject of commentary for weeks. The media ban may also have exacerbated the Sikh diaspora reaction. As news of the attack reverberated across the global Sikh community, rumors, innuendo, and suspicion began to fill the information void, a common occurrence when states lack a media strategy following a tragic political episode (Bensahel 2008). The episode also marked a critical turning point on the separatist question. According to Tatla (1999: 6), "a single 'critical event' seems to have alerted [Sikhs] to their minority position in a dramatic way, and encourage their sensitivities in a radical direction—the carving of a territorial state as a homeland." Operation Blue Star sparked the insurgency that would grip Punjab for the next decade, arguably the most serious territorial crisis within India since partition (Chima 2010). Although the insurgency had largely died out by the mid-1990s, the notoriety of Operation Blue Star has lasted to the present day among Sikhs.

Level of physical violence – The amount of physical violence that took place during this event by most accounts was staggering. According to the government's tally, 576 people died in the attack. However, Sikhs believe the Indian government dramatically undercounted or even concealed the number of civilians killed and estimated that at least 1,000 civilians lost their lives. Some third-party and Indian media groups have also questioned the government's number of people killed. As the next chapter will recount, Sikhs heard vicious innuendo of Indian soldiers beating Sikhs mercilessly, killing civilians, and mutilating the bodies. The attack also resulted in extensive physical damage to the complex interior. Heavy tank fire nearly destroyed the Akal Takht, while machine-gun fire maligned the façade of the Hamandir Sahib. The library caught fire during the attack, destroying thousands of religious and historic manuscripts including handwritten copies of the Guru Granth Sahib. Dead bodies littered the temple's sacred reservoir, and tank movement damaged various buildings and structures along the *parikrama*. In sum, the attack left one of the most important shrines inside the complex in ruins, damaged several other sections, and produced a higher death toll and casualty number than all the attributed militant attacks in the previous two years combined.[52] And without question, the operation led to further violence afterward. The attack also prompted a significant increase in tensions between Sikhs and Hindus, leading indirectly to the assassination of Indira Gandhi and retaliatory riots that killed thousands of Sikhs in Delhi. Tully and Jacob (1985) note that had Indira Gandhi realized

---

[52] On the eve of June 1984, Bhindranwale's militants had allegedly killed 165 Hindus and Nirankaris as well as 39 Sikhs who opposed Bhindranwale since the Akali morcha had begun in September 1982, this according to the government's estimates (Tully and Jacob 1985).

that Operation Blue Star could have led to so many casualties, she almost certainly would have never offered her go-ahead to the operation.

Level of symbolic violence – Operation Blue Star was a deeply symbolic event. Sikhs immediately recognized the attack on the Golden Temple as a bid by the Hindu majority to threaten their culture and way of life. The attack on the Golden Temple was steeped in the type of symbolism and symbolic violence that the Indian government should have been able to anticipate and avoid. Some of the symbolic significance —for example, carrying out the attack on the martyrdom anniversary of the fifth guru Arjun Dev — was painfully unnecessary.[53] The symbolism of the event was not limited to the attack itself. Sikhs saw Bhindranwale and his followers within the framework of their ethnic history only after they paid the ultimate sacrifice in perceivably defending the Golden Temple. They imagined the sacrifices of the Sikh militant as the latest in a long line of martyrs. The physical destruction of the religious complex, including the Akal Takht and library, was also highly symbolic, and convinced some Sikhs (and provided new evidence for Sikh activists to argue) that the state was attempting to destroy the Sikh nation, starting with its culture. As Fair (2008: 40) puts it, "Operation Blue Star and the ensuing massacres of Sikhs fostered a wider-spread militancy among the Sikhs in the Punjab by legitimizing the separatists' claims that India could not and would not protect Sikh interests."

According to Chima (2010: 27), there are three sets of Sikh ethno-religious practices that are highly rich in symbolic content, which Sikh leaders have used to mobilize large sections of

---

[53] In a statement to the press following the event, two retired Sikh generals of the Indian army explicitly criticized this decision and said it was a factor leading some Sikh soldiers to mutiny. One general noted, "The martyrdom day of Guru Arjun, being the epitome of supreme sacrifice in the face of extreme religious persecution, has a special significance for the Sikh solder" (Tully and Jacob 1985: 148).

the community: 1) the Sikhs' own narrative of their history, which tends to stress the contributions and sacrifices of its warriors and martyrs, 2) the constant fear of being reabsorbed into Hinduism, and 3) the Punjabi language and Gurmukhi script, which have become important markers of Sikh identity. As a traumatic event, Operation Blue Star evokes the first two criteria almost seamlessly: Sikhs saw the militants who died during the attack as martyrs who laid down their lives in defense of their religion, and interpreted the actions of the Indian government as a Hindu threat against the Sikh religion. And if the symbolism of the attack failed to directly connote the third set of mobilizing markers — a threat against the Punjabi language or Gurumukhi script — the attack furnished Sikh leaders with a more than able replacement: a full-scale military assault against Sikhism's most sacred shrine.

It is difficult to overstate the importance of the Golden Temple to Sikhism. It not only is "the highest seat of religious and temporal authority for the Sikhs (analogous to the significance of St. Peter's for Catholics)," but also functions for Sikhs as "the symbolic centre of a world without boundaries" (Cohen 1997: 113). The Golden Temple complex is also important politically. It houses the headquarters for prominent Sikh political and religious groups including the Akali Dal, the SGPC, and the All India Sikh Students Federation (AISSF). Its history traces back to the Sikh gurus who founded the temple and endowed it with its spiritual meaning. The temple's aesthetic beauty, historical connection to successive gurus, and centrality to most of Sikh history endow the shrine with special meaning. For all these reasons, the Golden Temple is the most powerful source of spirituality anywhere in the world for the Sikh:

The Harimandir, literally the House of God, represents a unique entity. Its buildings were built and dwelt in by several gurus, its sacred pool washed away a devotee's sins; at its center the Guru Granth was an embodiment of their gurus…

To sit in the inner sancto sanctum, listening to continuous hymn singing from

early dawn to dusk is a magical moment and mystical experience for the faithful.

(Tatla 1999: 28)

In short, the Golden Temple is one of the most beloved and sacred shrines in all of religion. The

Sikhs see it as perhaps their most enduring symbol and central to the practice of their faith; a

threat against its sanctity is therefore tantamount to attempting to destroy Sikhism.

In the years that followed, Operation Blue Star would become a rallying cry, a symbol of

an Indian state intolerant of Sikh culture, a galvanizing moment in the history of the Sikhs, and a

source of legitimization and justification for those who fought to break away from India and

form an independent Sikh state. In summarizing the attack, Tatla (1999: 28) touches on the

episode in both cultural and historical terms: "The Indian Army's assault on the [Golden

Temple], the holiest shrine in Sikh perception, constituted a "sacrilege" a slur on a nation's

dignity and integrity, an act of genocide... The Indian army's invasion of the Golden Temple was

seen as a third *ghallughara*, a historical term pregnant with the community's resistance to its

tyrants." As will be discussed in much greater detail in the next chapter, Sikhs interpreted these

events subjectively, as evidence of the governmental prejudice and pernicious intent against their

religion and way of life, rather than as perhaps an ill-conceived operation meant to forcibly

remove militants who were using the temple as their base of operations to conduct widespread

illegal activity.

THE DIASPORA AND THE SEPARATIST CAMPAIGN PRIOR TO BLUE STAR

During the Punjab Crisis, a favorite refrain of the Indian government as well as Indian

commentators was to allege that the Sikh diaspora played a hidden but powerful role in initiating

and then orchestrating the Khalistan campaign. While the rationale for making such denunciations had as much to do with placating domestic constituencies as it did properly identifying external threats, it is true that elements in the diaspora did attempt to rally support for Sikh independence, but these efforts in most cases failed to significantly amplify support for the idea among mainstream diaspora opinion or the states in which the diaspora members resided.

The earliest appeal for Sikh separatism from India appears to have taken place in 1954, when a Sikh activist in London named Davinder Singh Parmar lobbied other Sikhs for the establishment of an independent Sikh homeland to be called Khalistan, meaning "the land of the pure." Yet, Parmar's ideas attracted little support and by his own admission other diaspora Sikhs labeled him a madman. For example, when Parmar convened the first pro-Khalistan meeting in 1954, it drew only 20 participants, and Parmar acknowledged afterward that it had only persuaded one attendee (Fair 2005). Parmar continued to advocate for Khalistan, however, and by 1970 had aligned with a former Punjab government minister who was also working to build support in the diaspora for an independent state, Dr. Jagjit Singh Chohan. Parmar and Chohan launched a new publicity campaign for Khalistan. Fair (2005: 135) judges that Chohan and Parmar's collaboration was "widely perceived to be the meeting of minds that launched the Khalistan movement in earnest." While their vigorous campaigning failed to garner much support prior to 1984, it did ensure that thousands of Sikhs had heard the name "Khalistan" and knew of the idea. In 1971, Chohan made a highly publicized visit to Pakistan, and at a time when India was deadlocked in a war with the Pakistani state, he brashly advocated for an independent Khalistan to the Pakistani press. The coverage of these remarks ensured that many Sikhs in India learned of Chohan's demands, which for many in India was also the first time that they had ever heard the name "Khalistan" (Fair 2005). That same year, Chohan attempted to reach out to diaspora Sikhs and non-Sikh audiences alike by buying a half-page advertisement in the *New*

York Times declaring the need for Khalistan and declaring the Congress Party's deception of the Sikhs (Cohen 1997: 112). In 1974, several of the movement's future diaspora leaders met in Toronto and signed a blood pledge committed to the establishment of Khalistan (Kashmeri 1984). Chohan founded the National Council of Khalistan in April 1980 and became its president; three months later, Chohan proclaimed from London that Khalistan had been formed (Gupta 1990).

However, Chohan and Parmar ultimately failed to captivate the hearts and imagination of the global Sikh community with their appeals for an independent Sikh homeland, and most viewed Chohan, Parmar and their supporters as a "fanatical fringe" Fair, 2005). Most Sikhs continued to identify as "Indian." The fact remained that the vast majority of Sikhs still self-identified as Indian as well as Sikh, a dual identity that was hardly impossible to maintain given the historical and cultural linkages between Sikhs and Hindus, not to mention the Sikhs' own military service in the defense of India. Although the Akali Dal's Punjab autonomy campaign conducted throughout the 1970s and '80s gained diaspora support in many North American and British gurdwaras — enhancing the standing and legitimacy of community leaders who showed solidarity with the campaign (Biswas 2004) — diaspora support for Khalistan remained tepid even when Punjab became embroiled in the Nirankari clashes in 1978 and during the intensification of violence between Sikhs and the police services in 1982. However, it was during these years that diaspora Sikhs became increasingly concerned about the treatment of Sikhs in Punjab, which helped set the stage for what was to come.

DIASPORA MOBILIZATION AFTER BLUE STAR

Operation Blue Star "precipitated widespread galvanization," of the Khalistan cause in the United States, Canada and other countries with prominent Sikh populations (Fair 2005: 128). Following the attack, newly appointed diaspora Sikh officials met with high-level US government officials to protest the Indian government's action and eventually met with President Reagan at the White House to discuss the attack. On June 10th of 1984 alone, thousands turned out for protests in Vancouver, New York, Edmonton, Calgary, Toronto, San Francisco and Los Angeles (Tatla 1999). The attack marked the beginning of a prolonged period of lobbying activity by diaspora activists directed at US government officials. For example, a Khalistan proponent in 1985 enlisted North Carolina Senator Jesse Helms' support in lobbying the State Department to grant a visa request to Jagjit Singh Chauhan (Unna 1985). The following year, California Sikhs hosted a fundraiser for Senator Alan Cranston, and while condemning militant violence, expressed their solidarity with the senator that "fighting for oppression and fighting for justice is something we can understand" (Hicks 1986: para. 5). In June 1988, Sikh organizations took credit when California Congressman Wally Hearger offered an amendment in the House of Representatives proposing a freeze on US bilateral aid to India until the Indian government stopped violating human rights in Punjab; however, Hearger's amendment had little change of being passed into law and ultimately failed (Gupta 1990).

Importantly, Sikhs also formed several new diaspora organizations whose collective mission was to rally support and funds for the Khalistan movement, organize mass protests and demonstrations, lobby government officials and foreign policy actors, and plan an information campaign to present the Sikh position on what was happening in India. Diaspora leaders from New York to New Mexico called meetings and invited Sikhs from around the world to develop "a united front of Sikhs as well as a united strategy in dealing with the situation," according to one of the organizers of the New Mexico meeting (Howe 1984: para. 2). New pamphlets and fact sheets were produced and disseminated using local and national mailing lists. Sikhs also sought to influence how they were portrayed in American and global media. For example, Sikhs in Stockton and San Diego took up public campaigns urging local and national media to refer to the militants as "suspected Sikh extremists" rather than "terrorists" (Tatla 1999). Demonstrations were organized whenever and wherever significant Indian leaders visited the US or Canada, including at each stop of a multi-city diplomacy trip by Prime Minister Rajiv Gandhi in 1988. Other activists attempted to intimidate Indian diplomats based in Canada and the United States, such as in 1984/5 when protestors in San Jose pummeled India's San Francisco-based consul-general with eggs during a visit, or when activists in 1991 disrupted an Indian American fundraiser for a San Francisco congressman (Unna 1985; Tatla 1999).

Diaspora Sikhs in response to Blue Star also began raising funds and support for various Sikh charities and Punjab relief efforts. Although the exact level of diaspora involvement in the murky dealings of the Sikh insurgency is unknown, observers of the conflict generally agree that some of this fundraising may have benefited militant organizations operating against the Indian government. For its part, the Indian government accused the Sikh diaspora of facilitating a wide network of fundraising activity on behalf of several militant groups, and also alleged that certain groups such as Babbar Khalsa supplied militant outfits in Punjab with weapons or used their networks to smuggle weapon caches across the border from neighboring Pakistan (Fair 2005). The Indian consulate-general based in Vancouver in 1985 estimated that North American temples had provided $5 or $10 million to militants, the largest amounts of which originated from networks in Vancouver, Toronto and Yuba City (Unna 1985). While it remains difficult to assess these claims, the US Treasury Department's firearms division in 1985 investigated the smuggling of arms from the US to India, exploring the possibility that diaspora elements in the United States were using Canada as a staging ground for shipments. It failed to unearth any major or "smoking gun" evidence of widespread diaspora direct involvement — at least to the extent alleged by the Indian government (Unna 1985).

Although India's allegation of widespread diaspora complicity in Punjab unrest may have overblown its actual role, it remains true that some diaspora members offered direct support to the militant groups or even sought to join the insurgency directly. The most notorious case occurred in June 1985, when an Air India flight bound from Toronto and Montreal to London exploded off the coast of Ireland, killing 329 passengers and crew. Canadian authorities traced the attack to Sikh Canadian extremists affiliated with Babbar Khalsa, a Sikh separatist organization with a strong presence in Vancouver (Cohen 1997). In a different episode, the FBI in 1985 announced it had disrupted a plot New York and New Orleans-based extremists to assassinate Prime Minister Rajiv Gandhi and other government officials during a visit to the United States. Authorities also charged the alleged conspirators of planning guerrilla attacks against government buildings and a nuclear power plant in India (Unna 1985). The Canadian government in 1986 arrested five Sikhs in Montreal with Babbar Khalsa ties for possessing explosives and plotting to bomb another Air India flight (Marsden 1986). In one episode, airport authorities uncovered six unclaimed cases of arms on passenger flights originating in San Francisco and headed via New York to New Delhi (Unna 1985). Tatla (1999) also notes the existence of at least five Canadian Sikhs who between 1985 and 1990 died in encounters with security forces or other incidents in Punjab after enlisting in Sikh militancy. This list included Vancouver-based Talwinder Singh Parmar — a high-ranking member of Babbar Khalsa, who left Canada in 1988, joined the militancy in Punjab, and in 1992 was killed while in detention by Punjab police (Tatla 1999). Fair (2005) argues that besides serving as a source of diplomatic and financial support, the diaspora enabled Pakistan to become complicit in supporting Sikh militants such as Babbar Khalsa and the Khalistan Commando Force, primarily by allowing diaspora Sikhs to travel to Pakistan — ostensibly to make pilgrimages to its historical gurdwaras — and funnel financial and military assistance across the border (Fair 2005). It is important to note, however, that most Sikhs responded with nonviolent activity and by decade's end felt the militants' strategy had tarnished the community's image (Biswas 2004).

National and Local Sources of Organization:

Political organizations founded in the wake of Blue Star played a major role in shaping and facilitating the Sikh response. The highest profile Sikh group founded at the time was probably the World Sikh Organization (WSO), which according to its mission commits itself to "strive for an independent homeland by peaceful means." It has sought to fulfill this goal largely through lobbying and awareness-raising efforts and attempting to increase the visibility of human rights abuses against Sikhs in India (Biswas 2004). In the aftermath of Blue Star, the WSO started a weekly publication known as the *World Sikh News*, which editorialized in strong favor of Sikh independence and became the most widely distributed Sikh weekly in the diaspora and editorializes in strong favor of Sikh independence. The WSO grew into one of the largest diaspora organization by 1987, boasting more than 16,000 members. However, internal feuding, leadership rifts, and allegations of Indian infiltration have plagued the WSO (Tatla 1999; Biswas 2004). The WSO also found itself competing with rival organizations such as the Washington

DC-based Council of Khalistan, set up in Washington DC in 1986 by a former WSO member, which has gained influence among some governments through its lobbying efforts (Tatla 1999).

However, some diaspora elements have vilified both these professionals-led groups as being too moderate, and instead sought to establish organizations more willing to defend the right of Sikhs to employ violent tactics in Punjab and engage with militant groups. Probably the most prominent militant diaspora group is the International Sikh Youth Federation (ISYF), founded in August 1984 in Canada. The ISYF grew into a major rival of the WSO — during the height of the conflict, the two essentially competed for control of various gurdwaras in North America (Tatla 1999). In its heyday, many Sikhs perceived the ISYF as closely aligned with the Khalistan movement in Punjab. Like the WSO, factionalism and leadership rifts have also plagued the overall effectiveness of the ISYF. In 1988 it suffered a major rupture when members alleged that its upper tier of leadership had been infiltrated by "Indian intelligence," following an episode where several leaders apparently experienced a sudden change of heart about the need for Sikh independence (Ibid.).

The most notorious militant group operating in the diaspora is probably the Babbar Khalsa. Like its parent organization in Punjab, the Babbar Khalsa in Canada originally focused on spreading Sikh orthodoxy, but after Operation Blue Star began more overtly rallying around the Khalistani cause. Its strongest area of support is in Vancouver, where a large Sikh population resides; the group also has key support nodes in Toronto and Montreal (Tatla 1999). Both Canadian and Indian officials have alleged Babbar Khalsa involvement in a number of violent plots, including the bombing of an Air India plane in 1985 that killed 329 people, and a thwarted plot to blow up India's parliament buildings (Unna 1985). Other organizations, such as Jagjit Singh Chauhan's Khalistan Council, allegedly acted as charitable fronts for certain militant groups in Punjab, a role that allowed some diaspora members to channel funds directly to the militancy; the Khalistan Council denied these charges (Biswas 2004; Cohen 1997).

Notwithstanding the influence of these national networks, the most important source of organization in any Sikh community is the local gurdwara, where the Sikh *Sangat* ("congregation") meets in the presence of the collection of Sikh scriptures, called the *Guru Granth Sahib*. Gurdwaras normally function as the most critical institution in any Sikh overseas community; one observer described gurdwaras as "the only really influential and deeply rooted Sikh organizations in Canada" (Biswas 2004: 285). The gurdwaras are where Sikhs host mentor programs, community gatherings, and offer cultural learning and Punjabi language courses. Most Sikh organizations, including the WSO and ISYF, effectively exist through their affiliation with gurdwaras, and it is also where they hold most of their meetings (Biswas 2004).

Gurdwaras played a central role in mobilizing support for Khalistan, despite initial skepticism to the movement that immediately dissipated after Operation Blue Star (Fair 2005; Tatla 1999). Due to its status as a central node within any Sikh diaspora community — especially with regard to Sikh religious and political affairs — the gurdwara was able to promote "a highly stylized version of the conflict and of Sikh history" (Fair 2005: 132). In so doing, the gurdwara fulfilled its role of accessing an ethnic mythology to allow the movement to sustain ethnic members during times of hardship This activity is important not only because it promulgates the group's ethnic mythology, but also because it allowed group leaders to access the group's myth-symbol complex and enable a form of symbolic politics that can justify hostility, mobilization and fears of group extinction (Demmers 2012). The gurdwaras hosted prominent preachers and musical groups to extol the Khalistan movement and craft the images of its most prominent leaders. They arranged the photographs of Sikh militants alongside pictures of other Sikh martyrs, conferring religious legitimacy on the sacrifices of the militants who had died. Some may have even fundraised on behalf of militant groups, funneling their collections into a variety of organizations. It should be noted that not all gurdwaras became enjoined to the movement in such a way and that levels of support offered to Khalistani militants varied (Fair 2005).

CONCLUSION

This chapter has sought to establish a forthright accounting of what happened during Operation Blue Star as well as its consequences. It also qualified Blue Star as a traumatic event according to the framework introduced in chapter 3. Finally, it traced the growth of the Sikh diaspora, discussed the involvement of diaspora Sikhs in the Khalistan movement during its nascent stages, and examined the initial Sikh response to Operation Blue Star. The principal argument of this chapter is that a traumatic event of the magnitude of Operation Blue Star was successful in attracting new supporters from a previously inactive diaspora population to embrace the goals of the separatist movement and to mobilize these supporters to take action — which in this case took the form of mass protests and demonstrations, the creation of new organizations, lobbying activity, and the enlistment of a few individuals into the militancy. The next chapter, which examines the results of structured interviews conducted with American Sikhs about their views of Operation Blue Star, will allow this research to more ambitiously explore the process of perception creation in response to a traumatic event.

6

DIASPORA RESPONSES TO A TRAUMATIC EVENT: STRUCTURED INTERVIEWS WITH SIKHS IN YUBA CITY, BOSTON, AND WASHINGTON, D.C.

The previous chapter has highlighted some of the ways the Sikh diaspora responded to Operation Blue Star, including protests and demonstrations, political outreach and information campaigns, the creation of new but flawed organizations to champion the cause of Sikh independence, and the willingness of a small number of Sikhs to engage in violent activity. However, observers of the Sikh conflict — indeed, of most ethnic conflicts and policy issues in general — have too frequently passed over or taken for granted the dynamics through which significant political events lead to new interpretations, transform perceptions, and lay the groundwork for mobilization (Birkland 1998; Francisco 2004). This is unfortunate because it leaves unanswered the questions that can help predict the strength and composition of ensuing mobilization. To assess the possible repercussions of a traumatic event requires a more deliberate examination of the ethnic group's response.

This chapter focuses on the Sikh diaspora living in the United States and analyzes the reaction of these Sikhs to Operation Blue Star. To achieve this task, this chapter utilizes structured interviewing with American Sikhs, the intent of which is to allow analysis of perceptions surrounding Blue Star. This chapter focuses on fieldwork conducted by the researcher between November 2011 and August 2012 with Sikhs living in or around Yuba City,

California; Washington, DC; and Boston, Massachusetts. By examining the emotional response of these Sikhs to Blue Star, this research can help illustrate how — and under what conditions — do traumatic events have the potential to act as a catalyst for mobilization.

Through employment of the conceptual framework provided in chapter 3, this chapter analyzes the responses of 26 American Sikhs regarding their views of Operation Blue Star. First, this chapter focuses on how American Sikhs perceived the attack, including exploration of the impact of physical damage to the temple as well as symbolic significance attributed to the operation. Second, the chapter examines the function of Operation Blue Star as an "event galvanizer" — a political episode that distresses the ethnic community to the point of mobilization. Third, the chapter assesses how the attack may have transformed the perceptions of some diaspora Sikhs, leading to the embrace of new political positions largely in support of the goals of the Sikh separatist movement. At the end of this discourse, an analysis section examines the interview data more critically. I conclude by employing my hypotheses to analyze this event, add important caveats and qualifications, and assess broader implications as it concerns our scholarly understanding of ethnic conflict.

<u>Research Design and Selection of Interview Subjects</u>:

In selecting and then interviewing participants for this research, I employed a list of criteria that in the interest of disclosure I wish to make known. First and foremost, the identities of all subjects are kept anonymous out of concern for their privacy, and so this research will refer to the subjects by number — interviewee 1, interviewee 2, interviewee 3, and so on. All subjects were 18 years of age or older. Despite the researcher's attempts to include a greater number of women, only three (interviewees 12, 22 and 25) agreed to be interviewed — probably underscoring the degree to which traditional gender roles are still employed in Sikh communities. In terms of locational breakdown, interview subjects 1 through 13 live in or around Yuba City, interview subjects 14 through 18 live in or around Boston, and interview subjects 19 through 26 live in or around Washington, D.C. I sought purposefully to learn from a variety of perspectives about the Sikh separatist campaign by pursuing a mix of subjects who judged themselves as politically active, somewhat politically active, passive, or apolitical with respect to their awareness and involvement in Sikh politics. In conveying a coherent narrative based on these interviews, I have sought to make these discussions as representative as I possibly could. Where major agreement or disagreement exists on a given issue, I attempt to acknowledge and provide explanation. I also note important exceptions where a minority of respondents feels differently than the majority.

AMERICAN SIKHS AND THEIR PERCEPTIONS OF THE ATTACK

When he first learned news of the Golden Temple attack on June 5-6, 1984, Interviewee 5 of Yuba City was at his brother's high school graduation. "I just heard a little bit, and it didn't really sink in… Back then there wasn't twenty-four hour news," he said. "The news came slowly and you didn't get a lot of news… It was the next day when you realized what had happened." Interviewee 3 was at his local gurdwara in Yuba City and remembered panicked discussion suddenly coursing through the congregation. Interviewee 4 of Yuba City also recalled the frantic talk of Sikhs trying to understand what had happened.[54] In Boston, Interviewee 14 was at a

---

[54] Most American Sikhs learned of the attack through the local or evening news. Several also mentioned the impact of a news segment on the American television program "60 Minutes," which ran a few weeks before the attack. Imposition of a media curfew over Punjab meant that details were scarce and there was little information to report, and the ensuing lack of information made the situation worse by allowing the Sikh imagination to assume the community's worst fears. In the months following Blue Star,

company retreat when he first heard news of the attack over the radio, while Interviewee 15 saw it reported on television. Interviewee 16 of Boston had just arrived in New York City, and a family cousin greeted him with news of the attack. Interviewee 25, a college student in Washington DC at the time, remembered learning on June 2nd about the exchange of fire between militants and security forces, and discovering the next days that the Indian army had entered the temple. Back in Yuba City, Interviewee 8, who was also in college, learned of the attack from another student. The first thought passing through his mind was Indira Gandhi had just written her own death certificate. Similarly, Interviewee 1 remembered the folklore his uncle would tell him, that no person who attacked the Golden Temple had ever gone unpunished.

Other Sikhs interviewed for this project living in India or elsewhere at the time also reflected on their experience of learning about the attack. Interviewee 11, who was then a tenth grader in Punjab, remembered coming home from school one day and finding his father, uncle, and a local political leader all gathered at his home and deeply concerned about reports of a shooting at the Golden Temple. The next day, Indian soldiers chased Interviewee 11 home from school for violating curfew, which is how he learned the government had effectively declared martial law in the state. Interviewee 10 lived in the neighboring state of Haryana, and he recalled the Indian military passing through his city on the way to Amritsar. "Two, three days before, there had been a curfew [announced], so nobody could go," he said. "The media's all frozen — we didn't know for three, four days what had happened." Interviewee 9 of Sacramento resided in Fiji at the time. Following the attack, he noticed many Fiji Sikhs — who contrary to Sikh

---

eyewitness accounts from survivors would also come to fill in the gaps. Interviewee 14 noted that "slowly you have some relatives who had witnessed this stuff, or relatives who were actually killed and then somebody survived and they told you this is what they saw," which he attested was "quite shocking."

orthodoxy had always trimmed their hair and beard — began growing out the length of their beards and wearing traditional turbans, two of the most recognized symbols denoting a Sikh.

The Sikhs who agreed to be interviewed for this research reflected on a range of emotions about the moment almost thirty years ago when they learned the Indian government had ordered a military operation inside the Golden Temple. Perhaps the most widely shared sentiment was disbelief. Diaspora Sikhs were shocked the Indian government would execute an armed military encounter inside their holiest shrine. Interviewee 14 of Yuba City recalled his astonishment upon learning the news: "My immediate reaction was I just couldn't believe it. It's almost like, my God, how can somebody do that? It was almost to the point where I was thinking, *is somebody so foolish and stupid to do this? What were they thinking?*" According to Interviewee 5, "We had a very disgusted feeling. Helpless, but disgusted. How could these bastards do this to their own people?" Interviewee 23, who lived in Punjab at the time, said he felt "that I'm living in some other country," adding that "my military, which is supposed to protect me, which I called my army… now it's my army that's killing my people." And Interviewee 11 added: "Nobody ever imagined attacking the Golden Temple."

Interview subjects clearly viewed it as an assault on Sikhism itself. Sikhs felt betrayed. "I just couldn't understand how they would do it. How somebody would betray you outright like that," said Interviewee 14, who noted that in his youth in Punjab he had been raised to be "very nationalist, very pro-India." Interviewee 11 expressed a similar sentiment: "We fought two wars for India. [We had] so much pride. We are the protector of India. And they are turning on us." For Interviewee 2, the loyalty of Sikhs during India's own independence movement amplified their own sense of betrayal. "The Sikhs took such a part in gaining independence in the first place," he commented. "They sacrificed a lot of their lives. Then turn around, have this happen to them — the Indian government attacks the holiest place there is for Sikhs."[55] Interviewee 23

condemned what he said was the Indian government's lack of political will or constitutional

guarantee to protect the Sikhs. He contrasted it to the US government's response — which he

described as "prompt action" — to an August 2012 episode where an extremist in Wisconsin

entered a gurdwara and killed several Sikh worshippers.

If disbelief and betrayal were the first reactions, outrage ranked a close second. India's

own military staging an assault on the most sacred shrine of Sikhism weighed heavily on the

hearts and minds of most interview subjects. Several comments underscore how highly emotions

ran in response to Blue Star, which underscores the potential for emotion to function as a trigger

for ethnic conflict outbreaks (Petersen 2002). Reflecting at length about the attack, Interviewee 6

concluded, "My whole point is when [the Golden Temple attack] happened, I cried; I was very

much moved emotionally that this kind of thing happened to our Gurdwara." He later summed:

"It was devastating to my mind, emotionally, physically, in every way to the Sikh community."

Interviewee 11, who lived in Punjab, also surmised his response to the attack as "purely

emotional. Personally, I knew people that died. Those were good, young people, who had no idea

what they were fighting for. They just took up arms; they wanted revenge. They felt humiliated."

The Indian government's decision to shut down the media in Punjab during Operation Blue Star

also allowed innuendo and exaggeration to spread quickly, and in retrospect this was a grave

mistake on the government's part as it further enraged Sikhs in Punjab and the diaspora. Said

Interviewee 25: "Two or three days [after the attack] we were totally in the dark so we were

more outraged. We thought, 'She has bombed the Golden Temple!' We had no clue."

---

[55] Only one person, Interviewee 6, professed to being unsurprised by the Indian government's
decision to send the army into the Golden Temple, claiming that a family member who had made recent
trips to India was given information beforehand.

The fact that most Sikhs saw the operation as excessive and unnecessary, leading to hundreds of "preventable" civilian deaths, compounded the emotional toll the attack took on diaspora Sikhs. The thought of Sikh pilgrims killed in their place of worship intensely angered interview subjects, who wondered why the Indian government did not utilize a less severe approach such as cutting off food and electricity to the Golden Temple — a tactic the army successfully employed a few years later.[56] Said Interviewee 10:

> The Golden Temple is a very holy place, not just for Sikhs. Everybody goes; they believe it... We thought there was another way — if you think there are terrorists there, hiding in the Golden Temple, there must be a different way to get them out... Freeze the Golden Temple, cut off their electricity, give everybody the chance to come out, [or at least] the thousand people and kids to come out of the Golden Temple.

Significantly, the above interview subject assumes the Indian government possessed several options, yet selected the approach most resulting in civilian casualties. In fact, many respondents accused the government of targeting the Golden Temple because it would maximize the damage wrought to the Sikhs, and accused the government of intentionally staging the attack during a Sikh holiday — the birthday of Guru Arjun Dev — to significantly increase the number of Sikh pilgrims killed. Interviewee 3 is even more blunt: he states that the government was trying to "wipe out" the Sikhs. "My impression even today is the same, that [Operation Blue Star] was

---

[56] In May 1988, the Punjab police with support from the antiterrorist National Security Guards executed Operation Black Thunder, which again sought to remove militant forces from the Golden Temple. This time, however, security forces sought to prevent food and water from entering the temple and to cut electricity and other essential services in effort to lay siege to the temple rather than forcibly overtake it. They were also far more cautious in considering how operating in particular part of the complex would be perceived by the Sikh community, and offered periodic ceasefires to allow militants to give themselves up without fear of being fired upon. For a full comparison of Operations Blue Star and Black Thunder, see Fair (2008).

unnecessary, that it was cruel, and they just did it probably to do genocide [against] the Sikhs," he said. Interviewee 5 while criticizing several aspects of the attack also expressed deep skepticism of the government's motive behind its tactics and underscored a number of Sikh grievances. His words, since they touch on many of the dynamics discussed by interview subjects, is worth highlighting in full, and I have italicized parts for emphasis:

> They attacked the holy temple on a holiday in the middle of the night. Their excuse was that they were going to go and catch this terrorist [Bhindranwale]. People didn't buy it. They said if that's what they wanted and if he went out in the community and committed a crime, why didn't they catch him when he was out in the community? Why don't they come out with the tear gas or something? Why don't they wait for a time when there are not as many people at the temple? I mean *they planned it…* they planned it for days, kicking out media, bringing in hundreds of thousands of military men, the tanks. *And why on a holiday?…* Why attack on a holiday in the middle of the night when women and children are there? Why not wait until most of these people are out and let everybody start controlling people coming in and then when there [is a] smaller group [of] people, attack on that time? So that was what people were saying, that this wasn't to catch terrorists. *They just wanted to teach us a lesson* and wanted us to shut up and be second-class citizens.

Several interview subjects thus interpreted the attack as the culmination of tensions that had ebbed and flowed but always lingered for centuries between the Sikh and the Hindu. Sikhs cited their faith's historic rejection of the caste system, which they suspected made Hindu nationalists feel threatened. According to this interpretation, Hindus felt insecure and threatened not only by the basic tenets of Sikhism, which served at least as a symbolic rejoinder to the Hindu system of social hierarchy, but also the group's increasing demands for autonomy. Subscribers to this belief saw Operation Blue Star as the boldest attempt by the Hindu majority controlling India to bring Sikhs back under firm Hindu control. It should therefore serve as no surprise that Operation Blue Star led to new allegations that Hindus were attempting to "reabsorb" Sikhism.[57]

Finally, many Sikhs went a step further than interpreting the government's action as reflective of historical tensions, cultural insensitivity, political recklessness or Hindu nationalism run amok. Some deemed the attack an act of genocide — the initiation of a concerted campaign to kill Sikhs, beginning with Blue Star and climaxing in the rampant anti-Sikh riots after Indira Gandhi's assassination. However, applications of the term 'genocide' generally lacked definition, and those who employed it appeared to appreciate it more for its emotional resonance than its accuracy in describing the attacks.[58]

---

[57] For example, Interviewee 14 said that "even educated Hindus" believed that all Sikhs are really Hindus, "the sword arm of Hinduism." Interviewee 14 also linked the tensions to lingering Hindu prejudice going back to the British favorably treating the Sikhs, and also connected to Sikhism's founding as an anti-caste religion. Interviewee 6 suggested that many Hindus resented Sikhism because it "challenged their belief system and the value system of caste, and Interviewee 18 contrasted the schism in Hindu-Sikh relations with the historical conflict between Hinduism and Islam, arguing that Sikhism was seen as the graver threat because it challenged the supremacy of the Brahmans and appealed to the greater number by adopting Punjabi, "the common man's language."

[58] Multiple interpretations of genocide existed but none were deeply sketched out. Some suggested the level of violence waged by the government against Sikhs constituted genocide. Others believed the Indian government had enacted a devious scheme to limit Sikh population growth and significantly slow the Sikh birth rate. One interview subject, without using the word 'genocide,' discussed a stratagem where the government targeted Sikh youths as a means to decrease the number of Sikh males and thus slow the birth rate, as well as freeing criminals in Punjab so they could go out and kill Sikhs. In one case, and interview subject used the term, but then elaborated it meant, "trying to suppress this small minority in India." Another interview subject compared Gandhi's intentions to a Russian Pogrom and said she aimed to "finish off" the Sikhs.

<u>Physical and Symbolic Forms of Violence in Blue Star: What Resonated?</u>

The attack on militants inside the Golden Temple took on immense symbolic meaning due to a variety of factors, including the religious and political significance of the shrine and the shocking, unprecedented nature of the attack. The subjects whom I interviewed found it natural to compare Blue Star to other important historical events that startled and threatened a nation, including the Kennedy assassination, the Holocaust, and the September 11th terrorist attacks; for instance, Interviewee 1 commented that "I always use [September 11th] as an example because that was an attack on America, and that woke all of our eyes up, and made us, our military, everyone, get stronger." In part to illustrate to a non-Sikh the significance of the Golden Temple, multiple interviewees made direct comparisons to Vatican City and Mecca, while another suggested that an attack on the city of Amritsar was akin to a military assault on Jerusalem. When asked to reflect on the attack, Interview subjects enlisted a number of provocative, physically violent images and details. However, they also employed symbolic imagery such as scalping, mass graves, and the destruction of religious sanctuaries.

Although most respondents cited the occurrence of civilian deaths as the most disturbing element of the attack, subjects chose not to dwell long on the total number of people killed. Instead, they shifted focus to symbolic forms of violence, such as the brutality with which government forces are perceived to have treated Sikh pilgrims trapped inside the temple. This introduces an important point to make about the function of ethnic symbolism in influencing Sikh perceptions. Recall from chapter 2 that ethnic symbolism involves markers that resonate with and touch the core psychology of an ethnic community because they provide a crucial source of self-esteem and authenticity and a sense of the group's history (Eriksen 2002; Srubar 2007; Grün 2009). Symbolism is also crucial toward originating entire ethnic mythologies that can sustain the group during times of hardship and justify hostility or sacrifice (Demmers 2012). My interviews with diaspora Sikhs demonstrate a number of symbolic interpretations Sikhs made about the violence that took place during Operation Blue Star. Judging from the frequency of some of these allegations, a number have entered permanently into the canon of Sikh mythology.

For example, Interviewee 6 and several others referred to the same accusations: that the army made little attempt during the operation to distinguish between militants and civilians, shot dead any person who stood without permission, and in one notorious case, refused water to captured civilians, which led to a high number of deaths.[59] Interviewee 18 stressed repeatedly how Indian soldiers abused women and children during and after the attack, "to break the will of the Sikhs; to humiliate the women; to loot." Interviewee 5 said that he remembered seeing television images of police beating Sikhs in the streets, "their turbans falling off, their hair coming undone, blood running… it's just really disgusting to see." However, watching the violence unfold on television was impossible since the state had shut down all media coverage, and it is possible this respondent is conflating the Golden Temple attack with a later (or earlier) episode of violence. The images that came to mind for Interviewee 14 included "several hundred people with their hands tied behind their back, corpses they were dumping, and just the brutality of the whole thing." He also attested that he had seen a picture of Sant Jarnail Singh Bhindranwale's lifeless body, his head scalped. Interviewee 15 and a few others alleged the government buried its victims in mass graves: "Nobody came to claim those and they burned the bodies all day, even disintegrated the bodies in mass graves; there are pictures of that." He also

---

[59]According to survivors, the army locked approximately sixty pilgrims in a hostel room on the night between June 5th and 6th, locking their window, disconnecting their electricity and refusing to provide them with water despite extremely hot weather conditions. By the next morning, fifty-five of the sixty pilgrims had died, presumably from heat exhaustion. See Tully and Jacob (1985: 172).

recalled pictures showing children killed in the Golden Temple and blood spattered across its familiar marble floor.

In describing their perceptions of the attack, several respondents indicated mechanisms that helped shape their interpretations. For example, a few Sikhs referred to the colorful illustrations of the attack that emerged after Blue Star. These artistic renderings, which Sikh temples prominently display alongside portraits of other historical episodes, are drawn and painted in the distinct Sikh tradition of portraying overtly bloody battles and gruesome acts of martyrdom from Sikh history. An interesting comparison can be made between these illustrations and the conflict murals that appear in Northern Ireland, both of which attempt a narrative of the conflict to a specified audience. However, the murals in Northern Ireland invoke mostly symbolic imagery such as the likeness of Irish hunger striker Bobby Sands or the British Crown, connoting, respectively, the purity of the cause or British Imperial power. The Sikh illustrations by contrast are more literal and direct — perhaps owing to the Sikhs' collective desire to communicate the death toll and amount of carnage that took place during the attack.

A typical representation of Operation Blue Star would include dead bodies littered throughout the temple compound, multiple shrines destroyed, the holy water surrounding the main temple drenched in blood. At least one interview subject acknowledged these pictures helped inform his understanding of what happened during Operation Blue Star. Sitting on the floor of a California gurdwara, Interviewee 9 motioned to pictures adorning the walls when he described details about the operation that came to his mind:

I always see those pictures here… bloody pictures. When I spoke to my aunt in Punjab, there were bodies in the Sikh temple, [body] parts in the Sikh temple, the Golden Temple, for three, four months, rotting. They did that to show the world that this is what the Indian government did… those images will always stay in my mind.

Although Interviewee 9 acknowledged that he was never directly involved in the movement, the pictures nevertheless led him to allege the same claim made by others — that the Indian government deliberately hid the remains of Sikhs killed at the Golden Temple. It is important to note this claim has never been substantiated.

Violence waged against important religious and cultural icons during the attack also disturbed Sikh respondents due to their deep religious and cultural significance of artifacts. Interviewee 5, for example, stressed the destruction of the Akal Takht and compared it to the destruction of Vatican City, while others (Interviewees 2, 4, and 6) cited the burning of the library, which housed an impressive collection of religious documents. They questioned whether the army had intentionally targeted it to destroy those important religious scriptures. Even non-lethal details were remembered, such as when Interviewee 15 pointed out that Indian soldiers failed to remove their shoes during the operation, as is the custom when entering a Sikh gurdwara (the Indian government has disputed this charge). Asked to describe what images came to mind or might be symbolic about Blue Star, Interviewee 2 highlights violence committed against a number of cherished religious icons (emphasis added):

> It's more of a hatred than symbolic… shots being fired at the Golden Temple itself. *Priests being hit. The Holy Book being hit.* That was the biggest shocker I think. Because they actually didn't fire any cannons at the main temple, *but they did take shots [at the temple]*, machine guns and stuff like that. The book was hit.

Respondents also interpreted the decision to attack other gurdwaras simultaneously as an attempt to crush the Sikh spirit in one fell swoop. Interviewee 15 argued the government sought "to break the back of Sikhs and flush out the power" by attacking all the temples, "because that's where the congregation happens and that's where they talk about different things." He added: "If you want to control Sikhs and politically kill them, attack the highest seat and at the same time other gurdwaras and then bring them down."

These responses demonstrate how Sikh interpretations of the attack — what was important, what should be remembered, what lessons were imparted — could refer to acts of physical violence such as the civilian death toll, yet also conferred added meaning by embracing culturally resonant images describing how they were killed. For most subjects, these key details resonated as a threat to Sikhism's survival, and the employment of certain images such as scalping and mass graves conveyed as much symbolically as physically. One needs only to turn a few pages of Sikh history to find deeply powerful tales of Sikhs tortured and killed at the hands of a perceived foreign oppressor. Sikhs perceived the attack on the Golden Temple not as a military operation meant to neutralize a threat to the state, but as the state's assault against Sikhism in their homeland. The evidence of this perception can be found in the details about the attack that stood out to respondents – blood in the holy pool, the holy book being hit, Hamandir Sahib being struck by bullets, the Akal Takht destroyed, the burning of the library, a Sikh's turban torn from his head. These images resonate because they involve culturally significant monikers deeply cherished by the Sikh community. To wage violence against these icons is to threaten the Sikh's identity, her conception of self and cultural community, and as a consequence one should expect a deeply emotional and powerful response.

<u>A Grudge with Indira Gandhi</u>:

An unanticipated dynamic these interviews helped to illustrate was the degree to which several respondents came to loathe the late Prime Minister Indira Gandhi for her role in ordering the attacks.[60] More than any military officer, soldier, or politician, Sikhs associated Gandhi's name with Blue Star, to the point of their being virtually indistinguishable. For example, Interviewee 4 uses her name and the military forces carrying out the attack interchangeably, saying, "She should have never done that attack at the temple. There was uproar and outcry everywhere worldwide, when *she* attacked the temple." Interviewee 17 referred to her as the "Butcher of Amritsar."

Several Sikhs felt that Gandhi's motives included elements of revenge, insinuating she had held a grudge against the Akali Dal ever since the latter had organized resistance to Emergency rule in 1975. Said Interviewee 15: "During the [1975] elections, Sikhs were the only ones who went against [Indira Gandhi] and put her in jail. She would never forget that. She wanted to teach a lesson to the Sikhs." Asked if Operation Blue Star therefore constituted a form of punishment, he responded, "Oh, definitely," calling it "a very personal vendetta."[61] Interviewee 6 echoed this idea. "She was… very unhappy and not very pleased with that kind of behavior," the subject asserted, referring to Sikh resistance to the Emergency. "So she wanted to teach a lesson; that's what history tells us, or the books say. She wanted to teach a lesson and finish them off." Interviewee 25 interpreted her decision as a political maneuver meant to

---

[60] Given the level of abhorrence for Gandhi expressed in these interviews, it is clear that time has not much softened perceptions of Gandhi's culpability much since her assassination in November 1984, when, according to various media reports, some Sikhs allegedly celebrated in the streets of New York and elsewhere following news of her death, and a WSO official for Southern California proclaimed to local media, "We are ecstatic." See Sanger (1984) and Wedel (1984).

[61] Interviewee 15 asserted that his viewpoint was not only his opinion, but also the opinion of most Sikhs, "that since Indira Gandhi was put in jail, and she was demoralized and she felt so bad, she wanted to get back to Sikhs and to get revenge. [It was] a very personal vendetta."

convince Hindus that Sikhs were separatist so that Hindus would turn to Gandhi in her role as "Mother India." Interviewee 14 viewed Gandhi's intervention in Punjab as wholly political and manipulative, meant to make an example of the Sikhs: "If you look at the whole history of what she's done, it was all manipulating the politics of Punjab. That's really what it was she wanted to [do], it was one place where she felt threatened and that was one way to show to the rest of India that she can put these people down."

The degree to which diaspora Sikhs held Gandhi personally responsible for the attack perhaps derives from the need to simplify complex events and processes into familiar and personal frames. In general, interview subjects viewed Gandhi with a mixture of contempt, regret, and bewilderment that she would endorse the military operation in the first place — after learning about the operation, Interviewee 8 recalled thinking, "Oh my God, she's just written her death certificate, because nobody's ever gone in and attacked the Golden Temple." Some subjects described her assassination four months after the attack as a "relief" to Sikhs in the diaspora, since "she was responsible for those attacks" (Interviewee 11).[62] Asked the reason for ordering such a brazen attack, most of the interview subjects believed that Gandhi concluded that it was time to put the Sikhs in their place; indeed, "weaken the Sikhs" or "teach the Sikhs a lesson" became common refrains in almost every response on this topic. According to Interviewee 3, "the people at the helm, Indira Gandhi, I guess [they] wanted to teach Sikhs a

---

[62] In addition to conveying unflattering views about Indira Gandhi, some subjects such as Interviewee 5 were also quite critical about her son Rajiv, who assumed his mother's position following her death. Discussing the extensive rioting that took place in Delhi after Indira's death, Interviewee 5 said of Rajiv Gandhi: "His first job [was] 'let's s kill all the Sikhs and destroy their businesses.' He sends these guys out and they pay people. They get the poor people, the criminals, pay them and say 'okay, you go and kill as many [as you can],' and now [get] the police guard to make sure the Sikhs don't get away from these people." Like many of the interview subjects, Interviewee 5 thought that the Gandhi's family dominance within the Congress Party, which had allowed three members of the Nehru/Gandhi clan to serve as prime minister of India for most of its history, undermined India's claim to be a democracy.

lesson for being so independent-minded, who the authority is."[63] Interviewee 18 argued that "it was very clear from Indira Gandhi's mindset" that Sikhs "should be taught a lesson," leading Gandhi to label Sikhs as separatists and terrorists — "As the popular maxim goes, 'to kill a dog, you must first prove him mad.'" Said Interviewee 4:

> It was complicated for political and economic reasons, [but] the government always wanted to keep the Sikhs down, and so [the government] figured if they succeed they might try to get their own country... they know Sikhs are strong, they are fighters, and they'll retaliate.

This interview subject, like most other respondents, perceived Gandhi's desire as exacting a price on the Sikhs for their independence. Yet, the same person asserted it was the Sikhs' reverence for their main shrine that should have warned Gandhi to be more aware of the possible ramifications of attacking it: "That's why she was assassinated... I'm pretty sure [her bodyguards] were loyal to her; she trusted them. But they just couldn't stand her attack on the temple. The Sikhs are always, even in the past, the Sikhs retaliate. Somebody tries to destroy their religion, they'll go after them." All of these comments underscore two important perceptions about Gandhi's role: 1) the degree to which Sikhs held Gandhi personally responsible for the attacks, and 2) the widely held assumption among Sikhs that Gandhi owned a deep and poisonous grudge against the Sikhs, one that came to rival—and in the minds of Sikhs, justify—the level of animosity Sikhs clearly felt toward the prime minister.

In sum, Operation Blue Star shocked and threatened the Sikhs, many of whom suggested that it was their religion that was actually under attack. Indira Gandhi took on an especially

---

[63] Interviewee 3 went on to articulate a number of the demands made by Sikhs at the time, including that the government needed to designate Amritsar a sacred city, ban drugs and alcohol, and provide greater rights of self-determination to the state of Punjab.

villainous role for ordering the operation, and through this attack she became closely associated with the crackdown on Sikh nationalism. Sikhs perceived her motivation for ordering Operation Blue Star was to reassert Delhi's authority over the Sikhs, "teach them a lesson," and curb their growing influence through violence and intimidation.

OPERATION BLUE STAR AND EVENT GALVANIZATION

This section will assess respondent answers regarding the degree to which Operation Blue Star led to a significant transformation of Sikh perceptions, allowing mobilization to ensue. To later analyze if the Indian government's actions inside the Golden Temple galvanized the diaspora toward mobilization, however, first it is necessary to establish diaspora perceptions of that movement before the event. On this score, most respondents suggested that prior to Operation Blue Star, Sikhs in their communities did not care deeply or pay close attention to the ongoing push for the independence of Punjab. "I think more of the people here really didn't care much, didn't worry about it much," Interviewee 2 noted of the Sikh community in Yuba City, adding that in the weeks leading up to Blue Star, "[Local Sikhs also] never believed that the Indian government would send soldiers in there." According to Interviewee 14, a separate country was like "an alien concept," "was absolutely not in anyone's mind," and noted that Sikhs had been raised "to be a part of India."[64] Similarly, Interviewee 4 said that Sikhs "didn't care for [independence] that much." Interviewee 13 recalled that while recent Sikh migrants would occasionally discuss it, "the majority of the population who lived here didn't feel they needed Khalistan." Even Interviewee 13, who had visited India a few years before the events of 1984

---

[64] As an example, he mentioned that most Sikhs supported Indian athletes at the Olympics; however, he also suggested that the perceptions of some Sikhs of the Indian state were changing at least a year or two before Blue Star, due to the mounting tensions between Punjabi Sikhs and the center.

and observed the situation deteriorating, had not been persuaded by the goals of the movement prior to Blue Star. Said Interviewee 12: "We used to never hear about Khalistan."

Inasmuch as Sikhs even considered the prospect of independence, evidence suggests they appreciated the pride a country for Sikhs might bring, but understood how economic and political realities outweighed these and other incentives. Interviewee 8 suggested that there was a bit of sentiment that "It'd be nice to get it," but that no one actively supported the idea. Interviewee 4 suggested a certain level of political apathy in the diaspora existed when it came to homeland politics. "Sikhs [in America] knew… they [Punjabi Sikhs] were not getting fair rights, water rights, autonomy, political," he said. "They were not getting their fair share. It's just that nobody did too much about it." Geopolitical considerations also tempered expectations. "Some people thought it would be good to have your own country, but most people [thought] it's just not feasible," Interviewee 5 said. "A tiny little country, you have no port, it's a little island in the middle of India. It'd be good if you could have it, but it's not realistic." He did note, however, that a "small percentage" in the diaspora supported the idea. According to Interviewee 3, political and economic realities at least for some Sikhs always tempered the issue:

> Everybody has different ideas. I don't think anybody would have been unhappy if we got independent Punjab. But [Sikhs] were saying that, 'we are too small,' and what are we going to do with that? [We are] too poor, landlocked, and maybe they were used to that. In my [day], and I still think to this day, people talk about freedom. But when you're reduced to it, like right now, the Sikhs are worse off than they were under British rule.[65]

---

[65] Interviewee 3 went on to explain that Sikhs received greater respect and more benefits under British rule than they had during India's era of self-rule.

Some Sikhs professed their pro-Indian patriotism prior to 1984. Interviewee 18, who relocated from Punjab in the early 1990s, said that before June 1984, most Sikhs "never thought that India is not our country. We always thought that this is the land, for whose freedom, the forefathers had fought against the Afghans; they had sacrificed their lives, their family for the freedom of this land... The country was ours."[66] In sum, most respondents did not suggest the existence of significant support for Khalistan prior to the events of 1984, but portrayed Khalistan as the faint aspiration of a few individuals with little support in the larger community.

These views changed dramatically in the diaspora after Operation Blue Star. Respondents characterized the attack as "a shock" (Interviewee 4), "a wake-up call for the younger generation" (Interviewee 2), and "a huge mistake, a blunder by the Indian government" (Interviewee 5). Asked if Blue Star provided the separatist movement with greater credibility than it had previously enjoyed, most respondents answered that it almost certainly had. Sikhs realized that "if we had our own homeland, this wouldn't happen," in the words of Interviewee 4. Interviewee 5 expressed disbelief that the country's army would attack its own people, a moment he depicted as a game-changer: "That's not your army then, that's not your country... It's probably the only time you had a majority of Sikhs living outside [India], especially in the Yuba City area, feeling the need for a Khalistan." Asked directly if the attack made it more acceptable for diaspora Sikhs to support separatism, he responded, "Yeah. Definitely, there's no doubt about it." The attack motivated many American Sikhs to take a hard look at what was going on in Punjab for the first time. Where Sikhs as a community were once apathetic about the prospect for

---

[66] As an example, Interviewee 18 recalled how Sikhs in Punjab took special pride in the Sikhs' military contributions to the defense of India. "During the wars with Pakistan in 1965 and 1971," he said, "those were times when every plane shot down or advance made on every front, a mile or even smaller, was celebrated in our homes. Victory of the Indian army was like our own victory."

independence, they now expressed a full political awakening and an immediate hunger to learn more about what was going on in Punjab.

Operation Blue Star generated new sympathy for the separatist movement and provoked deep opposition to the Indian government. These reactions in Punjab and in the diaspora provided the movement with greater momentum and support than had previously existed. Said Interviewee 10: "I think after attacking the Golden Temple, everybody believed that Sikhs needed their homeland. Because if this government can attack a holy place, the Golden Temple, they can do anything. I think after 1984, everybody wanted to have Khalistan." According to Interviewee 8: "I think it united everybody. It's kind of like, 'oh my God, you just came into my house, and you just opened fire, and you killed.'" When asked if the attack had singularly convinced American Sikhs of the need for independence, he responded:

> Yes absolutely. [Sikhs] felt the government had stepped its bounds and reached too much. That was the reason. They felt there's no way. How would it be if someone went into the Vatican and attacked the Vatican and grabbed the Pope, because they felt the Pope had arms or something? ... Every single Catholic throughout the world would be angry and devastated, going, "how could you come in and attack our holiest shrine?"

As important about what Sikhs remembered about Operation Blue Star is what they had forgotten — or at least, which elements of the attack have over the years been discarded and are no longer remembered by a national community because they do not fit with the favored narrative of the conflict — what Behdad (2005) refers to as a national community's "historical amnesia." In this respect, it is noteworthy that few Sikhs attested how militants had engaged in an escalating campaign of violence in the run-up to Blue Star — frequently against other Sikhs suspected of being informers — or how they had destroyed cherished sections in order to fortify the complex, thereby also disturbing the sanctity of the Sikh shrine (Fair 2008).

Did Operation Blue Star justify the militancy and the employment of violence in the eyes of diaspora Sikhs? The researcher asked this question to most respondents, and it produced a variety of answers. Some condemned violence no matter the circumstance — Interviewee 15, a former official of the World Sikh Organization, offered his concise view: "No, you can never justify [violence]." Only a few readily agreed the attack had justified violence. However, several respondents implied they were now more empathetic than before of the challenges Sikh militants faced. Interviewee 14, for example, said violence "was the wrong way to do it. But of course the guys [who] were responding to the atrocities [thought they] are not the ones initiating it; but I am sure that wasn't always true." Some allowed violence *could* be morally just given the circumstances faced by homeland Sikhs. Interviewee 5, for instance, remarked how "violence is never right," but argued, "these people were pushed to the point where they didn't really have a choice… they had nothing to live for." He also volunteered that he might have made the same choice as the armed separatists, if he was in their place. Interviewee 12 — who was otherwise quite critical of the goals of the Khalistan movement — insinuated the decision to employ violence was reasonable given the trauma Sikhs had endured:

In my mind, not knowing all the details, but knowing that their holiest of holy places had been attacked by the government… Is it justified? I'm a believer in "let's talk this over, let's not use force." You know what I mean? But it's almost like it had gone beyond that. Where they crossed the line and the manner in which it was done, a lot of innocent lives lost… That goes against anything that I believe. But at the same time, when they were attacked in such a manner, maybe

in their minds it was justified.

She also drew inspiration from the American experience, framing the choice as the same faced

by the American founding fathers. Others felt that self-defense justified the use of force.

Interviewee 11 deflected attention back to India's treatment of Sikhs and drew from it this

lesson: "Any state, not just India, that uses violence to suppress the people, fails in every point of

social economic, and political justice. You then expect people to take up arms."

According to multiple respondents, attacking the Golden Temple was emotionally so

devastating that it overwhelmed Sikhs and drove them to make decisions that were decidedly

irrational. The fact that Operation Blue Star due to its emotional charge may have provided such

a sudden lift to the movement, but could not alone sustain support for the movement over the

long term, introduces a potentially important dimension to our understanding of traumatic events.

Gone were the concerns that Punjab lacked industry or a port. Said Interviewee 5: "People

couldn't think straight and they'd think, okay, we're just going to pick up arms. But how can you

win against tanks and armies... It was an emotional response in a situation where they saw no

other viable alternatives." Interviewee 13 made a similar connection: "Emotionally, everybody

felt that, yes, [Government officials] were getting what they deserved, because they attacked our

holiest place." However, respondents generally understood that the Sikh community eventually

would recover from the psychological trauma of Blue Star. When asked why support for the

movement seemed to wane within a few years, a common response was that Sikhs were ready to

move on with their lives.

It is important to note the reluctance of a few respondents to equate Blue Star with a

wholesale shift in perceptions, if only because they had other events in mind. While acknowledging that the Golden Temple attack "helped solidify" Sikhs in America, Interviewee 15 traced the Sikh desire for independence not to Blue Star, but to the crafting of the Indian constitution which failed to recognize Sikhism as a separate religion. Interviewee 3 was ambivalent about the overall effect of Blue Star on diaspora perceptions. When asked if it gave credibility to the independence movement, he responded that "everybody has different ideas" and "I don't imagine that there was any organized thing (after Blue Star), [but] there were little groups," presumably referring to factions in the community who championed the Khalistan struggle more fervently than others, perhaps even actively supporting militant groups, although he did not elaborate. According to Interviewees 12 and 13, Blue Star resonated more strongly with recent emigrants than with Sikhs whose families had lived longer in the US. Finally, Interviewee 6 commented that the militancy that followed Blue Star was neither for independence nor increased political rights, but derived from Sikhs' desire "for a little bit of revenge" for the attack itself.[67] However, most respondents saw Blue Star as having profoundly transformed diaspora perceptions in favor of Sikh independence, conferring the event with the potential to function as an event galvanizer. I will pick back up on this point in the analysis section of this chapter.

From Militant to Martyr: the Transformation of Bhindranwale:

Sometimes, traumatic events can take relatively obscure figures and transform them into inspirational if controversial figureheads, whose names become forever linked to the cause for which they have fought and sacrificed. This dynamic when it occurs enhances event

---

[67] His exact quote: "I think that the fight was not for independence or Khalistan... It was basically for a little bit of revenge and to convince the government that we do need something. Because when the agreement came, with Indira Gandhi, some of the things were agreed which we were asking... but then it really didn't come to a conclusion, it fizzled out."

galvanization because the imagining of new ethnic leaders — one for the current times — provides ethnic participants with a more intimate and personal access point through which to feel connected to the ethnic group's historically rooted mythology. Yet, the threshold can be high for gaining such prestige; it frequently has required leaders to sacrifice their lives for their ethnic cause, such as the Easter Rising martyrs or Michael Collins, or the nineteenth century Uyghur leader Yaqub Beg, who according to some ethnic fables died in combat with the Chinese, though it is more likely he was poisoned or assassinated.

So it was with Operation Blue Star and the creation of a martyr-hero in Sant Jarnail Singh Bhindranwale, who came to be conceived as one of a long line of "Saint-Soldiers" (Mahmood 1996).[68] Not dissimilar to how Indira Gandhi came to embody India's perceived attack on Sikhism, the martyrdom of Bhindranwale would eventually personify the movement and provide Sikhs with a valuable portal for linking the present with the past. Although I did not always identify Bhindranwale in my initial questioning, several interview subjects took it upon themselves to note his involvement, describing Bhindranwale as an important and historic figure and portraying him as the latest in a long line of martyrs. These respondents spoke of him with both admiration and religious reverence. Interviewee 4 identified him as "the leading guy, a religious person trying to promote the religion and trying to protect Sikh rights. He was exposing the government."[69] Interviewee 18 — who as head of a diaspora organization that promotes the cause of Khalistan, has something of a professional duty to safeguard Bhindranwale's legacy —

---

[68] The concept of the "Saint-Soldier" is rooted in militant readings of Sikh theology that ties Sikhism directly to militancy, arguing that to be a good Sikh one must seek to combine spirituality with military valor, and that those who condemn militancy are not "true Sikhs." For further discussion, see Mahmood (1996: 41).

[69] In the same breath, Interviewee 4 criticized the government's depiction of Bhindranwale: "The government was portraying a different picture of him, saying this guy's a radical saint. Because he was exposing the government, they didn't like that so that's why they killed him."

depicted his "Sant" as wise, humble, and fearless ("no grain of fear in his heart and soul"). He quoted widely from Bhindranwale's most famous quotes and parables — "A Sikh is not afraid of [death], and whoever is afraid of [death] is not a Sikh" — and portrayed him as the patriarch of the Khalistan movement even without having ever made an overt demand for independence during his lifetime. Indeed, Bhindranwale's martyrdom elevated his views and inspiration to unprecedented levels. Describing Bhindranwale's decision to stay behind in the Golden Temple, Interviewee 18 remarked:

> He had a full understanding of history, he understood his importance and the role he was playing and he understood what expectations the Sikh nation had for him. He knew that once this happens, he would sacrifice [his life]. He also knew that once he laid these prophetic words, the foundation of Khalistan would be laid.

Another respondent, Interviewee 14, who had traveled to India a few years before Operation Blue Star took place, saw Bhindranwale settle a dispute between two villagers. He was impressed by what he saw:

> My image of him was this real radical, firebrand of a guy, [but] when I heard him and saw him do his thing I said he's a pretty interesting guy and he's pretty sane. Within ten minutes he had those guys embracing each other and the whole dispute was settled... I said this guy, my image of him from TV, not TV but the news media, the newspapers and all that... was this guy was going to pull out a sword and cut this guy's head off or shoot somebody. But this guy was talking a lot of sense... everything he said was not illogical to me.

It was clear from the interviews that Bhindranwale's fame stemmed directly from his role and his death in Operation Blue Star. Had Bhindranwale not died at the Golden Temple, the controversial militant's fame likely would have receded. Only a few interview subjects before Operation Blue Star felt sympathetic to Bhindranwale and his cause; some had never heard of him. After the attacks, however, Bhindranwale became a celebrated figure, whose image was recognized widely and immediately in the global Sikh community. In the aftermath of Operation Blue Star, most in the diaspora came to recognize Bhindranwale as an important and historical leader. Explaining the transformative effect of Bhindranwale's death, Interviewee 1 attributes to Bhindranwale in death a symbolic strength that he could never have enjoyed while alive:

> A lot of people followed [Bhindranwale] like a martyr, which he was; he got killed. He himself even said, 'I don't care if they kill me. It's pretty much going to make me stronger for what they did.' And it did. After death, he became invincible because pretty much everyone wanted to follow what he was saying during that time.

Other Sikhs were more even-handed in their remembrance of Bhindranwale, yet they too appeared to recognize his legacy as a transformative Sikh leader from that period and a key figure in Sikh history. In the quote below, Interviewee 6 hints at an imperfect figure, but nevertheless one who sacrificed his life for the cause:

> A lot of people say, why did Bhindranwale sit in [the Golden Temple]? Well, it is his house, it's God's house, it's the Guru's house, and he is a Sikh so it's his right to sit there. People have different views about it, why wouldn't he do it in some other gurdwaras, but I think he, one thing about him, whatever his weaknesses, he was a very truthful man. And he knew he was going to die. He had already made a prediction that I want to become a martyr. I will die for this, defending it.

Interviewee 8 was more skeptical about Bhindranwale than his peers. However, he too recognized the importance of Operation Blue Star in cementing his legacy among the Sikhs:

> At that point in time, nobody really knew what Bhindranwale stood for, nobody really followed his day-to-day stuff. Who he was fighting, where was he getting the arms, why did you need to have arms in a holy place? In the gunfight, even if people didn't agree with his views, he came out as a martyr.

After Blue Star, the above respondent notes, portraits of Bhindranwale began to appear almost immediately in gurdwaras and people's homes — not unlike the photos of the 1916 Easter Rising martyrs that adorned the mantelpieces of Irish homes (Ussher 1949; Schmitt 1973). Pro-Khalistan slogans and signs began appearing across the Yuba City community praising his life and recalling his martyrdom. It was only in death that Bhindranwale attracted the type of global following that exists to the present day.

SIKH RESPONSES TO BLUE STAR: PRAYERS, PROTESTS... FUNDING?

As chapter 3 discussed, for a traumatic event to function as an event galvanizer, it must distress ethnic members and transform perceptions among a significant cluster of members to the point of mobilization. As part of this mobilization, ethnic members take actions in support of the cause, including participating in public demonstrations, political advocacy, making donations to, or joining movement organizations, including in some cases groups that are violent. For this research, interview subjects reflected on a variety of actions taken in response to Operation Blue Star. Some of the most frequent memories discussed were of special prayers held at the local temple. They also invoked the protests and demonstrations following the attack — Interviewee 3, for example, recalled Sikhs turning out in huge numbers for a demonstration in front of the

Indian consulate in San Francisco. One of those demonstrators was Interviewee 5, who traveled with other Yuba City Sikhs and reflected about the environment at the rally: "There was so much rage. We were so angry; it was 'Death to India!' 'Death to Indira Gandhi!'… 'Long Live Pakistan!' I didn't have any voice after that, [it was] so emotional." Similarly, New England Sikhs planned a demonstrations New York City and Washington. Interviewee 17 took part in a protest march in Boston, where he remembered Sikh demonstrators trying to light an Indian flag on fire only to discover that nylon does not burn very well.

In the wake of Blue Star, respondents described the process of becoming more organized and politically conscious. Many formed local groups to push back against the level of disinformation they perceived the Indian government to be spreading. Others took it upon themselves to push back against Indian propaganda – for example, Interviewee 14 remembered engaging on his own volition in several heated debates with Americans of Indian descent. In Yuba City, respondents recalled fresh slogans commemorating the Sikh nation (Interviewee 2), as well as a new float appearing in the local parade, honoring as martyrs those killed during the attack (Interviewee 1). There were growing pains along the way as Sikhs figured out how best to publicize the movement. Interviewee 25 helped organize "a big event" at a local university in Washington but was disappointed when "not a single non-Sikh came." Interviewee 15, already a well-known and respected leader in the Boston Sikh community, granted every media interview request he received to offer his reaction to Blue Star on behalf of Sikhs. For the first time, Sikhs in the United States began to engage the separatist issue by embracing the American political system at their disposal. Respondents such as Interviewee 4 wrote to his congressional representative asking the United States government to condemn India; others formed or joined American Sikh organizations committed to mobilizing support for the movement in the United

States; and Interviewee 18 founded a newsletter that grew to have a mailing list of Sikhs distributed across the United States and Canada.

According to the majority of respondents, the formation of the World Sikh Organization in July 1984 marked an important step in the Sikh diaspora's political maturation. However, some respondents — including Interviewee 15, a founding member of the WSO — lamented the organization's early rifts as a major blow to the movement's success at mobilizing, and these subjects believed the Indian government infiltrated and sabotaged the WSO's leadership ranks.[70] Despite these leadership woes, the diaspora claimed great pride in the WSO's activity and pointed to its successes in enlisting legislators such as Dan Burton, a Republican from Indiana who over the course of his career was known for possessing pro-Pakistan and anti-India views. Several respondents also portrayed the meeting of Sikh activists with President Reagan as a historic achievement for the Sikh separatist movement.

Respondents also described Sikhs participating in massive fundraising efforts as a response to Operation Blue Star. Some lamented it was all they could do. In most cases, Sikhs believed these funds were intended for medical purposes or financial stabilization for affected families. "We did collect some money to send back, through certain people, stuff like that," said Interviewee 2. "Certain groups, so they could have some medical treatments. People that were hurt, some families that were wiped out, help their kids that needed it." Interviewee 8 added his perception that Sikhs from all across California opened their wallets to provide relief to those in

---

[70] Interviewee 15 implied that the sense of urgency that Sikh activists felt in launching the WSO unfortunately had outweighed the need to conduct a more patient and thorough selection process. In fact, Interviewee 15 said his organization acted too hastily in appointing its leadership and alleged that some leaders were agents of the Indian government—a claim widely made by other Sikhs. Part of the evidence, he said, was the fact that certain leaders were allowed to later return to India at a time when the government was actively denying visas to known Sikh separatists.

Punjab: "Quite a bit of money went from here to non-profit organizations; a lot of money was given to them. Up and down the state, millions of bucks fed into the cause."

Did respondents think it was possible some of these donations eventually ended up in the accounts of violent extremist groups? This was a question I posed to almost every interview subject, and it yielded a surprisingly common response that some almost certainly had. Most of the time, Sikhs believed the donors had no intention of contributing to these groups, but that militants and supporters in the diaspora took advantage of an informal and unaccountable funding process. Sikhs were so desperate to find a way to support their co-ethnics in Punjab after Operation Blue Star that they unwittingly made contributions to the various groups now waging the insurgency. Said Interview 2: "We never knew if [the funds] got to the right people or not… Indian people are very generous to give. But sometimes they don't think where the money is going." Interviewee 13 referred to communal traits of generosity and naiveté that he and others say characterize the Sikhs:

> I think that Sikhs in general, Punjabis in general, are very giving in nature. Where they will, you know, [give] money. And that's their nature, right? But as far as looking at, is this money really going to get there? I remember it kind of put me off. I mean, wait, if you don't know if the money is going to get there, what's the point?[71]

Interviewee 13 also said he personally observed some militant fundraisers campaigning for donations at community meetings. He said supporters framed their fundraising appeals as an

---

[71] Interviewee 6 suggested that families that had lost loved ones to violence or were supportive of the movement were the most likely to have donated knowingly for the purposes of armed struggle, but it was not clear from his comments if he was referring to Sikhs in Punjab or diaspora Sikhs. He later added that there were probably "a lot of Sikhs outside" Punjab that disagreed with the tactics adopted by the movement.

imploration "to help the people who were trying to fight this cause back home" and to provide financial assistance to repair the Golden Temple and rebuild the Akal Takht. The respondent affirmed his belief, as did others, that "the money never made it where it was supposed to go." Interviewee 8 also indicated that while Sikhs hardly hesitated to give, the destination of these donations was not always clear: "When you're making contributions, you're making contributions somewhere, but they're not coming out saying, 'okay, this is what we're funding.' Did it go to arms? I'm sure it did. How much? I have no idea."

No interview subjects contradicted the claim that some funds may have unintentionally reached militant groups. However, some added that it was also likely — and relatively easy — for local Sikhs to donate knowingly and wittingly to militant organizations. For example, Interviewee 1 speculated that well-connected business owners knew exactly what they were doing when they contributed directly to militant groups. Asked if any Sikhs in Yuba City donated knowingly to militants, he responded:

> I can't speak for anybody, but I'm sure they did [provide funds to separatist militant groups]. Yeah. Monetarily, politically, whatever connections [local Sikhs] had over there. Any Sikhs that were here that had a lot of power over there. You know, lets say a big landowner or someone who had big bucks or a family that had big bucks. I'm sure they tried to push leverage to help out their brethren. Whether it's military stuff or whatever they need, I'm sure they did.

Asked to elaborate on his comment about "helping their brethren," Interviewee 1 replied:

> "I think it's one of those, 'we are few, but we are proud, type of things, so far as the Sikhs [are concerned]. You know, you have the turban, the beard, and we are

going to show that, 'hey, we aren't going to back down from anybody.' We're

going to fight for who we are, just like our gurus did during their time.

Interviewee 8 suggested that Sikhs wittingly donated to militant groups, stressing that giving to

the militants required only knowing through which donor networks to contribute:

There [were] a lot of organizations here set up. There was a group called Babbar

Khalsa and [Sikhs] knew that if you funded Babbar Khalsa money was going to

the war there. In fact, they were on the government's list as far as not travelling

and all that kind of stuff. So you knew what organizations you were funding, you

knew where the money was going to go. They were clear: "Hey, this is what

we're going to do, we need your help." They were die-hard fighter rebels, per se.

There were others who also believed some American Sikhs knowingly contributed to the

militancy, but their assessments were more tentative and qualified. Interviewee 14, for example,

suggested that he "would not be surprised" if contributions came from areas such as California or

Canada, where there were large populations of Punjabi Sikhs "who came recently and were

somehow either directly or indirectly involved in some militancy." Interviewee 16 remembered a

few in his community who had escaped the violence in Punjab at one point enticed other Sikhs if

they wanted "to support our people over there?" but he indicated that in the end only those exiles

"threw a dollar or two" at the Khalistan movement, and did so more as a face-saving gesture.

(The interview subject also indicated he knew of a family member who "was recruited and taken

over" to Punjab by the Khalistan movement, where he was killed.) Asked if it was his impression

that Sikhs had ever sent money explicitly to help fund militant groups in Punjab as opposed to

humanitarian organizations, a community leader in Washington DC replied cryptically that

"some groups might have… at that time they thought it was a genuine cause"

Sikhs who represented diaspora groups denied diverting funds to militants on behalf of their organizations. However, they acknowledged that some diaspora elements were in support of the insurgents. Interviewee 15, the former World Sikh Organization official, asserted that all donations to the WSO in the aftermath of Blue Star were made "in the name of people who had been killed and their families [who] were suffering," and that the WSO used these funds only for administrative purposes or to coordinate visits to the US by witnesses and survivors, movement leaders based in Punjab, or public figures such as Bhindranwale's wife. When asked if any Sikhs willingly donated to violent organizations, Interviewee 15 denied any personal involvement,[72] but acknowledged the existence of informal networks that may have supported insurgent groups: "Especially after the Delhi [riots]... a lot of money was given to organizations from India or people individually [who] knew this family, that family, and they may have used the money for themselves. Who knows what they did with the money." Interviewee 18, the pro-Khalistan diaspora official whose organization raises funds for a variety of Sikh causes, also denied that any group with which he had ever been affiliated employed funds to support militancy; he also made the somewhat improbable claim that separatist groups did not need or even want external funding.[73] A third interview subject who was active in diaspora politics at the time asked not to comment on diaspora fundraising for militant groups. No other interview subjects contradicted the claim that some funds may have reached militant groups intentionally.

---

[72] His full quote: "Not really. Most of the collection that I remember was to help the families; the people who got killed or people who were in jail, to fight for their release. Nobody ever approached [saying] they needed arms to fight. Nobody ever approached [on behalf of] this militant organization, at least not in the US... we never went out to people to say, 'Oh give us money to fight this, to fight that.'"

[73] Said Interviewee 18: "At no point in time did the armed struggle of Punjab go to that level, where it needed planes and tanks, something which needed money. In these years at least, I being whatever I am doing, neither I nor being in knowledge of somebody who through his personal contacts might have sent something."

In summary, Sikhs reflected on a variety of political activity in response to Operation Blue Star, which included planning protests and demonstrations, actively lobbying American government officials, raising awareness and grassroots support in the United States, and fundraising on behalf of the cause. On the issue of fundraising, no subject — except perhaps Interviewee 18, the diaspora organization official — denied that some Sikh funds probably ended up in the coffers of militant groups operating against the Indian government in Punjab. Most respondents assumed that militant supported diverted these funds without the explicit knowledge of the donors, who thought their assistance were going toward relief efforts in India. Other interview subjects professed to knowing of local Sikhs who wittingly donated to militant and violent organizations, and that doing so was relatively easy. Finally, it is important to note that respondents who formerly or currently worked for diaspora organizations denied that their groups ever directed funds toward militant activity.

ANALYSIS

This analysis section scrutinizes the interview data by assessing the value of my hypotheses identified in chapters 1 and 3 as it relates to this case study. This section also adds important caveats and qualifications based on this research, and assesses broader implications as it concerns our scholarly understanding of ethnic conflict. It begins with analysis of the physical and symbolic levels of violence and their effects on the Sikh diaspora.

Physical and Symbolic Levels of Violence:

Operation Blue Star devastated the Sikh community in profound and fundamental ways. While Punjab had seen a steady stream of increasingly violent events since 1982, no event in the history of the conflict compared to Blue Star in terms of physical violence — the death toll from Blue Star, alone, exceeded the number killed in the three years preceding it — or the symbolic violence embedded in the imagery of the Indian government attacking Sikhism's most sacred temple. Only when one understands the horror and fear that Sikhs felt when they learned the news of Operation Blue Star can the full breadth of the Sikh response be comprehended, a determination mirroring Horowitz's (2000) argument that a bloody phenomenon cannot be explained by a bloodless theory.

The relatively high amount of physical violence initiated during Operation Blue Star — the physical severity of the act as measured by human casualties and property damage — infuriated American Sikhs, and to some extent this encouraged them to increase their support of the goals of Sikh separatism. Respondents saw the operation as cruel and excessive; they cited the high death toll as the most outrageous legacy of the operation. In the years preceding Blue Star, no other event approached the number of people killed or the severity of destruction resulting from a single attack. The abruptness and perceived brutality of the government's actions shocked the Sikhs and initiated a transformation of their views on the conflict. Although I include some important caveats below about the utility of testing this hypothesis as a single case study, this analysis assesses that the response of Sikhs to the physical level of violence observed during Operation Blue Star provides at least tentative support for the first hypothesis:

H1a (physical violence): As the relative level of violent aggression or bloodshed involved in a traumatic event increases, separatist movements will attract new followers and persuade fence-sitters

As I have said, there are caveats in making this assessment. Principally, without comparison data to another case, it is difficult to determine if a positive relationship exists between the level of violent aggression and the movement's ability to attract followers. Blue Star needs to be compared to other events with differing levels of violent aggression, as I do in the next part of this research. Even when viewing Blue Star as a discrete event, one can reasonably assess that some features of the violence disturbed the Sikh community and impacted their perceptions of the separatist movement. Yet, boiling Blue Star down to its death toll and number of crumbled buildings does not capture the most significant dimensions of outrage suffered by the Sikhs.

The *way* that Sikh pilgrims died framed perceptions of the event to a far greater degree than the actual number of Sikhs killed, which is indicative of the symbolism the attack assumed. Sikhs interpreted the Indian government's actions to stand symbolically as an attack on Sikhism, a confrontation against its culture and way of life, easily equated to September 11 or the assassination of an American president. Allegations, reports, stories, and eye-witness accounts of widespread human rights abuses — including unproven claims that Sikhs were summarily executed, their bodies scalped and then thrown in mass graves — coursed through the diaspora in the aftermath of the attack, coloring the lens through which Sikhs envisaged the casualties. Blood staining the pool waters, shots striking Hamandir Sahib or the Guru Granth Sahib, the burning of the library, a Sikh's turban torn from his head — all impacted Sikh diaspora members emotionally and psychologically. Likewise, the destruction wrought against the complex — the near total destruction of the Akal Takht, bullets grazing the central shrine Harmandir Sahib, the burning down of the library — deeply upset respondents. Sikhs interpreted these events subjectively, as evidence of governmental prejudice and pernicious intent against their religion and way of life. Ethnic movement entrepreneurs were left with a much more favorable playing field on which to encourage a dominant frame of Operation Blue Star as symbolizing the Indian government's contempt for Sikhism, and many of the diaspora members interviewed for this research volunteered that they shifted their views after Blue Star to reflect these interpretations. The evidence presented by these interviews therefore offers greater support for the second hypothesis regarding the role of <u>symbolic violence</u> – acts of violence predisposed to significant cultural meaning:

> **H1b (symbolic violence):** When crucial details of a traumatic event gain symbolic significance or underscore specific and preexisting separatist frames from the conflict, separatist movements will attract new followers and persuade fence-sitters

Although respondents did not frame every occurrence in symbolic rather than physical terms,[74] Sikh responses frequently conferred violent acts with deeply symbolic meaning, suggesting symbolic violence constitutes a more potent vehicle to alter perceptions than physical violence.

<u>Event Galvanization and Mobilization:</u>

These perceptions of physical and symbolic violence enabled Operation Blue Star to assume the effects of an event galvanizer — a political episode that distresses the ethnic community to the point of mobilization. Before Blue Star took place, most American Sikhs did not care deeply or

---

[74] For example, most respondents associated the attack's occurrence on the birthday of Arjun Dev only with the fact it increased the number of civilians in the temple that day and thus the total number of civilian casualties, as opposed to highlighting the symbolism of attacking the Golden Temple on a cherished religious holiday. Respondents also did not emphasize the symbolism of the Punjab as the Sikhs' ancestral homeland as much as one might have expected, instead focusing on the threat and harm against fellow Sikhs and cherished religious shrines.

pay close attention to the ongoing militant and separatist campaigns, and respondents labeled the idea of Khalistan "an alien concept," "not realistic," and "absolutely not in anyone's mind." When Sikhs learned the upsetting news that their temple in Amritsar had been attacked, they described it as a "shock" and "wake-up call." Respondents viewed the attack as a sizable blunder committed by the Indian government; it represented a jarring escalation waged by the Hindu majority. The episode also created clear portrayals of a Sikh martyr-hero and non-Sikh villain, thereby increasing the attractiveness and romanticism of the separatist cause, which could now claim to be the latest in a long line of defenders of the faith. Most significantly, the attack underscored a threat to Sikhism that was consistent with how separatists framed the conflict. Operation Blue Star motivated thousands of Sikhs to side with the goals of separatism and favor independence, and many started following and sympathizing with the movement for the first time.

As perceptions of the Sikh separatist movement gained legitimacy, American Sikhs engaged in a variety of political actions in support of their separatist goals, even when their activism did not endorse the militants or their tactics. They organized hundreds of well-attended protests and demonstrations. They joined or founded local organizations committed to furthering the Sikh cause. Sikhs lobbied policymakers and tried to sway public opinion. Gurdwaras held prayer vigils and seminars to commemorate the attack, and Sikhs on their own volition made it their responsibility to debate and push back against developing North American perceptions of "Sikh terrorism." Perhaps most significantly, Sikhs opened their wallets and offered financial support to their co-ethnics in Punjab, mostly intended for humanitarian relief although some Sikhs may have wittingly given to violent militant organizations. Sikhs donated because they were angry about the attack and felt it was their responsibility to financially support Sikhs in

Punjab during their hour of need. They may have also felt a sense of shame for being absent from Punjab at a time it was perceived to be under attack and wanted to feel part of the homeland. All these actions describe a wide range of activity, but they all were undertaken in response to a traumatic event. The various activities outlined by the discussants provide tentative support for the third hypothesis:

H1c (event galvanization): As perceptions of the separatist movement improve and attract new followers, the likelihood of diaspora members providing greater levels of support to separatist groups in the homeland increases

Assessment of Overall Hypothesis:

The relatively high amount of physical violence involved in Operation Blue Star, combined with the symbolic violence interpreted in the event, underscored the preexisting frames already made by separatists, who attracted greater sympathy and attention after the attack, and whose claims were further buttressed by the anti-Sikh rioting following Indira Gandhi's assassination. Members of the Sikh diaspora, having sufficiently been "awakened," started following and sympathizing with the movement for the first time, and responded with a variety of political actions including protests, writing campaigns, involvement in new organizations, and perhaps most significantly, offering financial support to Sikhs in Punjab perceived to have included militant organizations. In sum, analysis of the above data and discussion offers some level of support to all of the hypotheses that were earlier posed. Although some important caveats are discussed below, overall the case of the Sikh diaspora response to Operation Blue Star offers general support to the prime hypothesis:

Hypothesis – A traumatic event in the homeland impacts ethnic members symbolically and emotionally and directly influences perceptions in the diaspora in favor of the separatist movement. It will motivate some diaspora members to aid or support co-ethnic separatist groups.

These relationships can be depicted on the explanatory model graphically as was done in chapter 3:

Figure 5.1 Operation Blue Star

Traumatic event	→	***Collective action frames***	→	***Diaspora perceptions***	→	***Ethnic mobilization***
Operation Blue Star						(protests/ demonstrations)
X		*(threat to Sikh survival)*		(lobbying)		
Physical violence		**X**				(formation of new organizations)
(Approx. 493—2100 civilian casualties)		Mobilizing structures				
(Approx. 100-200 militant casualties)		**X**				(fundraising)
(destruction of temple buildings/property)		Political opportunities				
X						
Symbolic violence						
(destruction of Akal Takht, library)						
(Shots fired on Harmandir Sahib)						
(Perceived abuse of Sikhs)						
(echoing the past)						

<u>Additional Comparative Findings and Observations:</u>

Although general support is offered for the above hypothesis, this part of the research has also pointed to some important determinants on mobilization that should be considered as possible mitigating conditions on the explanatory model. They warrant further consideration for developing a comparative understanding of how diasporas respond to traumatic events. The following variables emerged as potentially significant factors in the determination of diaspora mobilization and will be assessed in greater detail as part of the comparative analysis that makes up the next part of this research:

Diminishing Returns on Emotion over Time – While Operation Blue Star undeniably produced a powerful emotive response among Sikhs, the ensuing mobilization, forceful at first, lost its sense of urgency and priority among diaspora members over time. In her analysis of the importance of ideology and strategic choices to ethnic mobilization, Biswas (2004: 274) calls Operation Blue Star a "suddenly imposed grievance," which she defines as "a single event or set of events that dramatizes and heightens the political salience of a political issue." Biswas (2004) and Fair (2005) both argue that the Sikhs by focusing so intensely on a singular event were never able to sustain a platform that could transcend local differences or produce cohesion among the pro-Khalistan groups.

Generational Degradation – Many respondents indicated their belief that first generation American Sikhs or residents who were recent migrants from Punjab were more likely to embrace separatist activities than Sikhs whose families had lived in America for several generations. This indicates a relationship between assimilation or longevity in the new country and levels of support for the movement, though it could also be the case of mistaken perception. However, responses also indicated that a traumatic event as symbolically powerful as Operation Blue Star could penetrate this generational façade and emotionally stir ethnic members who were more assimilated than their parents or grandparents. For example, Interviewee 16 in describing watching Dan Rather's news coverage of Operation Blue Star with his daughter, "[who] had never been involved with anything Indian," recalled that during the telecast, "she got up, went into the bathroom, came back… she had been crying." This poses a provocative comparative question that this research will address in chapter 9.

Institutional Influences and Social Structure of Community – Sikhs identified the communal importance of the gurdwara as a formative influence on perceptions of the attack. In each community, the local gurdwara organized seminars and invited survivors to address the community. They honored Sikh militants as religious martyrs, and they were where Sikhs gathered as one community. Sikhs relied heavily on the gurdwara system to help assemble options and facilitate action, and gurdwaras became a principal vehicle both for fundraising and for channeling the funds into Punjab. The role of localized community institutions, as well as the impact of the Internet on facilitating action, will be addressed in the next part of the research.

OPERATION BLUE STAR AND THE PURSUIT OF A SYNTHESIZED APPROACH TO STUDYING ETHNIC MOBILIZATION

This case study provides insight into one of the fundamental debates concerning the causes of ethnic mobilization: the degree to which behavior inherently is instrumental and driven by rational decision-makers, or the product of value-laden, deeply embedded, emotional/psychological ties. Lichbach and Zuckerman (1997) argue that researchers need to embrace theoretical designs that synthesize between two or more of the research traditions — a "thick" research approach involving the adoption of a primary comparative approach but also utilizing one of the other schools to address inherent weaknesses therein. I have previously cited studies on ethno-national mobilization that suggest different starting positions but end with such a synthesized approach. Barreto (2009) contends that nationalists engage in collective action out of their desire for emotional satisfaction and a sense of belonging *alongside or combined with* the traditional rational goal of material gain. Similarly, Varshney (2003) argues that ethnic mobilization cannot proceed on either type alone, but stipulates that both instrumental rationality and a belief in values are required to explain most forms of ethnic behavior. The findings of these studies underscore the existence of multiple dynamics at work during the complex processes of ethno-national mobilization. This case study posits a similar finding: At different stages, the process of perception creation and mobilization operates based on values *or* rationality. Both are required to explain mobilization.

As this research has focused on traumatic events as an origin point for mobilization, it has often reflected Varshney's principal contention that value rationality does a better job of explaining the origin of ethnic mobilization than does instrumental rationality. A quick review of the history of the Sikh separatist movement in the diaspora can help illustrate this point. As early as 1954, diaspora activists such as Davinder Singh Parmar and Jagjit Singh Chohan sought to mobilize diaspora Sikhs to help support the establishment of an independent Sikh state, only to be rebuffed by most of the Sikh community. No doubt these elites were imperfect leaders who perhaps had personal weaknesses that left them unfit to motivate large sections of the ethnic population, but what is noteworthy is that most Sikhs prior to 1984 did not perceive a dire threat to their ethnic group in the homeland.

Instead, it took an event of Operation Blue Star's symbolic potency to access the ethnic mythology of Sikhism and lay the groundwork for the transformation of diaspora perceptions of the movement. When it did, Sikhs no longer believed India could ensure their ethnic group's survival, and the attack's symbolism and emotional resonance made Blue Star an especially effective catalyst for ethnic mobilization because it tapped into the community's psychological insecurities about the future survival of the ethnic group. This appears consistent with Varshney's above contention that analysis of emotions and cultural beliefs does a better job of explaining the origins of ethnic mobilization than does analysis of rational decision-making and ongoing efforts at manipulation. The instrumental paradigm cannot account for the widespread emotional distress caused by the Golden Temple attack, which provided the reservoir of raw emotion and trauma that powered the Sikh mobilization in the first place. Nor does it reflect the very real emotions of Sikh elites, some of whom I interviewed, as they sought to organize, rally, and fundraise. Only by taking into account the value-laden, deeply embedded, emotional/psychological ties does one come to fully appreciate how Sikh perceptions changed in the aftermath of Operation Blue Star.

Yet, this research also lends support to the general argument that instrumental rationality plays a significant role once mobilization reaches a critical stage. Respondents attested that some Sikh elites took advantage of certain charities and organizations by diverting funds intended for humanitarian purposes to militant groups and violent organizations in Punjab. If true, this level of manipulation in the Sikh diaspora would appear to lend support to the instrumentalist approach. The infighting amongst Sikh leaders and lack of a coherent strategy also lends support to the rational-instrumental perspective, since the occurrence of friction in the leadership ranks helps explain the separatist movement's inability to sustain its momentum a few years after Blue Star. The two dynamics consequently work in tandem — as Varshney and Barreto predicted — and the juxtaposition of these two dynamics helps to explain important dimensions of ethnic mobilization as a complex process-oriented transformation, beginning with changing perceptions and continuing into political action. Both forms must be understood to appreciate the full process.

CONCLUSION

This chapter has utilized extensive interviewing with American Sikhs to examine diaspora perceptions and responses to Operation Blue Star. The research offers general support for several of the hypotheses identified in chapter 3, although the case study has also helped clarify where the hypotheses require more qualification or specificity. The relatively high amount of physical violence involved in the attack did infuriate the Sikhs, but the symbolic nature of the attack proved an even more effective catalyst by tapping into deep-seeded fears about the ethnic group's survival within India. Sikhs therefore mobilized and responded in a variety of ways, including the extension of significant financial support mostly intended for humanitarian purposes but also deployed to violent militant groups in Punjab. This research has also raised important questions about the explanatory power of value rationality versus instrumental rationality. While values and rationalism both help to explain critical dimensions of ethnic mobilization, the values approach stressing the examination of emotions and cultural beliefs does a better job of accounting for the origins of ethnic mobilization and where movements can gain their sweeping power in the first place, whereas rationalism helps to explain mobilization once it reaches a critical stage.

The next few chapters will seek to place this research in a more ambitiously comparative framework by analyzing two other case studies and comparing them to the Sikhs. The next chapter enables comparison between Operation Blue Star and the Irish diaspora's responses to two traumatic events taking place in Northern Ireland. The ensuing chapter focuses on the Uyghur diaspora's reaction to the Urumqi riots in 2009. Comparison of these cases in chapter 9 will allow for further insights into the relationship between traumatic events, diaspora populations, and the prospect for mobilization, and should also enable the researcher to more fully grasp the role and limitations of the traumatic event in its function as an event galvanizer.

PART III

TRAUMATIC EVENTS IN COMPARATIVE CONTEXT

7

TRAUMATIC EVENTS IN NORTHERN IRELAND:
BLOODY SUNDAY AND THE IRISH HUNGER STRIKE

This chapter focuses on two traumatic events that took place during the Troubles of Northern Ireland: the 1972 Bloody Sunday killings and the 1981 Irish hunger strike. Relying primarily on scholarly research but also on a review of newspaper articles from that period, it assesses the impact of each event on the sizable Irish diaspora living in the United States. The ultimate goal of this chapter, however, is to place these cases and the Golden Temple attack into a more explicitly comparative context, using the traumatic events framework highlighted by this research to conduct a comparative analysis of these three events and their diaspora impacts.

First, this chapter examines the background of the conflict in Northern Ireland and explains the role played by the Irish-American diaspora. Second, the chapter identifies Bloody Sunday and the hunger strike as traumatic events according to the framework presented in chapter 3 and focuses particular attention on the relative levels of physical and symbolic violence for each event; it then examines the reaction and response of the Irish-American diaspora. This chapter finds that while all three events had galvanizing effects on the diaspora, the Irish hunger strike and Operation Blue Star surpassed Bloody Sunday as event galvanizers since both exhibited higher levels of symbolic violence.

BACKGROUND OF THE NORTHERN IRELAND CONFLICT AND IRISH DIASPORA

The conflict in Northern Ireland, known colloquially as the "Troubles," was a thirty-year era of political tensions lasting from 1969 to 1998 between Northern Ireland's Catholic/nationalist minority, who identified primarily as Irish, against the Protestant/unionist majority who saw themselves as British. Over the course of the Troubles, Catholic/nationalist paramilitary groups such as the Provisional Irish Republican Army (IRA), Protestant/loyalist paramilitary groups, and the British army waged a thirty-year battle that killed 3,700 people and injured 40,000 more (Ellis and McKay 2000; English 2003). Although republican interpretations of history link the Troubles to British imperialism in Ireland and the island's post-World War I partition, the genesis of the conflict can be traced to the late 1960s when the civil rights demands of Catholics led to intensifying political tensions and inter-community violence between the two communities, creating an opening for sectarian paramilitary groups to operate. From the ashes and destitution of severe rioting in the late '60s and early '70s rose the Provisional Irish Republican Army (IRA), a paramilitary organization determined to remove the British presence from Ireland and reunite the north with the south.

Intending to induce the British government to surrender control of Northern Ireland immediately, the IRA inaugurated a campaign of violence against the British that included tactical decisions to kill civilians, destroy property, detonate car bombs, assassinate political leaders and spread mayhem in pursuit of its political objectives. For its part, London in 1972 suspended Northern Ireland's Stormont government and ruled directly while the British army attempted to reassert order. British forces proved capable of reestablishing some order but were unable to extinguish the republican threat, leading to a political and military deadlock between the two sides. Further, the republican leadership by the late 1970s realized it could only drive out the British by engaging in a "long war" and thus adopted a new strategy whereby the IRA would eventually exhaust the British by targeting and destroying military, commercial and public sites. While the IRA gained international infamy as a type of terrorist organization, Northern Irish Catholic grievances widely seen as legitimate authenticated many of the goals of the republican movement, which helped to equivocate the IRA's characterization as a terrorist group among audiences at home and abroad.

Background of "Irish America":

Followers and participants of the Northern Irish Troubles have long viewed the Irish-American diaspora as offering an influential reservoir of support to Irish nationalism. During the years of the conflict, "Irish America" ranked among the largest ethnic diasporas in the United States: in the 1980 US census for example, 41 million Americans — 18% of the population — identified their heritage group as Irish.[75] On the basis of this extraordinary diaspora estimate for an island of fewer than 7 million people, many observers could be forgiven for assuming that "Irish America" functioned as one of the most influential diasporas in the world. However, some important caveats are in order. First, the total number of Americans claiming Irish ancestry proves misleading since it makes no distinction between those who are ethnically conscious of their "Irish-ness," as opposed to just being aware.[76] The number of Irish diaspora members who have taken a sustained interest in anything about their ethnic origin, including the status of the

---

[75] By comparison, Britain at that time claimed 13 million people of Irish descent, Canada, 5 million, Australia, almost 5 million, New Zealand, 700,000 and Argentina, 300,000. See Kearney, 1988; Arthur, 1991.

[76] Arthur (1991: 145-6) defines ethnic awareness as an ethnic group member's ability to recognize some cultural distinctiveness between groups as well as some orientation to it by their members, and states that ethnic consciousness represents "a continuum [entailing] a stronger sense of subjective orientation."

Northern Ireland conflict, has remained small.[77] Second, the 1980 census figure also does not account for the division between the Irish-Catholic community and those whose descendants were Irish Protestants. According to Guelke (1996), roughly half of those claiming Irish heritage were Protestant, many living in America's rural South or in Appalachia. In earlier generations they were often identified, and many self-identified, as "Scotch-Irish" (Leyburn 1962). For the most part, they no longer identify as "Irish" (Arthur 1991).[78]

What we commonly think of as the Irish diaspora in the modern context usually refers to the urban communities of Irish-Catholics who are concentrated in the urban northeast and north-central portions of the United States, whose descendants arrived in the US during the nineteenth century.[79] "It was in these areas that Irish-American working-class neighborhoods were to be found, where Irish bars provided a welcome to militant Irish republicans" (Guelke 1996: 523). Focusing on this dimension of Irish emigration establishes a clearer picture of the diaspora as it is traditionally perceived; it also offers insight into the psychological foundations of the community's later support for Irish nationalism. Although millions of Irish Catholics emigrated to the United States in varying waves between 1820 and 1900, Irish emigrants, regardless of the year they arrived, saw the occurrence of Ireland's great famine between 1845 and 1849 as the diaspora's *raison d'être*, embedding in the communal identity of these migrants the perception that the Irish had been forced involuntarily from the homeland. For this reason, Irish Catholics

---

[77] For example, the largest and oldest Irish-American group, the Ancient Order of Hibernians, claims a membership of only 80,000 (Guelke 1988, 1996). Arthur (1991: 145-6) suggests that Saint Patrick's Day may be the main manifestation of ethnic awareness for most Irish Americans.

[78] The first wave of Irish emigrants to the United States had actually been the Protestant Scotch-Irish, who arrived in the eighteenth century and played an important role in the formation of the country; Approximately 200,000 Ulster Presbyterians emigrated to the United States between 1700 and 1776; many would eventually settle the trans-Appalachian frontier. By the end of the century, one in six Americans claimed Scotch-Irish descent. See Arthur, 1991.

[79] According to the 1980 census, 70% of Irish-Catholic Americans lived in the urban northeast and north-central portions of the United States.

interpreted their status and their community with a deeply felt sense of grievance, and as a consequence, were more likely to self-identify in explicit political and religious terms. One should not exaggerate the effect of the famine as the sole determinant of Irish-American identity; it has also been effectively argued that Irish Catholics arrived right as America was undergoing its industrial expansion, ensuring the settlement of millions of Irish migrants in the growing urban corridors of America (Arthur 1991; see also Miller 1990).

Once the Irish-Catholics had arrived in America, however, it provided a new arena for Irish nationalism to flourish,[80] leading to a number of episodes when Irish-American communities began to influence events in the homeland. The first prominent example occurred during the latter-part of the nineteenth century, when the Irish Republican Brotherhood, a revolutionary secret society known also as the Fenians, staged several bungled raids between 1866 and 1870 from the United States into Canada. The Fenians intended a clandestine campaign meant to undermine Canada's defenses — cutting telegraph lines, destroying important railways, infiltrating the Canadian militia. Two of the ostensible purposes of these raids was to emancipate Canadians from British imperialism and perhaps spark a new war between Britain and the United States, although it may have also been the case that the Fenians — mostly Irish veterans of the American civil war — simply yearned for their own place in Irish mythology. In any event, Canada's border militias turned back most of their advances and the US did not come to their defense (Senior 1991; Wilson 2007, 2008). With considerably greater success, the Irish-American emigrant community also funded the Irish Land League to help end the Irish landlord

---

[80] This was a development that the British home secretary recognized as early as 1855 when he said: "In former Irish rebellions the Irish were *in* Ireland. We could reach their forces, cut off their resources in men and money, and then to [subjugate] them was comparatively easy. Now there is an Irish nation in the United States, equally hostile, with plenty of money, absolutely beyond our reach and yet within ten days' sail of our shore" (O'Brien 1980: 66; qtd. in Arthur 1991).

system, a development that Arthur (1991) describes as a more important revolution than Ireland's much heralded political revolution forty years later. During the Irish war for Independence, the Irish-American diaspora conducted a vigorous, ultimately unsuccessful campaign to persuade President Wilson to support Irish self-determination as an echo of his own Fourteen Points doctrine (Ibid.). American interest in Irish nationalism peaked when Ireland earned free-state status, but the Anglo-Irish Treaty of 1921 deeply divided opinions on both sides of the Atlantic, and the issue of Ireland soon faded entirely (Guelke 1996). From that time until the Troubles started in 1968, Irish America had very little influence on events in Ireland and lost its appeal as a political cause.[81]

Irish America, the IRA, and the Diaspora's Role During the Troubles:

The eruption of political violence in Northern Ireland in 1968 revitalized the interest of Irish Americans in the homeland. Thousands of Irish Americans joined Irish cultural groups and diaspora organizations, some of which supported the more radical tactics of republicanism, while others entered into more moderate international alliances such as the Northern Ireland Civil Rights Association. Probably the most influential group in the early years of the Troubles was the republican Northern Aid Committee, or Noraid. However, more mainstream alliances developed over time and facilitated the support of increasing numbers of Irish Americans for more moderate nationalist-Catholic forces in Northern Ireland such as the Social Democratic and Labour Party (SDLP). Cultural, familial and political linkages helped to sustain the diaspora's

---

[81] For example, an anti-partition resolution in 1951 was soundly defeated in the US House of Representatives despite intense Irish-American organizational pressure, and the author of a memo from the British foreign minister's office suggested that the defeat could be traced to the loss of appeal of the Irish cause, especially given Ireland's neutrality stance during the war and a wave of anti-Catholicism then plaguing the United States (Arthur 1991).

involvement during these years and helped overshadow trans-Atlantic differences: "The Irish Americans are tied to 'the old country' by a kinship network that shares a common romantic vision of Irish nationalism and traditional Catholicism, although it must be noted that the Irish-Americans are largely ignorant of the socialist agenda of many republican groups involved in the conflict" (Mumford 2005: 379).

Many spectators of the Northern Ireland conflict have noted the notoriously romantic interpretation among Americans of the IRA's political quest, which Irish Americans tend to perceive as Ireland's fight against the occupation of "the old country" (Mumford 2005). In the early years of the conflict, the IRA relied on Irish-American sympathy as well as American gun markets to strengthen its own organizational and tactical capacity. Until 1971, IRA agents stocked up on arms at Midwestern gun fairs and then relied on sympathetic East coast dockworkers and airline crews to smuggle these weapons back to Ireland. The first known IRA arms shipment, which arrived in Ireland in 1970, dramatically modernized the IRA's aging supply of weaponry.

The discovery of six unclaimed suitcases full of guns and ammunition at Dublin international airport in 1971 shut down these shipping lanes and forced republican supporters to improvise new ways to support the republican cause. It was in this context that the Irish-American organization Noraid — founded in 1970 by a former IRA member who had lived in America since 1927 — grew to notoriety as the suspected American wing of the IRA. Noraid's main activity on behalf of the republican movement was raising funds from within the Irish-American community. From 1969 to 1986, the group reported sending approximately $3 million of funds to its republican partners. Noraid relied on a host of localized community fundraising activities frequently steeped in the perceived "Irish tradition" — dinner-dance benefits, "whip-rounds" in Irish pubs, solicitation by direct mail, and ticket sales to annual testimonial dinners. The ostensible purpose of these funds was to provide financial relief to the families of republican prisoners; however, British and American authorities suspected that Noraid helped fuel the IRA by raising funds through its informal networks — additional to what it disclosed in accordance with legal requirements — to purchase weapons for the IRA (Guelke 1996). An American district court judge in 1981 ruled that Noraid was "an agent of the IRA providing money and services for other than relief purposes," and ordered the group to record the IRA as its foreign principal (Guelke 1988: 132).

Even without providing funds directly for arms purchases, the fact that Noraid supporters were contributing to republicans likely enabled the IRA to use its own funds to buy weapons. A leaked British army intelligence report in 1978 concluded that the United States served as the "PIRA's main weapon source" and estimated that overseas fundraising networks contributed approximately $240,000 per year toward the IRA's operating budget. Noraid accounted for more than half the total, which was also 25% above the amount declared to Department of Justice regulators (Guelke 1988: 133 note 7; Mumford 2005). Noraid's support for the IRA went far enough that Britain's Northern Ireland secretary made special visits to the United States to try to dissuade Irish Americans from supporting the IRA, and Prime Minister Margaret Thatcher urged President Reagan to crack down on the IRA's Irish supporters.[82]

Other diaspora groupings also formed in support of Irish nationalism, which showcased the diaspora's renewed interest in Ireland, but also demonstrated the diaspora's growing

---

[82] In one instance, the prime minister even pleaded with American tourists after an IRA bomb blast in London to "go back [to America] and tell them never to give money to Noraid because you see where it goes" (Associated Press 1981: 1; Associated Press 1982). Underscoring the same perception among moderate Irish Catholics in Northern Ireland, Bishop Daly in 1984 condemned Noraid's role in Northern Ireland as an arbiter of the IRA, remarking: "What we need from our American friends is not dollars for guns, but dollars for jobs" (Erlanger 1984).

moderation and increasing impatience with the tactics of more radical groups such as Noraid. The first major example of this came in 1974, when diaspora leaders who felt embarrassed by Noraid's activity founded the Irish National Caucus (INC), a lobbying organization meant to improve the image of the republican cause. Although committed to the nationalist cause, the INC gradually distanced itself from political violence and focused increasingly on human rights abuses. Congressional allies of the INC established the Ad Hoc Congressional Committee for Irish Affairs in 1977, which succeeded in pressuring the State Department to suspend sale of handguns to the Royal Ulster Constabulary two years later.[83] The most prominent alliance of leading Irish-American politicians was made up of Sen. Edward Kennedy, House Speaker Tip O'Neill, Gov. Hugh Carey and Sen. Patrick Moynihan; they became known as the "Four Horsemen." This influential group pressured the Carter administration, and later the Reagan administration, to become more deeply engaged in the Northern Ireland crisis and to support the position of its political ally in Northern Ireland, the Catholic-nationalist party SDLP (Mumford 2005). However, the Four Horsemen sharply condemned the activities of the Provisional IRA and encouraged Irish Americans not to give money to the republican cause (Guelke 1996; Arthur 1991).

These groups had limited success influencing American foreign policy. Before the Clinton administration embraced the Northern Irish peace process, America remained distant from the crisis in deference to the British government, its close Cold War ally. Nevertheless, diaspora groups were able to influence some policy decisions, such as when the diaspora succeeded in pressuring the Carter administration to prioritize Northern Ireland in American

---

[83] Chaired by Mario Biaggi, a conservative Democratic congressman from New York, the Ad Hoc Committee despite having no formal standing in the House of Representatives claimed a membership of over a hundred members of Congress, who like Biaggi were not themselves Irish-American (Guelke 1996).

foreign policy for the first time when Carter released a statement condemning the use of violence and promising American aid should a peace agreement be reached (Mumford 2005). However, the Reagan administration, despite taking occasional positions that broke with the British government, proved more resistant to interventionist policies that might upset London.

Finally, the diaspora's changing status in America complicated its capacity to mobilize support around the Irish cause. Throughout the second half of the twentieth century, Irish Americans gained increasing upward mobility. In theory, this might have provided the community with added influence and political weight, but in reality it narrowed the base of urban Irish-American support as families retreated to the suburbs. Irish-Americans as a group also proved to be more conservative and anti-communist than their Irish nationalist counterparts. At the same time, American audiences over the course of the Troubles proved less tolerant of terrorist activity than their Irish counterparts (Mumford 2005). These factors help explain Irish America's inability to mount a more cohesive pressure campaign on American public officials as well as the general absence of a "shamrock vote" during the 1970s and 1980s; they also illustrate why the diaspora was able to play a more constructive role as a moderating influence on republican activity during the 1990s peace process, this time endorsed by the Clinton administration.

TWO TRAUMATIC EVENTS IN NORTHERN IRELAND

This section analyzes the impact of two traumatic events in the history of Northern Ireland: the 1972 shooting of civilians by the British army that became known among nationalists as "Bloody Sunday," and the 1981 hunger strike for political status waged by republican prisoners. For each episode, I first focus on the event itself, its background, and its immediate impact on the trajectory of conflict. Next, I qualify the episode as a traumatic event and assess the levels of physical and symbolic violence that took place. These assessments are necessary to later examine what relationship exists between these events and diaspora mobilization. Finally, I examine the response of the Irish-American diaspora to the event.

Bloody Sunday

On January 30, 1972, British paramilitary troops opened fire on Catholic marchers in the nationalist Bogside area of Derry city, known to most Protestants as Londonderry.[84] Thirteen civilians were killed in the onslaught — a fourteenth victim would succumb to injuries a month later — and the soldiers' actions wounded several others.[85] The march had been organized by the moderate Northern Ireland Civil Rights Association (NICRA), which had planned for a peaceful protest against the British government's policy of internment against suspected paramilitaries. The soldiers, members of the British Parachute Regiment, later claimed they had received fire from elements in the crowd, but survivors of the attack have bitterly contested that anyone in the

---

[84] Derry/Londonderry's status as a city with two names is an example of a frequent occurrence in conflict zones, where rivaling communities refer to important locations by different names due to differing historical and cultural interpretations. In this case, Ulster's second-largest city historically was known as Derry but in the 1600s was renamed Londonderry during Ireland's plantation era in recognition of the city's connections to London livery companies (Byrnes 2010). In the present day, tensions over the name still flare up occasionally, as demonstrated by recent British and Irish newspaper editorials explaining their news organization's respective reasons for choosing one name over the other or employing each name in differing circumstances (Connolly 2011; Byrnes 2010; *Derry Journal* 2009)

[85] Due to the rising tide of violence at such events, British officials had barricaded the parade route prior to the march with the hope of mitigating the chance of sectarian rioting or paramilitary sniper fire. Most participants upon reaching the fortification had turned around without incident. However, a number of Catholic youths reportedly broke away and began attacking soldiers with stones and other missiles, which forced the military just after 4 p.m. to deploy tear gas and water cannons and begin making arrests. What transpired exactly in the next few moments is the source of considerable controversy, but end result was that soldiers fired upon the crowd, leading to a "brief, appalling period of violence [that] occasioned mayhem: confusion, shock, people running and screaming and diving for the ground – or falling, having been shot" (English 2003: 149).

crowd had been armed.[86] No weapons were found on any of the civilians killed, and later forensics and other evidence demonstrated that none of the dead civilians were carrying weapons or bombs that day. A government inquiry called the Widgery Tribunal released a report months afterward that mostly exonerated the soldiers of any wrongdoing despite acknowledging it had produced no evidence that civilians had been armed. The report's release shattered any remaining belief amongst nationalists that the British government could treat Catholic residents even-handedly, and many at this point turned to republican militias to protect their communities (English 2003; Conway 2003).

A look back at the deteriorating situation in 1972 helps one appreciate the ramifications of Bloody Sunday as a traumatic event. At the time, the British government was trying to pull off the difficult feat of aggressively countering the insurgent campaign of the IRA, while reassuring Catholics that British rule could protect their interests against loyalist violence and unionist overreach. Unfortunately, the growing strength of IRA activity had forced the British to upset this balance by rolling out a number of controversial security measures, including stepped up security of Catholic ghettos and "no-go" areas, as well as introducing its internment policy — the British government's decision to detain without trial suspected republican and loyalist participants in political violence. These policies from purely a security standpoint might have

---

[86] The paratroopers who discharged their weapons later claimed they were first fired upon from elements in or adjacent to the march. Survivors fiercely dispute this claim, and the victims' family members over the next two decades campaigned vigorously for an independent inquiry. According to English (2003), a member of the Official IRA, a group that splintered from the Provisionals, did fire a single shot from the Bogside just before 4 p.m. — "possibly" constituting the first shot fired on Bloody Sunday. English argues that while this may have confirmed the soldiers' belief that violence was being directed against them, " it cannot be taken as either explaining all of the soldiers' actions, or as justifying the fatal violence they deployed that day" (English 2003: 152). In 1997, British Prime Minister Tony Blair authorized the Saville Inquiry to investigate Bloody Sunday after the discovery of new evidence. After a sometimes quixotic fifteen-year investigation, the Saville Inquiry issued its report that the paratroopers had fired the first shot, and Prime Minister David Cameron issued a formal apology.

been necessary, but they were deeply unpopular among Catholic residents and significantly undermined the legitimacy of British rule. Groups like the NICRA adopted a strategy modeled on the American civil rights movement to counter internment — including scheduling demonstrations such as the rally that took place in Derry.

As the date of that parade had approached, the occurrence of several events in Derry — including a string of IRA nail bombings and the assassination of numerous British soldiers as well as recent inter-community rioting — left the British army skeptical that march organizers could keep the peace; further complicating matters, British commanders received intelligence reports indicating republican plans to plant bombers or snipers in the crowd. Responding to what they thought they knew, British authorities decided that cordoning off the parade route offered the best chance of preventing violence. They also called to Derry the British Parachute Regiment, a decision that in retrospect has been roundly criticized as shortsighted given the unit's reputation for "hard tactics."[87] When the soldiers who had been charged with keeping the peace instead chose to open fire on the marchers, their actions effectively severed the Catholic community's assumption that British rule could serve an effective arbiter or guarantee the protection of Catholic interests.[88] A few months after the attack, London suspended Northern Ireland's Stormont government and installed direct rule, which would last almost thirty years.

Bloody Sunday dealt a serious and lasting blow to the British government in its quest to reestablish order in Northern Ireland, as public fallout from the episode was considerable. The

---

[87] Deployment of the Parachute regiment for such a predictably sensitive mission was, in English's words, "profoundly ill-judged." Just a few days before the parade, in fact, other British Army units made requests to Army Headquarters to keep the Parachute Regiment out of their areas out of concern for their boorish behavior (English 2003: 154).

[88] On the day of the march, members of the Parachute regiment, in the words of English (2003: 154), were "…tense and anticipatory. And highly aggressive. The Parachute Regiment was hardly the gentlest collection of men, even for an army, and the soldiers were intent on preventing extended assaults."

Derry Journal reported that in the aftermath of the assault, "anger against British troops mounted to a new height" (English 2003: 150). The event horrified and mobilized Catholic audiences across the province. When the Derry community laid the victims to rest a few days after the attack, over 2,000 mourners attended their funeral at Saint Mary's Church and another 25,000 gathered outside (Ibid.). Northern Irish nationalist leaders such as Bernadette Devlin, who was present at the event, accused the British army of committing mass murder; in Dublin, Irish Prime Minister Jack Lynch called the conduct of the soldiers "unbelievably savage and inhuman" (Ibid.: 151). Angry crowds in the Irish capital set fire to the British embassy and petrol-bombed British-owned businesses, and the Irish government recalled its ambassador from London and announced a national day of mourning. Thousands of Dublin workers stopped work to show respect for those who died, and approximately 100,000 people marched on the British Embassy (Conflict Archive 2013). Back in the North, the decision of hundreds of angry youths to join the IRA provided a sizable investment in the organization's long-term prospects, with many of those new enlistees rising through the ranks of the IRA in the years that followed (English 2003; Conway 2003).[89]

Bloody Sunday was a watershed moment that probably benefited republicanism most of all. From a strategic standpoint, the fallout and public outcry generated by Bloody Sunday worked toward republican goals, as seen when London suspended Northern Ireland's Stormont government and declared direct rule only weeks after the attack. In an apparent retaliatory attack in late February, the Official IRA exploded a bomb at the headquarters of the Parachute

---

[89] In fact, one of the republican hunger strikers of 1980 was a cousin of Jim Wray, one of the victims of Bloody Sunday, who joined the IRA after what had happened that day. Bloody Sunday in the words of one IRA Provisional was a "turning point," leading "more young nationalists to join the Provisionals than any other single action by the British." Another Provisional commented: "A lot of people after that supported the IRA and empathized with what they were doing, engaging the Army on a regular basis and bombing the town." See English, 2003; 152.

Regiment, killing seven people (Conflict Archive 2013). Nevertheless, English (2003: 151-2) cautions against focusing too narrowly on Bloody Sunday, emphasizing the episode was "one event in an unfolding drama… for some it might have been decisive, but even here other events played their part."

<u>Bloody Sunday as a Traumatic Event:</u>

The events of Bloody Sunday meet several of the criteria identifying a traumatic event. The event constituted a sudden and unexpected form of violence committed by an unlikely source against members of the affected ethnic group. In the aftermath of the event, Northern Irish Catholics perceived the British army's actions as an act of government oppression. It shocked most residents and jarred the status quo. Bloody Sunday also attracted mass amounts of global and public attention and stayed in the limelight for several months afterward. Catholic perceptions that the ensuing government inquiry was a "whitewash" and cover-up assured Bloody Sunday its lasting notoriety. Finally, the episode marked a significant turning point in the course of the conflict: it simultaneously shattered the hopes of moderates that the British government could find a way to neutralize the worsening political situation, and offered a sizable boost to republican recruiting and fundraising at no penalty to the republican cause.

Level of physical violence – Placing Bloody Sunday in a comparative context, one can judge the relative level of violence to have been low. Even taking into account Northern Ireland's small population size, Bloody Sunday's death and injury tolls hardly rivaled the much larger casualty total from other traumatic episodes such as Operation Blue Star, where death totals numbered in the hundreds and property damage was extensive. Moreover, Bloody Sunday, while shocking, did not actually constitute a dramatic escalation of violence in the trajectory of the conflict: on December 4, 1971, just two months prior to Bloody Sunday, the loyalist paramilitary groups Ulster Volunteer Force (UVF) carried out a bomb attack in Belfast that killed 15 Catholic civilians. And on August 9, 1971 British soldiers had killed 10 Catholics — including a Catholic priest — and three Protestants during a series of raids across Northern Ireland (Conflict Archive 2013). It can therefore be concluded that the physical violence that took place on Bloody Sunday did not represent a dramatic escalation in either absolute or relative terms. Yet, no other event gained the far-reaching notoriety of Bloody Sunday, suggesting that other factors — such as symbolism — offer a better explanation of Bloody Sunday's meaningfulness to ethnic participants.

Level of symbolic violence – Nationalists symbolically interpreted Bloody Sunday as an event that demonstrated to Catholic residents not only that the British were fundamentally unconcerned about their welfare, but also reinforced republican arguments that Britain constituted a foreign force in Ireland (English 2003; see also Conway 2003). Several aspects of the attack strengthened its symbolic potency by activating certain cherished cultural markers. First, the attack's location in the city of Derry, known as a heartland of northern republicanism, signified the British state's perceived assault on the Catholic community (Conway 2003). The British paratroopers who fired on Northern Irish civilians did so in the deeply nationalist Bogside, one of several prominent Catholic "no-go" zones in Northern Ireland where social and economic disaffection and denial of basic civil rights had deeply alienated the population (Ibid.). The confrontation between civilians and soldiers took place at "Free Derry Corner," a local square and gathering place nationalists already cherished as a symbol of their defiance since the Battle of the Bogside.[90] Second, the episode resonated with other events from Irish nationalist history. Prior notorious episodes had also been dubbed "Bloody Sunday," and the common denominator connecting them all was the presence of a perceived British oppressor employing apparent randomized violence to kill Irish Catholics;[91] one does not need to be deeply imaginative to recognize the allegory and connections to the past these associations implied. Third, some crucial occurrences during the event, such as the lack of a clear threat against the soldiers, underscored the image of a dominant party intentionally targeting its rival; even the fact that January 30, 1972 took place on a Sunday likely enhanced the feeling among Catholics that their ethnic and religious identity was under attack.

However, Bloody Sunday lacked other enhancing details and images that might have further strengthened its appeal as a republican framing device. Probably the most crucial of these was the episode lacked a more explicit religious element or setting. Religious symbolism can be deeply powerful not only because religion serves as an ethnic markers, but also because it helps inform a society's values and moral compass. The intervention of a Catholic priest helping civilians reach safety during the shooting constitutes the closest representation of any overt religious presence — and it should serve as no surprise that a photograph of the priest crouched down, waving a handkerchief, shepherding civilians across the street became the most iconic image amongst Irish supporters (Conway 2003). However, during Bloody Sunday the British directed no violence against an important religious shrine or sanctuary; soldiers did not raid a

---

[90] During the Battle of the Bogside, which took place in 1969, nationalists rioted and fought the Royal Ulster Constabulary (RUC) in protest of a loyalist parade; it is considered one of the events that had spark the outbreak of violence leading to the Troubles.

[91] Other Bloody Sundays include an 1887 demonstration in London against British coercion; a climactic day of violence in 1920 between the British Cairo Gang and Michael Collins' Twelve Apostles, which ended with British forces killing civilians at Croke Park; and another outbreak of rioting in 1921 in Belfast.

Catholic Church or destroy Catholic relics, nor did they violate the sanctity of religiously sacred grounds. It is true that organizers of the march might have intentionally planned for the demonstration to take place on symbolic grounds, but Free Derry Corner was sacred only in a historic and overtly political sense, and not in a religious sense. The absence of a more explicitly religious element in the attack means that at a fundamental level, the assault did not constitute the same type of threat to Irish cultural identity.[92]

A second weakness of Bloody Sunday is the relative absence of casualties or sacrifices on behalf of the very organization claiming to defend the Catholic community against its ethnic rival: the Irish Republican Army. Bloody Sunday produced no martyrs for the IRA to claim and avenge; civil rights activists, not republican operatives, were the face of the march. If anything, the episode demonstrated the IRA's *failure* to protect residents. This is not to suggest that Bloody Sunday *hurt* the IRA or was ultimately counterproductive to its fortunes; as I earlier stated, it benefited republicanism most of all. As highlighted above, the event helped to swell republican recruiting, and also indirectly led to the suspension of local rule. However, this does suggest that Bloody Sunday failed to reach its full symbolic potential. Perhaps counter-intuitively, one can reach the conclusion that the nonexistence of an IRA death or casualty during the event may have surrendered some of the symbolic potential it offered, though by the same token the British would have had a much easier time claiming a republican threat had existed after all had such a thing occurred.

---

[92] One might argue comparatively that a Western society like Ireland's would be less susceptible to religious symbolism than a developing world society since the former can be expected to be more modern and the latter more traditional, but the argument here has less to do with one's religiosity. Rather, religious imagery does a better job connecting with and symbolizing one's ethno-national identity and character, even among the less religious.

Bloody Sunday — perhaps the most visible violent event of the Troubles across the Atlantic — shocked and appalled thousands of Irish Americans and emigrants, and evidence suggests it created newfound sympathy for the nationalist cause and led to some mobilization in the diaspora; however, it is less clear that Bloody Sunday attracted large numbers of new followers to the separatist cause. Irish groups such as Noraid benefited from increased Irish-American engagement on the Northern Ireland issue; Noraid founder Michael Flannery described Bloody Sunday as the organization's "first big publicity break" (English 2003: 152).

Perhaps its most immediate effect was sparking a record number of financial contributions to Irish cultural groups voicing support for the IRA. Noraid through the first six months of 1972 sent $312,000 to Ireland and took in a record $1 million in contributions for the year (Guelke 1988; Shannon 1984). Some of these funds may have gone toward IRA arms deals, many of which sympathetic supporters facilitated in the United States. In the years following Bloody Sunday, the IRA relied on American interlocutors to organize arms purchases and shipments from criminal gangs and professional arms dealers, such as in 1976 when a New York resident with mafia connections helped supply the IRA with a shipment of machine guns stolen from the US National Guard. An ensuing investigation uncovered an IRA arms supplier — a Brooklyn security guard whom the FBI estimates served as the IRA's main arms supplier and shipped over 2,500 weapons to Ireland — requesting $17,000 from Noraid chief Michael Flannery to purchase ammunition, grenade launchers and 20mm cannons (Mumford 2005).[93] While one should be careful not to exaggerate the influence of Bloody Sunday on these arms

---

[93] The FBI subsequently arrested both men along with four others, but all were acquitted when a jury accepted the defense's rather tenuous argument that the CIA had sanctioned the purchase to prevent the IRA from seeking arms from the Soviet Union.

deals, which came years afterward and involved American interlocutors active in the movement prior to 1972. Nonetheless, the boost in fundraising in America's Irish enclaves benefited the republican movement by strengthening the hand of individuals or groups such as Noraid willing to facilitate arms purchases for the IRA.

Bloody Sunday also reinforced Irish America's often-romantic perception of the republican movement, allowing radical republicanism to profit in the short-term from higher levels of diaspora enthusiasm and engagement. The establishment within years of Bloody Sunday of more hardline alliances such as the Irish National Caucus (INC) — which sought specifically to highlight the perceived brutality of the British security forces and social discrimination against Northern Irish Catholics — signified "the growing number of high profile Irish-American lobby groups with militant views on the Northern Ireland conflict that put them at odds with mainstream Nationalists" (Mumford 2005: 382). However, the boost to nationalist fundraising and activism appears to have been short-lived. As Bloody Sunday became a more distant memory and republicanism's violent tactics in Northern Ireland became too extreme for the taste of some of its American supporters, Irish America's activism and financial generosity began to ebb. Noraid membership by 1976 plummeted to just 2,000 members, and the group reported raising only about $160,000 that year (Hanley 2004).

The Irish Hunger Strike

The concept of self-immolation is deeply rooted in republican orthodoxy. During the Easter rising, Irish rebels now regarded as founders of the Irish Republic assured their own martyrdom when they rebelled against the British state and were subsequently executed. During the same era, the hunger strike had come into its own as a distinctly republican practice; between 1913 and

1922, more than 1,000 Irish prisoners — including future Irish president Eamonn de Valera —

took part in hunger strikes. Republicans solidified the status of the hunger strike in 1923 when a

remarkable 8,000 political prisoners engaged in a hunger strike that lasted several weeks.[94]

So when republican prisoners decided almost sixty years later to launch a hunger strike,

they adopted a maneuver that was deeply embedded in republican mythology (Beresford 1987;

O'Malley 1991; Sweeney 1993; Mulcahy 1995). In 1981, IRA and other republican paramilitary

members imprisoned in Northern Ireland's Maze or "H-Block" facility outside Belfast initiated a

hunger strike to try and force the British government to grant them political status. During the

hunger strike, which lasted from March to October of that year, ten republican inmates starved

themselves to death in protest of the government's refusal to accommodate their demands, and

three prisoners were elected to higher office. The leader of the republican prisoners was Bobby

Sands; he was the first to refuse food on March 1, 1981, and died 66 days later. However, Sands'

hunger strike was forever transformed when he allowed his name to be placed on the ballot for a

vacant British Parliament seat for Fermanagh/South Tyrone and eked out a narrow victory on 9

April, less than a month before his death.

Sands' election to Parliament, although incidental and unplanned at the beginning,

dramatically transformed the significance and impact of the strike. The fact that more than

100,000 people lined the funeral route for Sands' burial at Milltown cemetery — with recently

arrived camera crews from the United States, Europe, Japan and even Thailand looking on —

---

[94] One of the first significant hunger strikers of the twentieth century was Thomas Ashe, who died
on the second day of his strike after British authorities attempted to forcibly feed him using a tube. Only
one year removed from widespread skepticism of the Easter rising, tens of thousands poured into the
streets of Dublin to attend Ashe's funeral, demonstrating, in the words of one scholar, the hunger strike's
"long tradition and irrefutable power" (Sweeney 1993: 426). Three years later, the hunger strike of mayor
of Cork Thomas MacSwiney, which drew enormous attention and huge rallies, transformed the
republican into perhaps the most noted symbol of Irish resistance to British rule prior to 1981. See
Sweeney, 1993.

testifies to the status Sands had achieved by the time of his death. When the prisoners finally called off their strike seven months later after family members of the inmates had begun intervening,[95] the campaign had failed to achieve its immediate goals, but had succeeded in attracting considerable international attention while casting the British government in a deeply unflattering light.

Again, it is important to offer context to this event to ensure a full understanding of its impact. Prior to 1976, the British government had allowed internees the right to wear personal clothing, freely associate with other prisoners, and had not required them to perform typical "prison work." By stripping away the republican prisoners' political status, the British had meant to "delegitimize" the republican movement and signal the prisoners' status as ordinary criminals, while the prisoners considered themselves prisoners of war. The issue of prisoner status thus was critical for the detainees not because of the forfeiture of certain privileges, but because it represented an attempt to strip the republican cause of its legitimacy (Mulcahy 1995). Sands' election therefore represented a critical symbolic achievement and propaganda windfall for republicans because it showed, counter to British claims, that republicans enjoyed significant support from the people.[96]

The hunger strike in general and Sands' death in particular sparked widespread outrage and condemnation. As news of Sands' death spread, women began banging dustbin lids outside of their houses in West Belfast, an old community warning of an internment sweep. By 2 a.m.

---

[95] The strikers may have also called off their campaign in the face of decreasing public support as Margaret Thatcher showed no signs of wavering. Family members in August 1981 began intervening when the prisoners lost consciousness, and on October 3, the remaining hunger strikers called off their campaign.

[96] In the words of republican leader Gerry Adams, "[Bobby Sands'] victory exposed the lie that the hunger strikers — and by extension the IRA and the whole republican movement—had no popular support" (Adams 1986: 80; qtd. in English 2003).

that night, sections of Belfast were literally ablaze with burning barricades, while Catholic youths rioted and hurled Molotov cocktails at police (Beresford 1987). The IRA ramped up its activity throughout the strike, targeting prison officers and other government workers, although some republicans grumbled the IRA was not moving aggressively enough or mounting a sufficiently effective military response to the deaths of Bobby Sands and his associates (English 2003). The IRA according to its own words also sought to punish the British government for "torturing our prisoners" when in 1984 it exploded a time bomb at the British Conservative Party's yearly conference, narrowly missing the prime minister (Staniforth and Sampson 2012: 81). Thereafter, British Prime Minister Margaret Thatcher easily assumed the role of chief antagonist of Irish nationalists — in the words of English (2003: 207), "Mrs. Thatcher herself emerged from this episode as a republican hate-figure of Cromwellian proportions… But she too had helped, unwittingly, to inject life into the Irish republican struggle." The hunger strike, like Bloody Sunday, also provided a boost to IRA recruiting:

> As with internment in 1971 or Bloody Sunday in 1972, the IRA now enjoyed a
> larger reservoir of potential recruits than would have been the case but for
> probably ill-advised and avoidable choices made by the British government. And
> such reflections are all the more pressing when one considers the violence during
> and consequent upon the hunger strike. (English 2003: 207-8)

The hunger strike also caused a significant international stir. Following Sands' death, thousands of demonstrators in Paris, Rome and Milan marched in honor of Sands while shouting IRA slogans; some burned the Union Jack, while others chanted "freedom for Ulster." The Catholic *Ya* newspaper in Spain labeled Sands' death "subjectively an act of heroism," although a rival publication pronounced it political kamikaze and a misinformed strategy. Members of the opposition in India's Parliament observed a minute of silence for Sands, from which Indira Gandhi's ruling Congress Party abstained. Many international observers wondered how a Western government had allowed one of its own members of Parliament over the course of several weeks to commit suicide, slowly and painfully, without having tried to stop him. When the Queen visited Oslo shortly after Sands' death, demonstrators hurled at her a balloon filled with tomato sauce (Beresford 1987).

Reaction was especially mournful in the United States, where the hunger strike received immense media attention. Notwithstanding some scathing newspaper editorials condemning the terrorist violence of the IRA or the initial shock and lingering theological dilemma over the strikers' decision to commit suicide, the death of Bobby Sands and other hunger strikers shocked and angered Irish Americans, many of whom were taking an interest in Northern Ireland for the first time. Over 1,000 people in New York attended a special mass of reconciliation for Northern Ireland at Saint Patrick's Cathedral after Sands died, while across the country, a San Francisco news outlet reported the Irish community as "subdued, courteous enough, but curiously menacing, as if everyone is waiting for a message as yet undelivered" (Beresford 1987: 98). Similarly, the Boston *Globe* reported that predominant Irish-Catholic neighborhoods in South Boston mourned quietly and privately after Sands' death (McNamara 1981).

The Irish Hunger Strike as a Traumatic Event:

The Irish hunger strike was not a "typical" traumatic event. Unlike other events, it did not constitute a sudden and unexpected outbreak of political violence, but rather resulted from a deliberate and calculated campaign to build a crescendo of public pressure on the British government over the course of several weeks. Nevertheless, the hunger strike meets several of the criteria identifying a traumatic event. Although the event itself was not sudden, the novelty and severity of the hunger strikers' actions, and British government's refusal to compromise, shocked most residents. Like Bloody Sunday, the hunger strike attracted mass amounts of global and public attention, attracted journalists from all over the world, and stayed in the limelight for several months. Finally, the episode marked another significant turning point in the trajectory of the conflict. The hunger strike came to be perceived as an impressive show of force for militant republicanism at a critical moment, demonstrating how public support for the movement was far stronger than its detractors had suggested right as the British government was attempting to delegitimize the movement. By demonstrating the advantages of developing a more forceful political strategy to the IRA, it also presaged the gradual rise of its political wing Sinn Fein to political power in Northern Ireland.

Level of physical violence – Assessing the level of physical violence endured during the hunger strike is inherently more difficult to judge compared to other traumatic events. Without question, the deaths of the ten hunger strikers constituted acts of violence — as any person who observed the slow physical deterioration of the prisoners could attest — but violence in this case was self-inflicted. To determine the exact level at which the British government was responsible for this violence requires a great deal more interpretation, and is thus far more subjective, than understanding the government's culpability for British soldiers engaging Catholic civilians, or Indian soldiers storming a religious temple filled with worshippers. However, even in the worst-case scenario where the British government is judged to be fully responsible for the violence inflicted on the hunger strikers, the casualty toll would stand at ten republican prisoners who had lost their lives — fewer deaths than what took place during Bloody Sunday.

Level of symbolic violence – The Irish hunger strike was a deeply symbolic event that re-energized the republican movement. According to Sweeney (1993: 421), the hunger strike derives its power from its ability to echo "religio-political martyrdom and the pantheon of Irish heroes," allowing republicans "a weapon of last resort" to use against their perceived oppressor when other means have failed. It can ultimately be judged to have achieved a more powerful symbolism than Bloody Sunday, which has afforded it greater lasting power in republican theology. The sweeping symbolic power embodied in the hunger strike derives its strength from a number of important factors distinguishing it from Bloody Sunday.

First, the prisoners succeeded in emulating the Irish cult of self-sacrifice, which also allowed them to emulate previous republican icons. The Irish-nationalist cult of self-immolation served as "a passive means of defiance," and its cultural significance to Irish practice conferred legitimacy on its users and the cause to which they aspired (Sweeney 1993: 434). Irish folk heroes such as Cuchulain had also sacrificed their lives to allow other Irishmen to escape death, a motif Irish writers and poets incorporated into many of their works in the early twentieth century. By tapping into these deeply held cultural norms, they made a strong connection to an earlier generation of republican martyrs and standard-bearers who had also participated in the cult of sacrifice; in the words of English (2003: 211): "In this, as in much else, there are unavoidable echoes between 1981 and 1916. Icon-generating, quasi-religious martyrdom, the republican reaping of benefits from technical defeat, the Pyrrhic nature of the British victory and the intensification of Irish nationalist sentiment all point to such a comparison." By calling upon a maneuver historically embedded in the republican movement, the prisoners of 1981 enshrouded their actions in the mythology of republicanism and the likeness of its previous icons, legends and martyrs — all of whom were perceived to have selflessly laid down their lives for Ireland.

Second, the prisoners in adopting the hunger strike employed a means of political confrontation that drew upon Christian imagery and mythology — part of the reason the practice held so much appeal in the first place. According to Sweeney (1993: 421): "Although it can be demonstrated that the phenomenon of hunger striking is widely used as a means of political protest, particularly so within the last twenty-five years, it is equally valid to suggest that the hunger strike is an integral part of Irish history and mythology." Fasting, self-sacrifice, and suffering in Christ's image assumed a special status in the development of Irish-Christian traditions. Notwithstanding Catholics' unease regarding its morality, the symbolic and cultural value embedded in the hunger strike — in a society where ascriptive ethnic and religious identifiers "Irish" and "Catholic" had become virtually interchangeable — helps to explain the resurrection of this forlorn practice (Sweeney 1993; see also Larkin 1972). By adopting the hunger strike as a tactic, the prisoners were able to tap into several historical themes and Christian motifs embedded in in the Irish psyche, and to communicate with others about the urgency, necessity and unity of their cause, using a nationalist language understood without words.

Irish-American Mobilization after the Irish Hunger Strike:

Signs of increased activism in the Irish-American diaspora in response to the hunger strike emerged almost immediately after Sands' death; in the words of one prominent Irish-American activist, the strike "galvanized large sections of Irish-America in a way that no armed IRA campaign could ever achieve" (English 2003: 204) Demonstrators picketed outside British consulates in New York and Boston, and the International Longshoremen's Association in New York declared a 24-hour boycott of British container ships (Russell 1981). Irish groups pressured local and state governments to take action in response to the hunger strike. In Massachusetts and New Jersey, two states with large Irish populations, the state legislatures passed resolutions praising the "courage and commitment" of Bobby Sands; Boston city councilors passed similar legislation (McNamara 1981: 1). Others in the diaspora hinted at an increased role for Irish America as a result of the hunger strike. Following one relatively subdued protest, a Boston resident remarked to the local newspaper: "We understand very well what's going on… [and] we'll show our support with our wallets" (Ibid.). Irish-American organizations initiated a hard lobbying campaign pressuring President Reagan and other federal officials to intervene in the crisis; however, the president, who considered Margaret Thatcher an ideological and Cold War ally, resisted most of their entreaties. Irish groups found more support at the Congressional level, where members of the Four Horsemen worked closely with the government of the Republic of Ireland and denounced the British government for, in the words of Senator Kennedy, "its posture of inflexibility" and "intransigence that can only fan the flames of greater terrorism" (Archives of Irish America 2013).[97] Fulfilling a long-term endeavor, the Four Horsemen established the Friends of Ireland later that year "to promote the cause of constitutional nationalism on Capitol Hill" (Guelke 1996: 531; see also Canellos 2009).[98]

---

[97] For more on the Four Horsemen, see biographies on Sen. Ted Kennedy (Canellos 2009) and Speaker Tip O'Neil (Farrell 2002).

[98] Over the next three years the Friends of Ireland offered strong support to the New Ireland Forum embraced by the moderate Northern Ireland nationalist party SDLP; Thatcher's rejection of that Forum in 1984 infuriated its proponents in the United States, forcing President Reagan to drop his non-interventionist stance momentarily to pointedly praise the proposal's backers in America and the Republic of Ireland (Guelke 1996).

The 1981 hunger strike also helped to rejuvenate the republican movement among its American supporters, refocusing attention away from the IRA's tactics and back on British policy in Ireland. By several measures, its impact on perceptions in Irish America surpassed the impact of Bloody Sunday and created a more robust mobilization in response to the traumatic event. The hunger strike brought about a major revival in the fortunes of Noraid, which experienced dramatic increases in fundraising and membership (Mumford 2005; Hanley 2004). Noraid during the seven-month hunger strike reportedly raised $250,000, a significant increase from previous levels. The hunger strike also provided a boost to Noraid's membership, which raised its membership from 2,000 in 1976 to an estimated 5,000 by 1984 (Associated Press 1982; Hanley 2004).

However, a key difference separated the hunger strike from Bloody Sunday: instead of rallying the passions of only recent emigrants or first generation Americans as Bloody Sunday had done, the hunger strike prompted the interest of second, third, fourth, fifth, even sixth generation Irish Americans in joining Noraid and other groups. This marked a fundamental shift in Noraid's composition, and Noraid sought to capitalize and further entrench the interests of its members by organizing Sinn Fein-sponsored trips to Ireland especially for its American-born supporters who had never visited Ireland (Hanley 2004).[99] The hunger strike also emboldened Noraid and its allies to more willingly defy its detractors. For example, Noraid-aligned Irish cultural organizations selected Noraid founder Michael Flannery — who only the year before had stood trial for attempting to smuggle weapons into Ireland — and IRA-bomber Michael

---

[99] The trip caused considerable controversy — and led to the largest protest in front of the British Consulate in New York since the hunger strikes — when the RUC attempted to arrest an American Noraid official who had been barred from entering Northern Ireland, leading to a brief moment of chaos during a rally and the killing of an unarmed nationalist from a rubber bullet. See Erlanger, 13 Aug. 1984; Hanley, 2004.

O'Rourke to serve in consecutive years as grand marshal of the famed New York Saint Patrick's Day Parade. The nomination of Flannery in particular incited a backlash from the British government, and prominent American politicians announced their plans to boycott (Bierman 1983a, 1983b).

A flurry of arms-dealing also took place after the hunger strike, as evidenced by the number of cases that federal agents brought against republican gunrunners including Noraid-affiliated individuals. In one notorious episode, the FBI in 1982 charged Noraid founder Michael Flannery and four other Americans with conspiring to smuggle a cache of arms — 47 machine guns, a 20 mm cannon, a flamethrower and thousands of rounds of ammunition — to the IRA; however, the five were acquitted after stating their belief that the CIA had sanctioned their actions to dissuade the IRA from the Soviet Union (Associated Press 1982; Bierman 1983a; Guelke 1996). The next year, FBI undercover agents caught four IRA supporters including an American citizen attempting to buy surface-to-air missiles in a sting operation in New York; also in 1983, an IRA arms procurer detailed to FBI investigators the process whereby republican interlocutors returned Noraid funds to the United States for the purchase of arms and ammunition (Bierman 1982; Mumford 2005).

In perhaps the most dramatic seizure, Irish authorities in 1984 intercepted seven tons of weapons and ammunition from an Irish fishing trawler, which had transferred the funds from the American trawler *Valhalla* originating out of Boston (Mumford 2005; Guelke 1996).[100] In the aftermath of the hunger strike, Noraid officials were also far more blunt about the involvement of

---

[100] In the history of the IRA's various arms acquisitions, only the French navy's interception in 1987 of 150 tons of Libyan arms for the Provisional IRA surpassed the size of the *Valhalla*'s cache. As late as 1990, the FBI thwarted another major scheme when it uncovered the IRA's attempt to purchase surface-to-air missiles in Florida to use against British helicopters (Mumford 2005; Guelke 1996).

its organization and members in IRA activity; at one point, a Noraid spokesman proclaimed Irish Americans had "every right and duty" to send arms to Northern Ireland (Erlanger 1984: 1)

CONCLUSION

Bloody Sunday and the Irish hunger strike created a more hospitable environment for republicans to champion their cause in a general sense and more specifically to fundraise on behalf of the movement, some of which may have went toward the purchase of weapons. In comparison to Operation Blue Star, both events were able to accomplish similar effects on the diaspora despite significantly lower levels of physical violence. However, the status of the Irish hunger strike and Operation Blue Star as more richly symbolic events compared to Bloody Sunday increased their attractiveness to new followers of the respective ethno-separatist cause. This research therefore posits that while symbolic and physical violence both remain important determinants of diaspora mobilization, symbolic violence tends to trump physical violence as the more influential determinant because symbolism resonates with an overseas ethnic participant on a deeply emotional and psychological level and allows for more emotion-laden interpretations to take place. Both dynamics receive further attention in the next chapter analyzing the Uyghur diaspora and its response to 2009 rioting in Xinjiang.

8

TRAUMATIC EVENTS IN XINJIANG: THE URUMQI RIOTS

This chapter focuses on the ethnic diaspora of the Uyghur (pronounced *Whee-gur)* and its response to widespread rioting that took place July 2009 in Urumqi, the capital of the Chinese province of Xinjiang. It should be said up front that contemporary analysis of the Uyghur population—an ethnic minority of China found predominantly in the western province of Xinjiang—inherently faces certain difficulties, due to China's strict media constraints and attempts to control most public information. This chapter tries to bridge that gap by relying on eyewitness accounts, social media and Western investigative reporting from within China to provide a rudimentary sketch of what happened during the Urumqi violence. It further uses scholarly research and recent news articles to build an understanding of the Uyghur diaspora and how it has sought to respond.

This chapter is divided into four sections. The first section examines the background of Uyghurs in Xinjiang and the nature of its fraught relationship with the Chinese government and tense relations with Han Chinese, the second largest ethnic presence in Xinjiang. The second section traces the migration of the Uyghur diaspora from Central Asia to Turkey to the West, identifies notable exile groups such as the World Uyghur Congress, and examines China's claims that diaspora elements are responsible for fomenting terrorism and separatist violence in Xinjiang. The third section identifies the Urumqi riots as a traumatic event, again using the framework presented in chapter 3. This leads to an assessment of the Urumqi riots in terms of physical and symbolic levels of violence — and evidence suggests the riots endured a high degree of physical violence but only a modest degree of symbolism. Finally, this chapter analyzes the response of the Uyghur diaspora to the riots in the short time period since the riots took place.

This chapter argues the Urumqi riots led only to a modest mobilization of the Uyghur diaspora, partly because the event failed to gain much cultural or religious symbolism. Although the riots emboldened Uyghur exile groups, accelerated online activism, and propelled World Uyghur Congress leader Rebiya Kadeer to an unprecedented level of renown among Western governments, it does not appear to have had an equal effect at attracting a significant number of new supporters or increasing fundraising or grassroots support for the Uyghur cause. This chapter also considers the effect of the riots on Uyghurs involved in Islamic extremism and discusses how the riots—or perhaps a different traumatic event—might compel some Uyghur militants to seek resources from Islamic jihadist networks.

BACKGROUND OF XINJIANG AND THE UYGHUR DIASPORA

The Uyghurs until recently have been an understudied ethnic group due in part to China's historical isolation, although a number of scholarly works in the last ten years have helped reverse this trend. The Uyghurs are a Sunni Muslim, Turkic-speaking ethnic group concentrated in western China, where as of 2007 9.65 million Uyghurs reside according to official figures (Bovingdon 2010). The Uyghurs represent the largest ethnic group in China's resource-rich western province of Xinjiang—officially the Xinjiang Uyghur Autonomous Region—comprising about half the population of the province; however, they live alongside an expanding presence of

Han Chinese that as of 2007 had grown to 8.2 million (Bovingdon 2010). China's economic policies have driven a massive influx of Han Chinese, setting the stage for perpetual ethnic tensions between Uyghurs and Han and exacerbating the already fraught relationship between Uyghurs and the state. A Uyghur separatist movement has long dreamt of establishing an independent state—Uyghurs refer to their homeland not as Xinjiang but as East Turkestan—that would serve as a sanctuary for several ethnic Turkic tribes in Central Asia who believe they are ancestrally related. It remains difficult to assess the level of support in Xinjiang for independence, but the greater takeaway for scholars is that by resisting Chinese rule in some form for several generations, the Uyghurs through their defiance have retained a communal collective identity within China, constituting the signature act of a nation (Rudelson 1997; Ogden 2004; Bovingdon 2010).

Although the ancestral history of the Uyghurs is complex,[101] the Uyghur movement's push for independence, unsurprisingly, is a recent phenomenon, originating in the late nineteenth century. The Uyghurs first assertion for independence came in 1865 when Yaqub Beg, a military official in the employ of the Khanate of Koqand, established a Muslim state in Kashgaria that lasted from 1864 to 1877. Although the state ended with Yaqub Beg's death and the Chinese re-conquest of the region, his campaign set a precedent for future Uyghur separatist movements to appeal to religion and ethnicity, and Muslims in Xinjiang at the time felt proud of the brief establishment of a Muslim state, and considered Beg "a hero who brought their holy war to its

---

[101] The presence of Islam in Xinjiang can be traced back to the eighth century, although there is some scholarly debate about whether the population known today as the Uyghurs is ancestrally directly descended from the Turkic, nomadic steppe people to whom the term first referred. In the eleventh century, for instance, Mongols from the east invaded central Asia and defeated the Turks, a reason why many Turkish-speaking Chinese today actually descend from Mongol as well as Turkish tribes. Throughout history, the term *Uyghur* has also served as the names of communities influenced by Buddhism and Christianity before the Buddhist Uyghurs converted to Islam. See Rudelson (1997), Millward (1998), Gladney (2003) Bovingdon (2010).

completion by creating an independent and regionally unified Islamic kingdom" (Kim 2004; see also Fletcher 1995; Newby 2005).

During the first half of the twentieth century, Uyghur separatists attempted several times to break away from China, briefly founding the East Turkestan Islamic State at Kashgar in 1933, and with help from the Soviets in 1945, the short-lived East Turkestan Republic in Yining (Forbes 1986; Wang 1993).[102] Since the absorption of Xinjiang into the People's Republican of China in 1949, Uyghur discontent has made Xinjiang a constantly restive region under successive Communist regimes, which have had to deal repeatedly with sporadic episodes of ethnically motivated violence. Xinjiang's early volatility correlated with the fluctuating national policies of the Great Leap Forward and Cultural Revolution; according to Davis (2008), China's policies during the years of the Cultural Revolution were especially oppressive as the government cracked down on the practice of religion and ethnic languages, and restricted cultural cuisine and clothing. After Mao's death in 1976, the government lifted many restrictions on the Uyghurs as part of its liberalization and reform policies, but the provincial leadership, comprised primarily of Han Chinese, did not see eye-to-eye with the national authorities and preferred to continue implementation of strict prohibitions against Uyghur cultural and religious practices (Clarke 2008).[103]

---

[102] Some argue the ETR represented less a rebellion than an incident engineered by the Soviets. In this respect see Wang, 1993.

[103] In particular, provincial leaders feared that granting increased economic/social rights to ethnic minorities would generate demands for political autonomy. Additionally, world events at the time—such as the Iranian revolution, or the Soviets' continuing incursion in Afghanistan—were demonstrating the increasing power of political Islam, and likely gave local authorities second thoughts about relaxing their policies. Another scholar describes the Catch-22 for the Chinese government thusly: "Government religious reforms were intended to quell Uyghur disaffection with Chinese rule and cause Uyghurs to develop more harmonious sentiments for the Han Chinese. However, the Chinese [were] caught in a dilemma: when they allow or encourage it, Uyghurs become more content with the government but their

Several events in the 1990s solidified Xinjiang's growing reputation as China's "Wild West," including an armed uprising in Baren in 1990 and a wave of separatist bombings on the anniversary of Deng Xiaoping's death in 1997. [104] Both events aggravated tensions between the Uyghurs and the state to an unprecedented degree, and China responded with sweeping security measures that led to the arrests and accelerated trials of thousands of alleged Uyghur separatists (Clarke 2008; Davis 2008). Recognizing the changed security environment in the aftermath of the September 11 attacks in the United States, China began to make a public case of structural and ideological alignment between Uyghur separatists and Islamic extremists — the latter of whom the US was now battling in neighboring Afghanistan, a longtime Uyghur oasis and sanctuary (Chung 2002; Tyler 2003).

Beijing in 2002 released a report alleging a heretofore-unknown organization called the East Turkestan Islamic Movement or ETIM was a "major component" of al-Qa'ida's terrorist network, and China subsequently depicted Uyghur separatists as radical Islamists who aspired to launch a holy war and intended to set up a theocratic Islamic state in Xinjiang (Information Office 2002; see also Mackerras 2005; Davis 2008). The US, much to the disappointment of Uyghur exile groups, appeared to accept China's claims when in 2002 the State Department added the ETIM to its terrorism watch list. [105] However, ETIM has remained an elusive target for

---

strengthened Islamic practice leads them to feel more separate from and apathetic towards Chinese society." See Rudelson, 1997; 48.

[104] The 1997 bombings killed twelve people and the Chinese government executed eight alleged Uyghur terrorists in response.

[105] The State Department accused the ETIM of being responsible for "'numerous acts of terrorism' in China, including assassinations, arson attacks, and bombing of buses, cinemas, department stores, markets and hotels." It brought this action against the organization based on intelligence that ETIM had been planning to attack a US embassy in Kyrgyzstan. China produced its own version of a terrorist watch list in 2003 identifying the ETIM, the Eastern Turkestan Liberation Organization (ETLO), the World Uyghur Youth Congress (WUYC), and the Eastern Turkestan Information Center (ETIC), as well as eleven individuals, all from the Uyghur community. See Ogden

specialists and academics to study—some have even questioned its existence—and analysts who have examined the group have reached different conclusions about the capability and level of threat it poses (for example, see Reed and Raschke 2010; Cunningham 2012).

In recent years, separatist activity in Xinjiang by groups such as ETIM appears to have actually cooled even while China increasingly mounted a public case against Uyghur terrorism. While it is notoriously difficult to ascertain the exact level of separatist unrest in Xinjiang due to the lack of access to the region, Millward (2009) notes that between 1997 and 2008, there were not any reported incidents of separatist violence — "certainly nothing most people would call 'terrorism,'" in his words (348); likewise, Bovingdon (2010: 112) concludes in his recent book that "A careful and critical review of the evidence reveals that Xinjiang has been far quieter since 2001 than has any part of China proper." The Chinese government in 2008 did blame a number of attacks staged in the run-up to the summer Olympics Games on the ETIM, but Western media and Xinjiang scholars have expressed skepticism about several of these claims. In the most prominent of these violent episodes, two attackers drove a truck into a Kashgar police station and threw two grenades into the station, killing 16 policemen (Wong and Bradsher 2008).[106]

During the same period, however, larger ethnic communal tensions between the Uyghurs and Han Chinese have risen. The Chinese government has attempted to placate the Uyghurs through its Great Western Development plan to the region, believing that enhanced economic prosperity would cultivate in the Uyghurs a sense of Chinese national identity (Davis 2008;

2008.

[106] Two Uyghurs eventually were sentenced to death for the attacks; however, some independent eyewitness accounts challenged parts of the official version of events. The nature and source of this attack has been widely disputed. The Chinese government has produced little evidence proving that the attack was indeed the work of Uyghur terrorists. Additionally, video of the attack taken by a bystander at the scene appears to show two men of Han Chinese rather than Uyghur descent, casting further doubt on the government's claims. For more on the disputed nature of this case, see Wong, 2008a, 2008b.

Bovingdon 2010). However, this may have only exacerbated the situation. The most critical issue from the point of view of the Uyghurs is not the economic development of Xinjiang but the Chinese government's suppression of its cultural and religious freedoms. In fact, many Uyghurs perceive the government as deeply suspicious of the Islamic character of Uyghur identity, and thus more willing to repress its traditions or allow the cultural uniqueness of the Uyghur community to erode. In this sense, many Uyghurs interpret China's development policies as a cynical attempt to dilute the Uyghur culture by facilitating the migration of Han Chinese to Xinjiang (Mackerras 2004, 2005; Ogden 2004).

THE UYGHUR DIASPORA

There are roughly one million Uyghurs who make up the Uyghur diaspora, making it comparable in size to the Sikh diaspora. Yet, an important distinction in this regard is that while the Sikhs have settled primarily in Western countries, the largest concentration of Uyghurs outside Xinjiang—fully half the diaspora—can be found in the "western Turkestan" Central Asian states of Kazakhstan, Kyrgyzstan, Turkmenistan and Uzbekistan, as well as significant clusters in Pakistan and Afghanistan (Chung 2002; Wang 2003). The largest Uyghur population beyond China resides in Kazakhstan, where 300,000 Uyghurs have lived for several generations (Golovnina 2009; Leonard 2009). However, Soviet-era repression during the twentieth century constrained the ability of these clusters in Central Asia to become more organized, and modern-day cooperation between these states and China—facilitated in part by the regional security conference known as the Shanghai Cooperation Organization—has continued that trend since the end of the Cold War (Shichor 2007).

The next largest presence in the diaspora resides in Turkey, where Uyghurs claim ancestral links to the Turks. Moreover, Turkey's status in NATO made it the most attractive destination for Uyghurs looking to escape the influence of Communism. As a result, Turkey was long the most influential node in the Uyghur diaspora during the twentieth century, and also why Turkey since the 1950s has provided Uyghur activists a primary haven to help shape an East Turkestan independence movement (Shichor 2007). Early diaspora leaders such as Mehmet Emin Bughra and Isa Yusuf Alptekin were the early pioneers of the Uyghur movement and first to publicize the case for East Turkestan independence, primarily by publishing widely about their cause and appealing directly to international leaders and organizations; however, they failed to attract significant media attention, in part because of China's imperviousness to external pressure during the Cold War. However, China since the 1990s has pressured the Turkish government to restrict Uyghur national activism as it has become more sensitive to separatist activity within its borders, and this combined with growing economic relations between the two countries has dampened Turkey's enthusiasm in hosting the Uyghur community (Shichor 2007).

As the twentieth century came to a close, Uyghur groups thus felt the need to move westward again, this time to Europe and eventually the United States — the latter of which is where the balance of power in the diaspora now resides despite only about 1,000 Uyghurs living in the entire country (Shichor 2007; Eckholm 2009a). Mirroring the Uyghurs' move to the West, a new crop of Western-oriented diaspora leaders—many of whom are younger, better educated, more web savvy, fluent in English, and left Xinjiang willingly and legally in the 1980s—have assumed control of the cause and set about establishing a more realistic and pragmatic course for the Uyghur struggle (Shichor 2007). The new Uyghur agenda is less likely to stress the need for East Turkestan independence, but instead emphasizes the community's more modest desire for greater Uyghur autonomy within China and the protection of cultural and religious rights. Uyghurs believe Western governments will find a human rights platform more palatable than an assertive independence campaign, since, as Shichor (2007) points out, it manages the balancing act of conforming to Washington's value-laden quest for democracy without deeply upsetting the Chinese.

Today, the most prominent Uyghur organizations are headquartered primarily in the United States and Europe, and despite occasional fractures over tactics and strategy as well as the presence of too many organizations (see Shichor, 2007), these groups have managed to represent the Uyghur population to Western governments with a generally unified voice. The most influential organization is the World Uyghur Congress, which serves as the umbrella for 51 exile groups around the globe. The Congress, which is headquartered in Munich but operates mainly from Washington, regularly accuses Beijing of human rights abuses and a campaign to erode Uyghur culture (Asia News 2011; Millward 2009). It is headed by Rebiya Kadeer, a deeply inspirational figure among Uyghurs who China banished to the US in 2003 after she fell out of the government's favor. The Chinese government accuses the Congress and its affiliates of abetting Islamic terrorism and fomenting unrest in Xinjiang, but the Congress has rejected all of these charges and proclaims its interest is only in promoting human rights issues affecting the Uyghur population (Times Topic 2009; Millward 2009).

The public profile of the Congress has grown in recent years, thanks in part to Kadeer's stewardship of the organization and China's decision to publicly blame her for several incidents of ethnic unrest in Xinjiang. Kadeer in 2006 also became president of the Uyghur American Association, which represents the approximately 1,000 Uyghurs in the United States; other prominent groups include the East Turkestan National Congress, the Eastern Turkestan National

Freedom Center in Washington DC, and the Eastern Turkestan Union in Europe (Chung 2002; Eckholm 2009a).

Scholars disagree about the extent to which the diaspora has influenced or facilitated violent activity in China. Rohan Gunaratna and Kenneth George Pereire, two terrorism experts with the Institute of Defense and Strategic Studies in Singapore, allege that the Uyghur diaspora covertly funds terrorist organizations in China (see Gunaratna and Pereire 2006). Separately, Pereire (2006) accuses diaspora groups of placing members in Europe to study the tactics and technologies of the terrorist group al-Qa'ida in Iraq, and has depicted the Uyghur diaspora as serving as a robust source of support for the ETIM and other militant groups, "enabling these groups to survive." Chung (2002) also indicates that Uyghur groups such as the East Turkestan Opposition Party, the Revolutionary Front of Eastern Turkestan, and the Organization for the Liberation of Uyghurstan are linked to guerilla cells operating in Xinjiang's Taklamakan Desert. However, Chung ultimately contends that most Uyghur separatist political organizations do not advocate or encourage violence but are more likely to organize conferences or lobby members of Congress.

Most academics that study Xinjiang reject claims of Uyghur links to Islamic fundamentalism as exaggerated (Gladney 2003; Millward 2004, 2007, 2009; Shichor 2006; Clarke 2008; Fletcher 2008; Bovingdon 2010). These studies point out that most of these groups have foresworn violence since 9/11 and are only "pressing for a peaceful resolution of ongoing conflicts in the region" 2Gladney 2003: 458). Most exile organizations provide support to Uyghur political groups, not to groups advocating violence and terrorism. They are also quite skeptical of the Bush administration's decision in 2002 to nominate ETIM as a terrorist organization, a move they viewed as accepting at face value China's claims of a Uyghur-al-Qa'ida link.

In sum, the Uyghur diaspora based in Turkey helped to shape the modern day separatist movement during the second half of the twentieth century. The diaspora has since shifted westward to Europe and North America, where it has lobbied Western governments to press for human rights. China in the meantime has made multiple allegations about the level and type of support that Uyghurs receive from the outside. Beijing since September 11 has argued the Uyghur movement is aligned with Islamic Uyghur extremists allied with al-Qai'da, and in more recent years has alleged that World Uyghur Congress leader Rebiya Kadeer and other diaspora elements are linked to Uyghur terrorism. However, the Chinese government has not put forward much evidence in support of these claims, and diaspora leaders have asserted they are only interested in the rights and well being of the Uyghur population.

THE URUMQI RIOTS

On the night of 5 July 2009, large-scale rioting broke out on the streets of Urumqi, the capital city of Xinjiang, leading to widespread inter-ethnic violence, looting and "revenge killings" over several days, killing at least 197 people. Due to media restrictions and China's attempt to control most public information, we do not know with certainty how these events played out, but eyewitness accounts and social media, in addition to what China did allow to be reported, have enabled journalists and scholars to provide a rudimentary sketch of what happened. The origin of these riots appears to have been a demonstration that took place on the afternoon of July 5, at or near the People's Square in the heart of the city. The Uyghurs who attended had gathered to protest a factory riot in Guangdong Province a few weeks earlier that resulted in the deaths of

Uyghur employees. The protest, though it remained peaceful for some three hours, by 7 p.m. had grown into a mob, one that was angrily confronting Han residents passing by, according to witnesses (Bovingdon 2010; Branigan 2009a). The exact moment that violence broke out is unclear, but we do know that Chinese police arrived at some point around 7 p.m. to end the demonstration, and some allege they used violence to put down the protest (Branigan 2009a, 2010; Watts 2009).[107] What is clear is that police sought to end the demonstration, at which point a crowd of demonstrators moved toward the south and southwest portions of the city, including the Shanxi Hang shopping district and a mixed Han and Uyghur neighborhood along Zhongwan Street (Millward 2009).

From 8 p.m. that night to 2 a.m. the next morning, these areas suffered through some of the worst interethnic violence China had seen in years. Uyghur mobs smashed store windows, erected barricades, and intimidated residents. Roaming gangs torched shop fronts and erected barricades to keep out the police. Photos that emerged after the riots showed images of blood-soaked cars overturned in the streets and residents wielding shovels as a weapon. Reports indicate that Uyghurs began questioning passing drivers about their ethnicity, identifying Han and dragging them from their vehicles and beating them. The destruction that took place in these parts of the city is well documented because China invited Western journalists to survey the violence, an unusual move from Beijing. In other sections of the city, Chinese police and military forces pursued and arrested hundreds of Uyghurs, and fragmented and unconfirmed reporting has indicated security personnel opened fire on Uyghur demonstrators while they fled (Branigan

---

[107] Bovingdon (2010) also calls attention to two pervading but contrary rumors: that police may have arrived too late to stop the violence, or that they waited too long to take action while awaiting instructions from Beijing.

2010).[108] Then it was the turn of the Han Chinese. Groups of Han vigilantes armed with homemade weapons began targeting Uyghur residents for indiscriminate revenge killings. According to one particularly harrowing press report:

> At first the talk was of self-defense. Then it turned to vengeance. A respectable-looking middle-aged woman carried a plank with a nail poking from it; a younger woman in a colorful top and white diamante mules clutched a metal pipe. A father, passing with his family, held his young son with one hand and a length of wood with the other. Then, a roar in the distance. They walked, then ran, toward the Uyghur part of town, where many would smash up stores and threaten residents. It would take round after round of teargas and thousands of riot and paramilitary police to disperse them (Branigan 2009a: para. 2-3).

The government the next day shut down the Internet and cell phone services, and continued to call in more security forces to quell the unrest in Urumqi. The government reported no casualty figures for these attacks, which nonetheless attracted significant international media attention (Bovingdon 2010). On July 10, Security forces used truncheons on a group of protestors that appeared to be marching peacefully.

All told, at least 197 people died during the violence, and over 1,700 were reported injured (Millward 2009). However, the World Uyghur Congress has estimated the death toll to be 1,000 killed, based on eyewitness reporting (World Uyghur Congress 2013a). In the months following the riots, the Chinese government claimed to have arrested 1,400 Uyghurs, sentencing

---

[108] The Western journalists whom China had invited to survey the damage in Han areas also observed signs of Uyghur abuse the following day. They reported encountering a Han mob attacking a Uyghur man and then turning on the journalists themselves as well as a large group of women who demanded that the government release their male relatives who had been picked up the previous night. See Bovingdon, 2010.

35 to death for their role. Again, the World Uyghur Congress estimates those figures to be higher: 10,000 Uyghurs detained, 4,000-5,000 Uyghurs disappeared, and 4,000-5,000 Uyghurs killed since the Urumqi riots (Radio Free Europe 2011). It is of course impossible to independently verify any of these claims.

The riots stemmed from Han-Uyghur tensions generally, but were sparked by ethnic violence on 25 June in a toy factory in Guangdong Province, 2,000 miles away from Urumqi. What led to this unrest is unclear, but the confrontation may have resulted from a "cultural misunderstanding" after an employee alleged six Uyghurs had raped two Han workers at the factory (Millward 2009). Following this allegation, which was posted to an Internet bulletin board, violence broke out at the factory, and Han employees, armed with clubs, iron bars and machetes, stormed the Uyghur dormitories. Officially, two Uyghurs were killed and 118 were injured, but videos of the violence that the diaspora helped circulate on the Internet seemed to suggest a level of violence far beyond what the authorities had described. A Han man's proclamation that he had killed seven or eight Uyghurs and that he estimated the number to have perished at 30 also attracted mass attention in the Uyghur global community (Millward 2009; Watts 2009). Suspecting that a Chinese cover-up was underway, Uyghur exile groups mobilized its supporters both inside and outside China, leading to the July demonstration. It is thus both tragic and ironic that the disturbance that sparked the demonstration in Urumqi and violence that followed transpired thousands of miles away, resulted in far fewer casualties, and was facilitated by the Uyghur community. The toy factory incident was also heavily promoted by the Uyghur diaspora and has become irrevocably linked in the Uyghur mind to the violence that followed.

Governments around the world professed shock at the scale of the violence and urged China to show restraint. The chief of human rights at the United Nations professed "alarm" at the large number of casualties and called on all sides to show restraint. Both the United Nations chief of human rights and the White House expressed deep concern and also urged restraint, as did the European Union and the governments of France, Germany, Australia, Switzerland, Singapore, and Taiwan (Associated Press 2009a; Central News Agency 2009; Channel News Asia 2009a, 2009b, 2009c; United Nations News Centre 2009). American House Speaker Nancy Pelosi, a long-time critic of China, criticized Beijing for its "harsh policies" and urged dialogue with the Uyghurs, and the Organization of the Islamic Conference condemned the violence while criticizing China for "the disproportionate use of force" (Channel News Asia 2009b). In the Islamic world, Uyghur exile groups lobbied governments to take a tougher position against China for mishandling the unrest. These efforts bore the most fruit in Turkey, where Prime Minister Recep Tayyip Erdogan at the behest of Uyghur exile groups and opposition parties compared the violence to genocide and threatened to raise the issue of China's ethnic violence against Uyghurs at the UN Security Council (BBC News 2009). Sixty Turkish lawmakers resigned from a Turkish-Chinese inter-parliamentary friendship group, and a government minister called on Turks to boycott Chinese goods, although the government stopped short of officially sanctioning such action (Associated Press 2009c, 2009d). Iran also sought to push back against China, petitioning Beijing to "observe the rights of the Muslims in Xinjiang" (Panda 2010: 12). However, the Turkish government eventually backed off these threats, and neither country appears to have taken a permanent interest in pressuring China more firmly.

While Western governments urged caution and Islamic nations expressed their indignation, the global Uyghur community declared its outrage and rallied supporters to protest against China. As a result, demonstrations took place in front of Chinese embassies all over the world, a few of which lapsed into violence. Protestors in the Netherlands forced the Chinese mission to close temporarily, and Dutch police arrested 142 protestors after they started throwing rocks and stones at the mission (RTE News 2009). Suspected Uyghur activists in Munich launched three Molotov cocktails overnight at the Chinese consulate, setting a Chinese flag on fire (Channel News Asia 2009b). Authorities in Oslo summoned a large police force in riot gear to separate approximately 100 Uyghurs from China's Embassy (Associated Press 2009b). For its part, the World Uyghur Congress organized a peaceful march to the Chinese embassy in Washington that attracted roughly 100 Uyghur exiles (Eckholm 2009b; Montgomery 2009).

Countries with sizable Uyghur and Muslim populations saw the largest demonstrations. Turkey with its large Uyghur diaspora presence endured daily demonstrations, and hundreds of Turks and Uyghurs protested daily in Ankara and Istanbul, hurling eggs at the missions and setting Chinese flags on fire (Associated Press 2009b). In Kazakhstan, 5,000 Uyghurs protested against China's indiscriminate use of force, the largest regional gathering of Uyghurs in several years and also something of an anomaly since Kazakhstan maintains tight control over its Uyghur community (Leonard 2009). In Jakarta and other Indonesian cities, several dozen protestors briefly clashed with security forces and issued calls for jihad or "holy war" outside the Chinese Embassy (AFP 2009b).

The riots in Urumqi constituted the deepest unrest that Xinjiang had ever experienced and recalled memories of the violence that had taken place in 1989 at Tiananmen Square (Millward 2009; Bovingdon 2010). It has also come to reflect the rising tide of ethnic tensions between the Uyghur and Han communities. In the aftermath of the Urumqi riots, the Chinese government accused Rebiya Kadeer and the World Uyghur Congress of triggering the violence and claimed to have a phone recording of Kadeer discussing the demonstrations in advance; Kadeer has denied any role (Montgomery 2009; see also Bovingdon 2010). Ironically, the government's decision to hold Kadeer publicly responsible may have backfired on the government by elevating her status in Western countries as the undisputed leader of the Uyghurs. Xinjiang remained quiet in August, but in September tensions flared again when Han residents claimed to be the target of "syringe attacks" presumably conducted by Uyghur terrorists, leading to hysteria among Han residents in several Xinjiang cities (Economist 2009; Bovingdon 2010). The Chinese government removed Urumqi's police chief and the top Communist Party official for Xinjiang was also fired in September, almost certainly in response to the unrest that by that point had engulfed the province for three months. It is less clear if the government's decision to replace the provincial secretary of Xinjiang the following April was also due in pat to the late-summer violence the year before; but if so, it would mean the violence in Urumqi eventually laid claim to all three of the top posts in the provincial leadership.

Urumqi Riots as a Traumatic Event:

This episode meets several of the criteria qualifying a traumatic event. The riots swept over Urumqi with suddenness and ferocity, shocking the international community and enraging the global Uyghur population. The episode was extremely violent, representing perhaps the greatest unrest in China since Tiananmen Square. The riots drew mass amounts of international attention and concern — Western newspapers such as the *Guardian*, the *New York Times*, the *Washington Post* and the *Boston Globe,* among others, covered the episode for several weeks, providing unprecedented news coverage for the Uyghur cause. Further, the Internet and social media allowed Uyghurs and media outlets alike to circulate photos of the violence, some of which were quite horrifying and undercut the government's narrative that the Uyghurs were completely to blame. Without having great insight into internal perceptions of the government's role following the episode, it seems generally clear that Uyghurs perceive the Chinese government to have botched its handling of the episode and to have employed abusive tactics and indiscriminate force, which has conferred a lasting notoriety to the event.

In spite of these similarities to other traumatic events, some noteworthy differences distinguish this case as far as its impact on Xinjiang's internal security is concerned. Foremost among these is that the Urumqi riots — unlike Operation Blue Star, Bloody Sunday, and the Irish hunger strikes — do not appear to have sparked increased militant activity within the country in which it occurred. Although reliable reporting from China's western areas are scarce, it seems probable that China would not have hesitated to report more incidents of militant activity to strengthen its case unless it felt doing so would endanger stability. However, there have been only a few reports of militant attacks, and the most reviled Uyghur separatist group in China, the ETIM, went into a period of prolonged inactivity after the attack, at least according to Chinese reporting. Admittedly, we cannot know for certain all of Xinjiang's political dealings given China's restrictions and control of information, but there is not much evidence that groups like the ETIM received a boost in funds, recruiting, or local support in the aftermath of Urumqi. This event, unlike the other, also involved both of the ethnic communities participating in violent acts, and at least according to official estimates it can be said that the Han community suffered the most.

Level of physical violence – By most accounts, the amount of physical violence taking place during the riots was staggering. The violence clearly affected a huge sum of people. All sides agree that *at least* 197 people died and 1,700 people were injured, but Uyghurs believe that China has downplayed or even concealed the actual number of Uyghur deaths and actually put the death toll at approximately 1,000. According to reports, Uyghurs beat Han residents mercilessly on the night of July 5, with metal pipes and jagged wooden clubs. Gangs of Han Chinese used similar tactics during reprisal attacks a few days later, and Chinese security forces also adopted rough tactics and opened fire on civilians, according to eyewitness accounts. Photos of the violence spread on the Internet depicting harrowing images of bloodied residents nursing serious head trauma and walking in an apparent daze. Other photos show graphic images of dead bodies scattered in the streets (Boston Globe 2009). The amount of property damage — which one estimate put at 3 million *Yuan,* or roughly $480,000 (*Bloomberg* 2009) — was also extensive as Uyghur gangs destroyed multiple shops and storefronts, and invaded cross-community areas. The riots also prompted a significant increase in tensions between the Uyghurs and the Han, including ensuing violent episodes such as allegations of Uyghur-orchestrated syringe attacks that led to mass hysteria in the province.

Level of symbolic violence – It is difficult to know the extent to which Uyghurs in China symbolically interpreted the Urumqi riots, but reasonable to speculate that Uyghurs saw the event as emblematic of China's perceived repression of the Uyghur population. The killing of mass numbers of civilians — confirmed or not, it is what Uyghurs believe — will have reinforced the Uyghur perception of China as a cruel, dictatorial and foreign force imposing its will. Uyghurs may have seen China's disruption of the march at the People's Square as representative of the government's overall suppression of the Uyghur right to free expression, and the factory violence that inspired the demonstration as further evidence of the economic inequality and lack of opportunity that all Uyghurs face. The fact that the protest took place at the People's Square — a public center symbolizing the state — could itself epitomize for the

Uyghurs their willingness to confront the state in the face of insurmountable odds; alternatively, it could represent the Uyghurs attempt to resolve their issues peacefully only to be crushed by the Chinese government. Even the government's decision to invite Western journalists to tour Han devastated areas of Urumqi but not the Uyghur areas will have implied the state's priorities—demonstrating its concern for Han residents and efforts to protect them from current harm, while at the same time containing all evidence of Uyghur suffering. The point here is not to conclude which symbolic interpretations did take place, but to demonstrate that the potential for symbolism did exist. Historically, the riots also epitomized previous acts of government violence against the Uyghurs, including China's attempted manipulation of a hereditary struggle in 1931 that plunged the region into chaos, the unrest surrounding both attempts to establish independent states prior to Communist rule, and the instability and bloodshed that accompanied the Great Leap Forward and Cultural Revolution (Rudelson 1997).

Yet, the Urumqi riots fail to tap into a richer allegory for Uyghurs, mainly because the event does not access any of the cultural or religious anxieties that fuel the Uyghurs' campaign against China. Indeed, nothing that transpired during the riots — the government's suppression of the demonstration, the possible use of force by security forces on Uyghur civilians, or the Han-Uyghur violence that followed — stands out for its cultural or religious symbolism, thereby limiting the potential to emotionally impact a diaspora member. The demonstration took place at a public square in the town center, not a mosque or religious shrine similar to the Red Mosque in Pakistan. China's policies restricting Islam or the Uyghur language played no immediate role in the confrontation. The episode touches implicitly on ethnicity only in the sense of determining the different communities involved, but the violence does not incorporate the type of cultural meaning that Uyghurs would recognize by virtue of their identity and socialization. It is also possible that the participation of some Uyghur residents in violent acts against Han Chinese, which most Uyghur leaders do acknowledge, may have blunted the symbolic cache of the riots.

DIASPORA MOBILIZATION AFTER THE URUMQI RIOTS

In the three years since the riots, Uyghur organizations have rallied around the leadership of the World Uyghur Congress, which in turn has led engagement efforts with Western governments on behalf of the Uyghur population. The Congress has also played a central role in coordinating and publicizing the activity of its affiliate groups, including protests, press events, and demonstrations held on the anniversary of the riots and other historic events. For example, the Congress in July 2012 helped publicize events commemorating the third anniversary of the Urumqi riots in fourteen different countries, including the United States, Canada, Australia and much of Western Europe (World Uyghur Congress 2013b). The Congress has found itself at the epicenter of all this activity because: 1) the Congress through its umbrella of affiliated groups has the greatest global reach, and 2) the Chinese government elevated the stature of Rebiya Kadeer when it alleged she was the main conspirator behind the riots but failed to offer persuasive evidence. The Congress during this time has grown more assertive in criticizing China, frequently framing the Urumqi riots as just the clearest and most well known example of the state's recklessness. Kadeer has consistently sought to rebut Beijing's version of events and provide the Uyghur perspective on what caused the violence. For example, in an Op-Ed piece that ran in the *Wall Street Journal* three days after the riots, Kadeer wrote "it is years of Chinese repression of Uyghurs—topped by further confirmation that Chinese officials have no interest in observing the rule of law—that is the cause of the current Uyghur discontent" and that "China's brutal reaction to [the] protest will only reinforce these views" (Kadeer 2009: A17).

Since the riots, the Congress and other Uyghur organizations have been especially effective at harnessing the Internet and social media to disseminate information, trade online YouTube videos, coordinate action, and energize supporters. This thesis has already cited the ability of Uyghur organizations to rapidly circulate video of the factory riots in Guangdong Province. In the period of time since the Urumqi violence, Uyghurs have enhanced their usage of the Internet by coordinating marches, rallies and demonstrations for maximum global effect. The World Uyghur Congress has also regularly posted "press releases" to its web site condemning the Chinese government for various current or historical acts, and since 2009 almost all of these announcements have referenced the Urumqi riots. As recently as February 2013, a press release announcing the anniversary of a suppressed protest in China in 1997 compared it to the Urumqi riots and committed as much space to condemning China for the Urumqi riots as it did the event being commemorated, thus underscoring the event's continuing symbolism. The end result is that Uyghurs since the Urumqi violence have enhanced their usage of the Internet not only to coordinate organizing efforts for maximum global effect, but also to ensure a common narrative regarding its details and causes. This in turn has allowed the riots to serve effectively as a microcosm of all of China's injustices against the Uyghurs.

This level of online activity provides an instructive discussion point regarding diaspora movements in the twenty-first century. Vergani and Zuev (2011) argue the Internet provides a critical political medium given the size and diffusion of the Uyghur diaspora, because it is one of the few resources the Uyghurs can use to create a "spatial togetherness and expression of transnational loyalty" (228). Further highlighting the role of the Internet in coordinating actions and perceptions, they analyze a series of uploaded YouTube videos about the Urumqi violence and determine the intended audiences for the majority of these videos is Uyghur diaspora communities residing in other states — not the domestic non-Uyghur audience of the new country. This focus on the Uyghur online community is not new; Gladney (2005: 458) that "the growing influence of 'cyber-separatism' and international popularization of the Uyghur cause" had long concerned China. In sum, the Uyghur movement's use of the Internet since the Urumqi riots represents the acceleration of a decade-long trend of increasing online activism by the Uyghur community, but the power of the Urumqi riots within this web of online activism is to function as a single symbolic episode encapsulating the grievances that Uyghurs carry against the state overall.

Although the riots have rallied Uyghurs around the World Uyghur Congress and ignited the passions of the ethnic group's cyber-community, it has not led to a demonstrable increase in terms of either fundraising or membership for these Uyghur organizations; few if any investigative or media reporting indicate that the Congress or other Uyghur groups has increased its membership or received greater fundraising contributions since the Urumqi riots, according to several database searches. Based on limited information, we can therefore tentatively conclude that this traumatic event appears to have functioned effectively as a rallying point for Uyghur diaspora members already involved in the movement, but failed to make significant gains in growing its membership base or attracting new members.

A number of factors can help explain this. The Congress has adopted a public relations strategy that overwhelmingly concentrates its resources at pressuring Western governments to take a tougher stance on China, and it is likely to see very little use in collecting funds to send to the homeland because of China's tight control of the region. It already receives external financial support from human rights organizations, which partially negates the urgency of raising funds for its own activities. Finally, Uyghurs in the West might perceive the danger of sending cash when

Uyghur separatists operate in a shadowy environment that may include association with Islamic fundamentalists in Central and South Asia (a possibility I discuss in greater detail below). These factors all discourage diaspora members from radical options such as seeking to support armed separatist groups, but encourages them to operate in the relative open by lobbying their new state governments. It is also true that not enough time has passed to fully assess the global impact of the Urumqi riots on the Uyghur population.

The Uyghur Diaspora and Islamic Extremism:

To this point, we have primarily analyzed the activity of Uyghur exile groups in response to the Urumqi violence, and concluded that the event energized the efforts of activists without necessarily attracting many new supporters. In discussing the impact of this traumatic event on Uyghurs in the diaspora, however, we must also view reaction through an entirely different prism: the threat of Uyghur Muslims who might be involved in Islamic fundamentalist activity or have access to jihadist networks. This introduces a difficult analytic overlap between ethnic identity and religious dogma, two ideologies that are not always distinct but encompass very different political goals. The Uyghur diaspora, human rights organizations and practiced Xinjiang observers have long clashed with the Chinese government regarding the government's claims of a supposed linkage between the Uyghurs of Xinjiang and Islamic extremism.

Indeed, there are good reasons to cast doubt on most of the Chinese government's claims. First, the goals and agenda of the Uyghur movement do not align easily with Islamic fundamentalists. Most Uyghurs practice the Sufi rather than Salafi form of Islam adopted by many fundamentalists, and previous research consistently points to nationalistic and separatist ambitions rather than ideological fervor as the primary motivation of Uyghur militants (Ogden

2004). Second, China in a practical sense offers neither the relative openness of a Western society nor the lax control of a weak or failing state that has attracted Islamic militant groups in the past; Islamist groups would find it difficult to operate amidst the state's tight security grip in the region. Third, China has been effective at isolating Xinjiang's Uyghur population from the global Islamic community, further limiting inroads between Uyghurs and Islamic groups.[109] For these reasons, the Uyghurs and Islamic jihadists are unlikely bedfellows.

Yet, the possibility of even a small minority of Uyghur separatists turning to jihadist groups cannot be ignored — especially if the Chinese government were ever to engage in action that Islamists might interpret as an attack against Islam. Although the firm organizational links claimed by the Chinese government between al-Qa'ida and the ETIM likely does not exist, it remains true that some Uyghur militants undeniably have found safe haven in Afghanistan and Pakistan or had involvement with jihadist activity outside of China. For example, US forces in 2001 and 2002 captured 25 Uyghur separatists in Afghanistan during the initial months of the Afghanistan war, which boosted China's claim that Uyghur separatism was allied with al-Qa'ida. However, the Pentagon later rules that the detainees, subsequently held at the US's military prison camp at Guantanamo Bay, presented no threat to the United States and could be released (Wright 2005). Perhaps more noteworthy is the Pakistani army's reported killing of ETIM leader Hasan Mahsum in al-Qa'ida's sanctuary in South Waziristan, which would also seem to indicate institutional ties between ETIM and al-Qa'ida (Clarke 2008). In July 2010, a year after the Urumqi riots, Norwegian authorities uncovered an al-Qa'ida-linked terrorist bomb plot and

---

[109] Although Beijing has recently made efforts to provide Uyghurs with slightly greater freedom of movement, including limited and controlled opportunities to carry out *Hajj* pilgrimages to Mecca, the level of restrictions on travel and access outside Xinjiang prevents the Uyghur community from building ties outside their own ethnic group. For all of these reasons, the chances of Islamic fundamentalist groups embracing the Uyghur cause as one of its own are unlikely.

arrested three individuals — one of whom was a Chinese Uyghur — claiming to belong the Turkestan Islamic Party, a possible offshoot of the ETIM (Wong 2010). In July 2011, following a weekend outbreak of "knife and bomb" attacks in Kashgar that killed 22, the government alleged that ETIM militants were to blame and that they had trained in the tribal regions of Pakistan — an unusually specific accusation possibly signaling China's growing impatience; overseas Uyghur groups disputed the ETIM connection and held the government responsible for the attacks (Wines 2011a, 2011b; Barriaux 2011). While this fragmented evidence over the course of ten years stops well short of affirming the Chinese government's version of events, these associations do suggest the possibility that some Uyghur militants have access to global jihadist networks and could attempt to build support under the right circumstances — especially in the event of a traumatic episode that galvanized the Islamic community against China.

In the wake of the Urumqi riots, this was exactly the fear of a few analysts despite the ideological disconnect separating their movements (See Panda 2010). A threat did emerge after the riots where the Algerian-based al-Qaida in the Islamic Maghreb threatened to retaliate for the slaughter of Muslims, and the Chinese embassy in Algeria warned companies and workers to take precautions (Branigan 2009b). However, the general lack of evidence of widespread Islamic anger indicates the Urumqi riots failed to capture the imagination of the greater Islamic community, probably because the event did not involve an explicit affront to Islam that would have been most likely to spur a larger backlash. With the exception of the lone threat report on the Chinese embassy in Algeria (which passed without incident), no evidence of increased ties between Islamist terrorist groups and Uyghur separatist militants came to pass.

CONCLUSION

This chapter has analyzed the Uyghur diaspora and its response to the Urumqi riots, which created immediate international sympathy for the Uyghur movement and propelled World Uyghur Congress leader Rebiya Kadeer to an unprecedented level of renown among Western governments. This emboldened Uyghur exile groups in some ways, particularly their coordination with each other and their efforts to appeal to Western governments to see the plight of the Uyghurs as an issue of human rights. However, the Urumqi riots, though certainly a devastating event for those committed to the Uyghur campaign, does not appear to have attracted a significant number of new supporters or increased fundraising or grassroots support for the Uyghur cause. It also failed to strike a nerve in the shadowy world of Islamic fundamentalist violence despite the apparent involvement of a small minority of Uyghurs in Islamic militant networks. In the next chapter, I will further analyze this event and its effect on the diaspora through comparison to the other case studies that this research has undertaken.

9

COMPARATIVE ANALYSIS OF THE FOUR EVENTS

This chapter brings together the traumatic events examined in chapters 7 and 8 and analyzes each event in comparative context with Operation Blue Star. The aim of this chapter is to provide comparative analysis of these events using the framework outlined in chapter 3. It assesses what factors help explain important variations in the diaspora's mobilizing response to each event. No traumatic event solely influenced the activity of its diaspora members, but Operation Blue Star, Bloody Sunday, the Irish hunger strikes, and the Urumqi riots all undeniably created opportunities for diaspora mobilization. These events fostered a more hospitable environment for separatist diaspora activists to champion their cause, allowing diasporas to attract new supporters, lobby foreign governments, and fundraise on behalf of the movement. Yet, levels of mobilization in response to these events varied in important ways. Comparative analysis of all four events can help illustrate how violence and symbolism involved in each event directly influenced perceptions and partially shaped the response of diaspora populations.

TRAUMATIC EVENTS IN COMPARISON

Both traumatic events in Northern Ireland effected tangible, affirmative responses from the Irish diaspora: donations increased, demonstrations were larger, and communal anger infused lobbying efforts with more grassroots support. In the case of Bloody Sunday, an event that led to outrage and further violence on both sides of the border in Ireland and widespread condemnation throughout the world, Irish America reacted mournfully and angrily to what had happened at Derry. In response, fundraising for groups such as Noraid increased dramatically, and some of these funds probably benefited militant republican groups. However, Bloody Sunday appears to have mainly galvanized Irish emigrants or 1st generation Irish Americans, but was less successful at attracting the support of ethnic members from longer established families. The boost to international sources of fundraising provided by the event also appears to have been short-lived. As Bloody Sunday became a more distant memory and republican violence in Northern Ireland increased too dramatically for the taste of some American supporters, Irish America's activism and financial generosity began to ebb.

The hunger strike generated a similarly strong response — public demonstrations, lobbying efforts, and a powerful fundraising boost to diaspora groups — but with an added dimension: the hunger strike motivated thousands of previously inactive Irish Americans, many of whom were multi-generation Americans, to become active in the movement at least temporarily — through such activities as joining a diaspora organization or participating in overseas trips to Ireland. The hunger strike also emboldened republican organizations such as Noraid to take more controversial political actions in open defiance of the British government or even its more moderate critics in the diaspora.

The Urumqi riots succeeded in mobilizing Uyghur diaspora and exile groups to protest the violence in Xinjiang and actions of the Chinese government in the near term. During the weeks following the riots, Uyghurs protested in front of Chinese embassies all over the world, and some of these demonstrations turned violent. However, the event did not enable Uyghur organizations to attract significant amounts of new followers. It may have acted as an effective rallying cry for Uyghur activists, but there is little evidence indicating it significantly enhanced fundraising for these groups or grew their membership bases. Perhaps even more importantly, the Urumqi riots failed to galvanize much outrage within militant Islamist channels, to which some Uyghurs have access and could garner greater attention if groups such as al-Qa'ida took a significant interest in the Uyghur conflict.

It is therefore reasonable to conclude that Operation Blue Star and the Irish hunger strike functioned more effectively as traumatic events than Bloody Sunday or the Urumqi riots. The hunger strike's ability to motivate into action new supporters previously uninterested in the Irish question, as opposed to Irish emigrants, ultimately sets it apart from Bloody Sunday as the more influential event in Ireland. It compares favorably to the effect of Operation Blue Star on the Sikh diaspora, of which many members — including several Sikhs whom I interviewed — reported becoming more religious and involved in the Sikh community after the attack on the Golden Temple. Operation Blue Star also affected the Sikh diaspora on a fundamental and deeply emotional level, galvanizing it to organize protests and demonstrations and contribute money for humanitarian relief. Blue Star increased the appeal of the separatist movement, attracting new followers and increasing the level of fundraising.

Despite dramatic differences between the events in terms of scale, political significance and cultural meaning, Blue Star and the hunger strike outperformed Bloody Sunday and the Urumqi riots in attracting and mobilizing new supporters. Comparative analysis of all four events and testing the hypotheses guiding this research helps to explain how violence and symbolism involved in each event directly influenced perceptions and partially shaped the response of diaspora populations.

Using the framework outlined in chapter 3 allows us to assess the level of physical violence for each of the traumatic events. Here, we will use the framework to compare the Uyghur event and both Irish events to Operation Blue Star. Regarding the Irish cases, both events exhibited relatively low levels of physical violence. Fourteen people died as a result from Bloody Sunday. Ten people voluntarily died on hunger strike. Property damage was minimal during Bloody Sunday—perhaps the slight scarring of a few buildings from shots fired—and virtually nonexistent for the hunger strike. Both events therefore offer a sharp contrast to Operation Blue Star in terms of physical violence. During the assault at Amritsar, several temple buildings were badly damaged, and estimated deaths ranged from 493 to almost 2,100. The level of physical violence for either Irish event also did not represent a radical escalation of bloodshed from the conflict's previous levels, another departure from Blue Star.

The Urumqi riots compares more favorably to Operation Blue Star than either Irish event. One judges the level of physical violence in the Urumqi riots to have been high — perhaps not approaching the 587 official casualties witnessed during the Golden Temple attack, but certainly well above the number killed in Derry in 1972 or at Maze Prison in 1981. The Urumqi riots, like Operation Blue Star, included a death toll that numbered in the hundreds. Both events led to allegations of the government's security forces mistreating or killing civilians, and the government after each event was accused of facilitating the disappearance of ethnic members. The level of property damage from the Urumqi riots compares to the destruction in Amritsar of several buildings in the complex. The level of physical violence demonstrated during the Urumqi riots also sparked an escalation of ethnic tensions from the conflict's previous levels, though perhaps not to the same degree as the course of events in Punjab following Operation Blue Star.

Figure 8.1 Exhibited Physical Violence in the Four Cases

Event	Operation Blue Star	Bloody Sunday	Irish Hunger Strike	Urumqi Riots
Physical violence	Approx. 493—2100 civilian casualties Approx. 100-200 militant casualties Destruction of temple buildings/property	14 civilians killed little property damage	10 prisoners killed no property damage	197-approx. 1,000 killed 1700 injured Destruction of shopfronts, buildings, vehicles; approx. $480,000 in damage

Figure 8.2 Relationship between Physical Violence and Mobilization for Four Cases

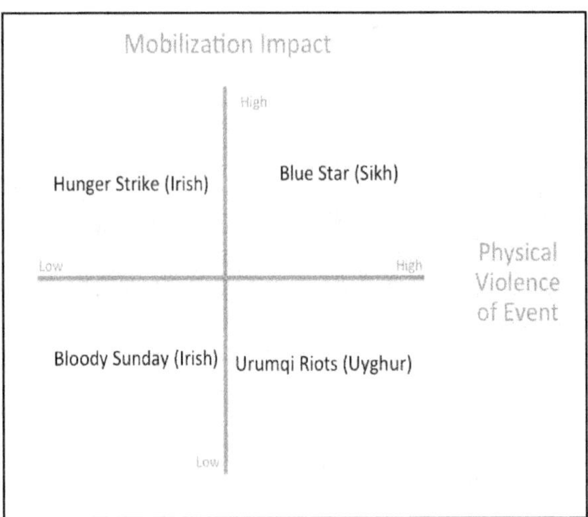

In sum, the traumatic events affecting the Sikh and Uyghur diasporas exhibited greater levels of physical violence than either traumatic event affecting the Irish diaspora. Therefore, regarding

the first hypothesis on physical violence, these inputs hypothetically should result in the Sikh and Uyghur diasporas experiencing a stronger mobilization than the Irish diaspora:

H1a (physical violence): As the relative level of violent aggression or bloodshed involved in a traumatic event increases, separatist movements will attract new followers and persuade fence-sitters

Yet, we know this not to be the case. The response of the Irish-American diaspora to the hunger strike—despite a substantially *lower* input for physical violence—is comparable to the Sikh reaction to Operation Blue Star. In spite of the high level of physical violence exhibited during the Urumqi riots, the response of the Uyghur diaspora is weaker than Blue Star or the hunger strike. Therefore, the inputs for physical violence do not produce consistently strong diaspora responses, offering weak support for the first hypothesis when viewed in isolation. This suggests that when it comes to creating a nationalist saga the actual body count can be but a minor variable, as it was during the Boston massacre, when only four people were killed, or perhaps during the Alamo attack when 200 Americans were killed as compared to over 400 Mexicans.

Symbolic Violence:

I will now perform the same exercise for symbolic forms of violence, starting again with the Irish cases. The Irish hunger strike eclipsed Bloody Sunday as the more symbolically violent episode. The event — perceived by some Irish Catholics as a "crucifixion" — was also more symbolically violent than the Urumqi violence, and compared favorably with the high level of symbolic violence witnessed during Operation Blue Star. Despite stark differences in scale and the number of people harmed, important similarities can be drawn between the hunger strike and Blue Star. Irish Catholics perceived the hunger strike to represent just the latest stage of the British cruelty and neglect exhibited toward the Irish, just as Sikhs immediately recognized the attack on the Golden Temple as a bid by the Hindu majority to threaten their culture and way of life. Both Sikh and Catholic saw the participants of each event within the framework of their ethnic history, imagining the sacrifices of the Sikh militant and the republican prisoner as the latest in a long line of martyrs. Like the attack at the Golden Temple, the hunger strike had the powerful effect of linking its ethnic participants to the past in part by employing a recognizable cast of republican "heroes" (Bobby Sands) and British "villains" (Margaret Thatcher). It is interesting that Thatcher was involuntarily cast into the same villainous role that Indian Prime Minister Indira Gandhi occupied three years later — while the Sikhs' attempt on Gandhi's life succeeded, republicans narrowly failed in their attempt to assassinate Thatcher when in 1984 they detonated a powerful bomb in her Brighton hotel room. This allowed ethnic observers to perceive the hunger strike, like Operation Blue Star, in emotional and symbolic terms.

Bloody Sunday did not experience a similarly high level of symbolic violence, in part because the event did not become as immersed in nationalist mythology as the hunger strike or Operation Blue Star for Sikhs. Similarly, the Urumqi riots failed to offer the same type of potency for symbolism because it failed to access any sort of nationalist Uyghur mythology as well as the religious and cultural practices that Uyghur Muslims perceive are under China's assault, or alternatively, militant Uyghurs connected to international jihadist networks could interpret as attacks on Islam.

Event	Operation Blue Star	Bloody Sunday	Irish Hunger Strike	Urumqi Riots
Symbolic violence	Destruction of Akal Takht, library Shots fired on Harmandir Sahib) Perceived abuse of Sikhs Echoing the past	Setting/location Some religious overlap – priest, Sunday Echoing the past	Martyrdom/self-immolation Echoing the past	Suppression of the demonstration Location at People's Square Epitomizing previous acts of randomized violence

Figure 8.4 Relationship between Symbolic Violence and Mobilization for Four Cases

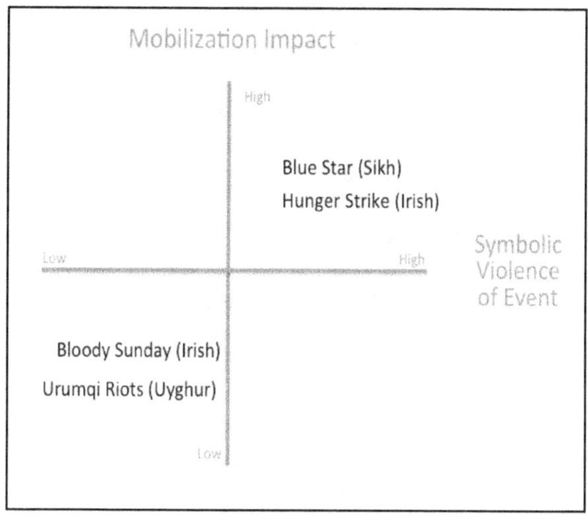

In short, The Indian government's perceived sacrilege in storming the marble courtyard of the Golden Temple complex outweighed the symbolic potential of possibly hundreds of Uyghurs dying in riotous violence in the darkened streets of Urumqi, and the campaign of prisoners to starve themselves to death more deeply affected a generation of Irish America whose familial connection to Ireland was remote than did the events that took place in Derry nine years earlier. Between the four cases, the hunger strike produced an effect similar to the level of threat perceived by American Sikhs as a result of Operation Blue Star. This offers greater support for the second hypothesis:

> **H1b (symbolic violence):** When crucial details of a traumatic event gain symbolic significance or underscore specific and preexisting separatist frames from the conflict, separatist movements will attract new followers and persuade fence-sitters

This should not be misconstrued to mean that nothing about the violence of Bloody Sunday or the Urumqi riots was symbolically evident. As I have argued, Bloody Sunday transpired in a symbolically rich setting and came to symbolize the perception of Britain as an unsympathetic foreign occupier. Bloody Sunday also retained greater symbolism among Catholic residents in Ireland than in the diaspora because Northern Irish residents arguably were more likely to see the heart of the conflict as the abuse of the Catholic community's civil and political rights, while diaspora members were more likely to frame it as a struggle to remove the British and reclaim the island's northern section as belonging to the Irish people. The Urumqi riots provided a rallying cry for the Uyghur diaspora at dozens of demonstrations since 2009, and also enlivened exile groups that are continually lobbying Western governments under the guise of human rights. However, Bloody Sunday and the Urumqi riots in comparison to the other two events lacked the same level of ethno-religious indicators that connected with co-ethnic participants on a deeper, more psychological level, and therefore failed to invite ethnic members to make more emotion-laden interpretations about the threat to the ethnic group's survival.

This research has thus far assessed that Operation Blue Star and the Irish hunger strike exhibited stronger symbolic qualities than Bloody Sunday or the Urumqi riots, which enabled both events through their impact on ethnic perceptions to galvanize the diaspora into mobilization more effectively. These cases also indicate that fluctuating levels of physical violence do not necessarily influence diaspora mobilization to the same degree, which suggests that diaspora populations are less responsive to the absolute amount of physical damage or casualties than to an event's symbolic potential. In sum, these four cases demonstrate that diaspora observers are more likely to make emotion-laden interpretations when confronted with symbolic forms of violence as opposed to physical forms. This research therefore assesses that an event that is more symbolically violent has greater influence on a diaspora than an event that is more physically violent; if true, this finding represents an important qualification to the research model.

Event Galvanization:

Event galvanization is the process where a political episode distresses the ethnic community to the point of mobilization. The above findings underscore the importance of symbolism to the process of event galvanization. Symbolically powerful events such as Operation Blue Star or the Irish hunger strike, and to a lesser degree Bloody Sunday or the Urumqi riots, create a fertile environment for elites and movement entrepreneurs to increase levels of support for the movement.

In the case of Northern Ireland, both events allowed diaspora republican activists such as Noraid chief Michael Flannery to conduct more explicit, high-level activity on behalf of the republican movement, including channeling funds to the IRA and facilitating the purchase of weaponry and ammunition. Lobbying activity, participation in protests and demonstrations, and membership enrollment in cultural groups also increased as a result of the hunger strike. Despite the significant disparity in terms of physical violence between the two events, the hunger strike produced a diaspora response comparable to the effect of Operation Blue Star on Sikhs in America.[110] In response to these events, both diasporas engaged in widespread activity on behalf of the separatist movement including fundraising, lobbying efforts, and organizing protests and demonstrations.

These activities also occurred in response to Bloody Sunday, but to a lesser degree. Bloody Sunday sparked an immediate uptick of financial contributions to Irish cultural groups voicing support for the IRA, some of which may have been channeled into IRA arms deals facilitated by its supporters abroad. However, the boost to nationalist fundraising appears to have been shorter-lived than the boost that followed the hunger strike, and Bloody Sunday additionally failed to significantly expand the movement's strength internationally by attracting new supporters.

The Urumqi riots created immediate international sympathy for the Uyghur movement and propelled World Uyghur Congress leader Rebiya Kadeer to an unprecedented level of renown among Western governments. The riots emboldened Uyghur exile groups in coordinating their actions with each other as they sought to appeal to Western governments and frame the

---

[110] It is also noteworthy that in both the Sikh and Irish cases, the principal antagonists whom both diaspora populations grew to revile as a result of these events were women. This might speak to the role of tradition in the formation of ethnicity and the implicit threat a powerful female leader represents to tradition.

Uyghur cause as an issue of human rights. However, the Urumqi riots, though certainly a devastating event for those committed to the Uyghur campaign, does not outwardly appear to have attracted a significant number of new supporters or increased fundraising or grassroots support for the Uyghur cause. It also failed to strike a nerve in the shadowy world of Islamic fundamentalist violence despite the apparent involvement of a small minority of Uyghurs in Islamic militant networks.

In sum, the Sikh response to Operation Blue Star constituted the most intense form of event galvanization among the four cases, followed by the Irish hunger strike, Bloody Sunday, and the Urumqi riots. This offers tentative support to the third hypothesis:

H1c (event galvanization): As perceptions of the separatist movement improve and attract new followers, the likelihood of diaspora members providing greater levels of support to separatist groups in the homeland increases

OVERALL ASSESSMENT OF THE PRIME HYPOTHESIS

Having investigated each of the hypotheses, let us now return to the prime hypothesis guiding this research framework:

Hypothesis – A traumatic event in the homeland impacts ethnic members symbolically and emotionally and directly influences perceptions in the diaspora in favor of the separatist movement. It will motivate some diaspora members to aid or support co-ethnic separatist groups.

Although the testing of hypotheses has tentatively suggested the need to further qualify the model so that symbolic levels of violence influence diaspora mobilization to a greater degree than physical levels of violence, the results appear to generally conform to the model (See Appendix). For these four cases, plugging in the respective data inputs into the research model (using the sub-hypotheses to make more qualified assessments) has — with caveats — accurately predicted which traumatic events would most effectively galvanize the diaspora. Operation Blue Star generated the most widespread diaspora response since it exhibited the highest levels of physical and symbolic violence. The hunger strike, which matches Blue Star in exhibiting a high level of symbolic violence but does not approach its level of physical violence, generated a weaker overall diaspora response than Blue Star but stronger than the others. Bloody Sunday generated a weaker diaspora response because it lacked potency for symbolic and physical violence. However, and somewhat surprisingly, it produced a more observable effect than the Urumqi riots, which as a traumatic event led to an immediate outpouring of grief but appears to have failed at igniting any long-term trends in support of the Uyghur movement except to raise the public profiles of certain leaders and groups. This is a surprising finding because the Urumqi riots produced a starkly higher level of physical violence than Bloody Sunday, further underscoring the potency of symbolism over physical destruction. Unsurprisingly, the most powerful form of violence during a traumatic event is violence that is both symbolic and destructive. Operation Blue Star exemplifies this trend.

BEYOND THE EVENT: OTHER DETERMINANTS

Although this analysis has offered support for the above hypothesis, this research also points to important determinants of mobilization that should be considered as possible mitigating conditions on the explanatory model. As I alluded at the end of chapter 6, these additional causes warrant further consideration for developing a better comparative understanding of how diasporas respond to traumatic events. The following variables emerged as potentially significant factors in the determination of diaspora mobilization:

Diminishing Returns on Emotion over Time – The influence of traumatic events diminished over time for all four traumatic events analyzed — as measured by fundraising levels and ethnic participation in diaspora organizations, indicating the diminishing returns of a traumatic event's influence. Scholars and governments alike would be wise to take note of this trend. As has been argued, Operation Blue Star distressed Sikhs emotionally and psychologically, leaving a powerful wound on the communal Sikh psyche. So too, to varying degrees, did the Irish hunger strike, Bloody Sunday, and Urumqi riots affect the Irish and Uyghur diasporas. However, wounds heal over time, and while traumatic events can produce an incomparably powerful emotive response among ethnic members, it may be the case they are less effective at fueling a movement over a sustained period of time.

Part of the explanation is the lag in time for diaspora populations to observe how their support is being used and not liking what they saw. Sikh respondents attested that although their emotional devastation after Blue Star was genuine, they had grown weary of the militancy within a few years due to the violence and the amount of disarray between the various groups. Similarly, after an initial surge in fundraising following a traumatic event, Irish-American donations to Noraid dried up within a few years as terrorism-averse Irish Americans became more aware about the IRA's tactics. Traumatic events afford rare opportunities to reset perceptions of the separatist movement and mobilize new supporters, but it is incumbent that movement leaders use these chances only to initiate support, not to sustain it.

In her analysis of the importance of ideology and strategic choices to ethnic mobilization, Biswas (2004: 274) describes events such as Operation Blue Star as a "suddenly imposed grievance," which she defines as "a single event or set of events that dramatizes and heightens the political salience of a political issue." Suddenly imposed grievances can be fundamental to efforts at mobilizing support, Biswas contends, but they cannot sustain mobilization absent other mechanisms. Biswas (2004) and Fair (2005) both argue that the Sikhs by focusing so intensely on a singular event were never able to sustain a platform that could transcend local differences or produce cohesion among the pro-Khalistan groups.

Irish diaspora leaders probably did a better job of building more self-sustaining infrastructure, including the founding of new diaspora organizations such as Americans for a New Irish Agenda that eventually surpassed Noraid's influence. However, these new alliances by the 1990s acted as a moderating influence on the movement and the incentive of maintaining their support helped push republican leaders further down the road of the 1990s peace process (Guelke 1996). It remains to be seen what will happen in the Uyghur case, but the fact that these separatist movements traced so much of their support to traumatic events may shed some light on why levels of support tapered off to varying degrees after a few years.

Generational Degradation – The effect of a diaspora's transmigration to a new country over the course of several generations can over time weaken the emotional connections of its members, leaving them less inclined to care about events taking place in a distant homeland. Less affluent and recently-arrived diaspora members will feel the greatest impact because they identify more strongly with the ethnic group; compared to others, their identity is relatively uninterrupted by processes of assimilation and their loyalties are not as tied to the new state. More affluent members, judged to be further along in the assimilation process, might respond differently because their sense of ethnic identity is weaker and sense of loyalty to the new state stronger. They might also feel like they have more to lose in the new country by participating in or contributing to a separatism campaign. In sum, recent emigrants from these cases tended to be more susceptible to the emotional impact of events in the homeland; multi-generational ethnic members tended to be less impressionable.

In the case of the Sikhs, many respondents indicated their belief that first generation Americans or recent migrants from Punjab to the United States were more likely to embrace separatist activism than Sikhs whose families had lived in America for several generations, suggesting levels of support for the movement may have varied according to assimilation. As they explained it, more recent transplants would have taken greater interest in the movement due to family connections, economic interests, or the feeling of a more direct connection to the homeland — pre-assimilationist emigrants, in other words. The Irish diaspora's assimilation and cultural integration over several generations has weakened the Irish identity over time, a problem that has not nearly been as pervasive for the less-established Sikh-American community or for the Uyghurs, who suffer more from a lack of numbers.

However, the capacity to penetrate this generational façade and engage new ethnic members has become the hallmark of violent events that are also religiously or culturally symbolic. Sikh respondents were clear that an event with enough symbolically tragic power such as Operation Blue Star caused even the most established and assimilated of Sikhs to rethink their views of the conflict and of the Sikh separatist movement. And the marvel of the Irish hunger strike was that it accomplished what Bloody Sunday (and the Urumqi riots for Uyghurs) had failed to achieve — attracting support from those whose ancestral identity lay dormant.

Mobilizing Structures and Institutions – All of these case studies have helped illustrate the sweeping power of traumatic events on diaspora perceptions, but each case in its own way also acts as a powerful reminder that a traumatic event plays only a partial role in explaining the success or failure of a diaspora mobilization. As was discussed in chapter 3, there are two other sets of factors in addition to collective action frames that also drive groups to engage in collective behavior: mobilizing structures and political opportunities. At least as much as collective action frames, these variables also determine the diaspora's mobilization response to a traumatic event. In some cases, these added factors overshadow the effect of traumatic events and can act as an amplifying force or a constraint on the diaspora's prospects of staging a successful mobilization.

In the case of mobilizing structures, preexisting institutions and social structures play a crucial role in providing options for mobilization and helping to facilitate the community's response to a traumatic event. Once the community — or even individual members — take the decision to engage in some form of political action or activism in response to a traumatic event, preexisting institutions and networks afford them with readily available resources, such as meeting venues, links to other communities, connections to the homeland, or networks through which to divert funding. In a sense, these institutions can act as an amplifying force or as a constraint on mobilization even after event galvanization has already provided the necessary spark for mobilization to take place.

In the Sikhs' case, the communal importance of the gurdwara ensured it would play a formative role in influencing Sikh perceptions of the attack, such as by organizing seminars and inviting survivors to address the community or by honoring Sikh militants as religious martyrs. Sikhs relied heavily on the gurdwara system to help assemble options and facilitate action, and gurdwaras became a principal vehicle both for fundraising and for channeling the funds into Punjab. However, some scholars argue the movement relied too much on gurdwaras instead of building a sustainable base of support outside gurdwara politics.[111]

Perhaps secular organizations such as the World Sikh Organization might have done a better job of leading the diaspora if they had existed prior to Operation Blue Star. Sikh organizations such as the moderate World Sikh Congress or more militant International Sikh Youth Federation essentially were startups in the aftermath of Operation Blue Star, which undoubtedly affected their capacity to function. In comparison, Noraid had been founded a few years before Bloody Sunday, which meant the group was more organized and better established when Northern Ireland's traumatic events took place. Exiles had also founded the World Uyghur Congress along with other groups prior to the Urumqi riots, and this strengthened the ability to organize and coordinate an effective global response. While this may not have resulted in Uyghur separatists receiving a groundswell of new support, prior operational experience and functionality allowed the Congress to hit the ground running and execute its strategy — focused mainly on rallying support in the West — more effectively than if it, like the WSO, was only coming into existence. On the other hand, the combination of too many organizations and the

---

[111] Biswas (2004: 281) points out: "The focus on Sikh temple or gurdwara politics, rather than an outward-looking orientation, meant that personal and caste rivalries became more salient determinants of the nature of Sikh politics," and combined with an over-reliance on a single event to ultimately divide the movement.

concentration of the Uyghur overseas population in countries that limit their ability to organize restricted the overall capacity of the diaspora to act forcefully and collectively.

Interaction and Networking – Many ethnic studies tend to challenge the statist interpretation of "nation-state building," which contends that populations as they assimilate and grow more prosperous will lose their ethnic identity. Ethno-nationalism scholars have characterized these ideas as simplistic and proven wrong by events (Connor 1994; Varshney 2002). Apart from whether assimilation leads to the evaporation of ethnic identity in the manner that nation-state scholarship claims, snapshots of the three ethnic communities that this research has examined provide some support for the claim that the amount of physical interaction among ethnic members positively influences the strength of identity in the community. In particular, the disappearance of many Irish neighborhoods during the second half of the twentieth century, along with other assimilation traits such as increased education and higher income, probably weakened the communal identity of the Irish diaspora, thereby reducing the emotional leverage of a traumatic event. Mobilization scholars such as Tilly (2002) point out that groups respond differently during mobilization based on the "detached" or "embedded" nature of their identities — the latter of which is invoked every day and clearly provides a more potent source for mobilization, and is most common among first-generation, unassimilated transmigrants. "Dense within-group social interaction" strengthens the diaspora's capacity for mobilization (Ross 1997a: 323). As diaspora populations assimilate, they become significantly less likely to live in neighborhood enclaves.

The evidence or absence of social networks also facilitate intra-group communication and dialogue which lead to a more unified and coherent response. Social networks provide a mechanism for generating social capital (in the form of enhanced group solidarity) in response to a real or perceived threat (Portes and Sensenbrenner 1993; Portes 1998; Sanders 2002). Through these networks, members move greater amounts of information, facilitating the ethnic group's response to events. Less interaction among ethnic members would also cripple the development of some of the important facilitative and communication networks needed for when the diaspora does rally around a specific cause. Of course, the Uyghur case demonstrates how the Internet and social media are facilitating the creation of new networks made up of disparate nodes all over the world.

Political Opportunities – As for political opportunities, both the Irish and Sikh diasporas notwithstanding some successes were unable to significantly alter US foreign policy at the time of these events, an outcome that has as much to do with the limiting realities of the Cold War as it did the overall effectiveness of either ethnic movement. The Irish diaspora had considerably greater success fifteen years later during the Clinton administration, when Irish diaspora leaders were able to persuade the US government to grant Sinn Fein leader Gerry Adams an entrance visa into the United States over the vehement objections of the British government. The Uyghur diaspora's battle with the Chinese government after the Urumqi riots came later, but the movement's decision to shift its emphasis from independence to human rights reflects the lack of opportunity Uyghur leaders saw in challenging the territorial integrity of China. The US position on Xinjiang is not unlike its position on Tibet, where the US has been critical but circumspect of China's treatment of the population.

CONCLUSION

The overall findings of this comparative analysis underscore the role of cultural symbolism in mobilizing the diaspora in response to a traumatic event. This chapter has provided comparative analysis of the four traumatic events highlighted by this research and concluded that symbolic levels of violence tend to influence diaspora mobilization to a greater degree than physical levels of violence. The final chapter will consider the implications of these findings for policymakers and for certain theoretical debates, and will suggest future courses of study that can build on this research.

10

CONCLUSION

Traumatic events in the homeland have the capacity to mobilize ethnic supporters overseas. They can rally the diaspora population into action using preexisting channels, or even foster the creation of new structures of organization such as the innovation of new groups and networks. The occurrence of a traumatic event can help separatist movements attract new supporters and mobilize the diaspora to take action in support of the core objectives of the separatists. Yet, not all traumatic events influence diaspora populations in the same way. The case studies presented in this research has shown that the effects of traumatic events on diaspora populations — including the decision by diaspora members to protest, fundraise, endorse violence, or enlisting in the collective efforts of a violent organization — can depend on a variety of factors and conditions. So when is a traumatic event most likely to transform diaspora perceptions of the separatist movement and lead to the diaspora's galvanization? The explanatory model I developed in chapter 3 and ensuing case studies have allowed me to make a number of key findings with respect to this critical question.

First, *Traumatic events exhibiting high levels of physical and symbolic forms of violence have the potential to mobilize previously inactive diaspora populations by tapping into deep-seeded fears about the ethnic group's status or survival.* The comparative case studies allowed me to analyze different events using comparison data and assess with greater confidence if a positive relationship exists between levels of violent aggression and the movement's ability to attract followers. Comparative analysis of these cases revealed that the symbolism of violence waged during an event surpasses the influence of actual numbers injured or killed during the event in determining the strength of diaspora mobilization that follows the event. These diasporas engaged in mass protests and demonstrations, lobbied foreign governments, created new political organizations, and fundraised on behalf of a variety of causes related to the separatist movement. These results are largely consistent with what the research model and hypotheses predict, although caveats and additional considerations underscore the need for further refinement of the theory.

Second, *symbolically powerful events are especially effective at mobilizing previously inactive diaspora populations by creating fertile environments in which movement entrepreneurs can increase levels of support for the movement.* Symbolic events have the potency to access the ethnic mythology of the group and lay the groundwork for the transformation of diaspora perceptions of the movement. In each of the case studies this research has examined, the diaspora group's response to a traumatic event has fluctuated according to the degree of symbolism and level of symbolic violence the event exhibited. Highly symbolic events that tapped into an ethnic group's understanding of its own history and mythology — Operation Blue Star and the Irish hunger strike — led to more robust forms of diaspora mobilization and succeeded in attracting new supporters. Events that could only credit their notoriety to the sudden eruption of violence as measured by deaths, injuries or property damage — such as the Urumqi riots, and to some degree, Bloody Sunday — will probably lead to widespread anger and calls for revenge in the homeland, but are less likely than highly symbolic events to spark mobilization in the diaspora. The reason for this differential is the ability of a symbolic event to signal to the diaspora population an imminent threat to the ethnic group's culture and identity. The killing of 10, 100 or even 1,000 ethnic members — while tragic — is not as likely to lead a diaspora member to perceive an irrevocable threat to the ethnic group's culture or existence. In contrast, the destruction of a holy shrine can forever affect the ethnic group's future and self-conception, and the emergence of events or actors that can claim their place within the ethnic group's mythological narrative will likewise have the potential to inspire diaspora members to engage in collective forms of action.

Third, *comprehending diaspora mobilization in response to a traumatic event depends on appreciating a group's cultural values as well as the underlying rationality of political actors.* In the early stages of mobilization, understanding the values, group identity, and interpretations of the group's historical mythology shed light on the starting point of actions taken in response to a traumatic event. Analyzing the diaspora's response to traumatic events according to the emotional connection it shared with the homeland and cultural beliefs that shaped the group's interpretation did a better job than analysis of rational decision-making at accounting for the origins of ethnic mobilization and where movements gain their sweeping power in the first place. However, rationalism helps to explain mobilization once it reaches a critical stage. In the Sikh case, the efforts of activists and the damning effect of leadership infighting on the Sikh diaspora's ability to respond underscores that rationalism too helps to explain mobilization once it reaches a critical stage. In other cases, diaspora leaders such as Michael Flannery and Rebiya Kadeer played critical leadership roles for their respective organizations that helped to organize the diaspora and facilitate its response following a traumatic event.

Finally, *there are other explanatory determinants that also influence and condition the strength of mobilization that takes place in the diaspora in response to a traumatic event.* The generational degradation of a diaspora population's identity can weaken the emotional connections of its members, leaving them less inclined to care about events taking place in a distant homeland. Preexisting institutions and social structures play a crucial role in providing options for mobilization and helping to facilitate the community's response to a traumatic event. Physical interaction among ethnic members and the presence of strong social networks also helps to determine the strength of the diaspora's response. Whether these organizations have the strength and leadership to sustain the movement is critical because the effect of the event on diaspora members, while sweepingly powerful, is short-lived, and will wane over time as the nearness of the event fades. Finally, political conditions can act as either an amplifying force or a constraint on the diaspora's prospects of staging a successful mobilization.

POLICY IMPLICATIONS

While support from the diaspora may not determine the overall outcome of an insurgent campaign, the role diasporas can play in response to traumatic political events in empowering violent anti-state movements, prolonging its campaign through fundraising or publicizing the case against the government's treatment of the ethnic group in the realm of international opinion can drain the overall resources and prestige of the state. Policymakers should be interested in strategies that can effectively curb, mitigate, reduce or otherwise resolve the problem of ethnic insurgencies in their state. Policymakers must also recognize when an ethnic group has been treated unfairly or has made legitimate demands. In light of this research on traumatic events and diaspora mobilization, how can governments take appropriate measures to either prevent traumatic events from happening, or manage the diaspora's response event more effectively when it occurs? Although I do not mean to construct an exhaustive list of specific strategies, the following suggestions may help governments to facilitate more constructive action that can create pathways not only to peace and stability within the state but also the achievement of fairness and justice for the afflicted ethnic group.

<u>Preventing a Traumatic Event:</u>

To try to prevent traumatic events from occurring, governments must first have the cognitive ability to assess whether a counterinsurgency proposal could have the kind of "symbolic" impact that these pages have described. Based on this analysis, events exhibiting a high level of symbolic violence, including attacks on shrines, sacred spaces, or events that allow militants to utilize culturally resonant practices such as a hunger strike, may reshape diaspora perceptions and mobilize some diaspora members to engage in anti-state activity. Governments must have a deep understanding of its minority population that extends to the minority group's cultural and political values, perceptions of its status in society, and how it views its own treatment. In light of the role of perceptions, policymakers need to identify the most prominent influences in a community, map out social networks, and understand which groups enjoy the greatest amount of strategic influence (Forest 2010). Government leaders should stress the need for cooperation and communication with the ethnic group during times of rising tensions, and must acknowledge the legitimacy of the ethnic group's grievances and demands even during tense negotiations.

Second, in situations where the use of force may be required, governments must proceed with extreme caution and be willing to modify their actions when attempting to engage separatists in temples, shrines, and other cultural and religiously significant places. They have to approach each scenario with a level of flexibility — instead of rigid standard operating procedures — according to the nature of the specific situation. In planning the operation, governments should assess the different levels and degrees of sacredness. They should determine areas or entrance points where an operation would be less provocative (Bensahel 2008). Governments should also be cognizant of the possible symbolism of large crowds gathering in public plazas or historic squares. Using the police instead of the military whenever possible could help governments avoid unnecessary bloodshed since most police services are trained to use force only when necessary and to avoid indiscriminate killing (Bensahel 2008).

Third, governments must implement an effective public relations campaign targeted at the minority population. The government's communication strategy with the ethnic minority is paramount. A striking number of traumatic events took place in part because of poor communication by the homeland government. The Indian government during the Blue Star attack commented on neither the purpose nor the execution of the Blue Star attack while it was happening. The violence in Urumqi resulted in part over confusion and a lack of transparency regarding factory unrest against Uyghurs in Guangdong province. And the British government lost touch with its public message to Northern Ireland's Catholic population, leading to the violence that preceded Bloody Sunday. And since popular support is a crucial element of any counterinsurgency operation, governments must understand how an operation is perceived lest they risk minority or popular opinion blaming all damage on the state (Bensahel 2008). To mitigate these risks, governments should make clear their commitment to diversity, tolerance and respectful debate.

Fourth, states must exercise patience in dealing with insurgents who frequently are trying to "bait" the government into taking ill-advised actions. Using force imprudently affords insurgents the chance to attract popular support, whereas movements that are already employing violence are likely to alienate their own bases of support so long as the government does not overreact. Qualitative analysis indicates that broad terror campaigns often backfire, whereas restrained terror attacks that do not kill civilians allow insurgents to make significant gains (Connable and Libicki 2010). Contrary to popular belief, it may be the case that governments are really trying to outlast insurgencies rather than the other way around. Governments at a minimum should attempt mediation first even if it judges a peaceful outcome unlikely. If the government engages in violence without first attempting to mediate the situation, the affected ethnic population is even more likely to hold the state responsible (Bensahel 2008).

Fifth, governments must ensure that intelligence related to any proposed counterinsurgency action is timely and accurate. Improved intelligence can help to prevent needless traumatic events from happening, whereas intelligence failures help to explain a number of government blunders leading to traumatic event occurrences. For example, better intelligence might have avoided the Indian army's lack of knowledge about the defenses of Sikh militants inside the Golden Temple, or the British parachute regiment's uneasiness on Bloody Sunday amid probably false intelligence reports of an impending attack.

Managing a Traumatic Event:

No matter how many preventive measures a government might put in place, the reality is that groups engaged in ethnic conflict are at a high risk of encountering a deeply violent and distressing episode that increase the probability of diaspora involvement. Governments can try to contain the impact of the diaspora's mobilization against it via a number of strategies. Probably the most frequent strategy is to pressure the countries where the diaspora population resides to control its anti-state activities. China did this in the 1990s when it exerted pressure on Turkey to crack down on its Uyghur population. More recently, India asked Canada to pay greater attention to Sikh dissident groups operating within its borders (*Hindu* 2010). However, relying on other states to "control" these populations subjects the state's security to the interests and whims of bilateral relations with that other state, and can also result in blowback if the state in question refuses to cooperate or forces the government to trade favors in exchange for its compliance (Byman *et al.* 2001). It also is not likely to provide the most equitable strategy to resolving the ethnic group's concern.

There are other methods that governments can take to avert or reduce the diaspora's alienation and anti-government mobilization following a traumatic event. First, governments must develop a sophisticated communications strategy and engage the diaspora populations of their ethnic minorities directly. Governments also need to be transparent and communicate the specific priorities of the government's involvement, explaining the reasons for the government's actions during the traumatic episode. Transparency is critical during these stages. Outreach will be key. One of the most important goals of the government's communications strategy is to provide accurate information on the traumatic event to thwart myths and misperceptions. In effectively communicating to both domestic and foreign audiences, governments need to engage militants with counterarguments and diminish the credibility of their message (Forest 2010). An effective public relations strategy can counter insurgents' claims to legitimacy, and information campaigns can decrease popular support for insurgents by holding them publicly accountable (Bensahel 2008). Of course, governments cannot achieve this level of engagement without preexisting relationships with the diaspora communities. Governments embroiled in ethnic conflict must do a better job of reaching out to the diaspora populations of their ethnic minorities, not only to conciliate following a traumatic event, but also to enlist possible facilitators of peace.

Second, in seeking to engage the diaspora population, governments should seek to strike a public posture that balances sobriety with empathy and avoids any defensiveness about the government's position. Showing compassion for the views of the minority can also help defuse some of the diaspora community's fear and anger. In contrast, defensiveness and attempting to place blame on the ethnic minority will only exacerbate tensions in the diaspora and increase the likelihood of diaspora mobilization. As this research has shown, diaspora members intervening in the conflict most often perceived the ethnic group's culture or identity to be under assault by the homeland government or its majority ethnic population. Acknowledging the pain experienced by diaspora members when they learn about the deaths of co-ethnics or destruction of a cherished emblem can help nurture a common understanding and lead to further opportunities for cooperation.

Third, governments should create organizations or foster alliances that will help to make clear the state's commitment to diversity, tolerance and respectful debate. When possible, governments should embrace new and innovative groups committed to confronting hostile ideologies and seeking nonviolent pathways to peace (Forest 2010). Governments should create within certain embassies permanent forums dedicated to cross-cultural liaison during times of crisis. Rather than alleging the diaspora's culpability, these groups should work with diasporas to facilitate collaborative partnerships that can help to stabilize the situation. Governments should also promote interethnic civic groups and organizations where it is possible in the diaspora so that different overseas ethnic populations originating from the same country increases the chance for interethnic collaboration and decreases the likelihood of hardened political views of an opposing ethnic group. Supporting inter-communal organizations and civic ties, especially in diverse urban population areas, can help to mitigate anti-state mobilization and create new, dynamic alliances to counter the forces of extremism.

THEORETICAL IMPLICATIONS

At the beginning of this dissertation, I identified three spheres in which this research could contribute to the scholarly literature on ethnic conflict. I shall now revisit each of these. First, by concentrating on diasporas this research sought to contribute to our scholarly understanding of ethnic identity as an increasingly globalized phenomenon. The animated response of diaspora members to events in the homeland highlights the extent to which these communities are able to recreate ethnic identity in the diaspora. As Danforth (1995: 79-80) states, "In this era of globalization, national communities are being 'imagined' in a new way... National communities are not being replaced by transnational ones; they are being constructed on a transnational scale." Symbolism proved an especially important feature in mobilizing diaspora members into action as it allowed diaspora members to compensate for the lack of any remaining physical connection to the homeland. The children of Sikh exiles may not have ever visited Punjab, but the outbreak of violence there can nonetheless devastate them if it lends itself to symbolic interpretation. Even in a diaspora such as Irish America that had endured some generational degradation over time, a symbolic event such as the Irish hunger strike attracted the previously uninitiated and facilitated their engagement in activities related to the Irish republican movement that most Irish Americans associated with the cause of their ancestors.

There were also dynamics that were unique to the diaspora in that they exposed ethnic members to pressures and dualities that homeland ethnic members never face. As diaspora communities become more established in the host state, the ethnic identities of its member evolve and become more complex. The diaspora member's self-perception — "Who Am I?" — grows into an amalgamation of ancestral and new state influences, thus enabling multiple Sikh respondents to remark proudly on the first Sikh-American elected to Congress, or an Irish American from South Boston to attempt to smuggle arms to Ireland years after serving in the US military and fighting in Vietnam. Sometimes residual guilt may also influence the diaspora's group identity. When a traumatic event signaled worsening tensions in the conflict, it made many Sikh respondents feel guilty for having "escaped" the fate of their brethren. This residual guilt likely helped motivate some diaspora members to donate their time and money to the cause — from the relative safety of Canada and the United States.

Second, this research sought to boost our theoretical understanding about the causal mechanisms involving ethnic identity. This research raised important questions about the explanatory power of value rationality versus instrumental rationality, and as I have argued, this research lends general support to the case made by other scholars who favor a more creative understanding of ethnic mobilizing determinants that moves beyond pure rationality. However, it is important to also note the role of institutions in shaping the diaspora response once kindled. Exile groups, diaspora organizations, ethnic networks within the new state and webs of global exchanges all helped facilitate the diaspora's response. Technological advances also accounted for how diaspora members learned about events in the homeland — from official media, social media, through text or pictures, and through interactions with each other. In the case of the Uyghur diaspora, activists used web sites and online social networks to create a response to the Urumqi riots that was more globally coordinated — but not better resourced — than either Irish case or the Sikh response to Operation Blue Star. The ultimate inability of the Uyghur movement to attract significant membership growth despite these added technological innovations serves as a useful reminder — particularly in the era of Twitter and the Arab Spring — that technology is no replacement for the dynamic interaction between events, symbolism, emotions and identity.

Third, this research sought to add a new perspective to our theoretical understanding of ethnic identity as a determinant of group violence. Recent studies (Collier and Hoeffler 2000; Fearon and Latin 2003; Kalyvas 2006) have attempted to refute the "conventional belief" that the occurrence of ethnic grievances is the most important predictor of political conflict, instead arguing that violence is determined by rationalism and opportunity-seekers on a playing field shaped by environmental conditions such as a weak central government, poverty and political instability. These studies are important and add much to the literature, but they do not sufficiently account for the emotional and psychological underpinnings of ethnic identity, nor does it account for the ethnic member's symbolic interpretation of political phenomena inspiring and inspired by this identity. This research has shown that a symbolically powerful traumatic event can motivate thousands of diaspora members to offer support for homeland insurgencies and separatist movements not out of calculation of their own personal safety, security and profitability, but because the emotional connection and shared understanding of identity has the power to animate ethnic members thousands of miles outside the homeland. This is an crucial aspect when discussing the collective action of groups involved in ethnic conflict and the literature must capture it.

CONCLUSION: LOOKING TO THE FUTURE

This analysis represents an initial attempt to increase our understanding of the relationship between traumatic political events, diaspora populations and ongoing ethnic conflict. The interview data and comparative case studies presented in this research has helped to shed light on the nature of these relationships, but they have also kindled ideas for other pathways to examining the dynamics of ethnic and diaspora group behavior. This study raises several important questions and topics that future research should consider.

Chief among these is the need to examine the growing and multi-faceted relationships between diasporas and ethnic or religiously-based insurgencies in the present-day, including a number of Islamic fundamentalist groups receiving financial support and resources from sympathizers in the West. For example, the militant group al-Shabaab since 2007 has tried to recruit dozens of US citizens from the Somali diaspora in Minnesota, while Kurdish nationalists residing throughout Europe have recently provided financial aid and sanctuary to members of the Kurdish Worker's Party (PKK), which for several decades has been engulfed in a guerrilla campaign against Turkey (Forliti 2012; Mazzetti 2013; Eccarius-Kelly 2008, 2011). In May 2010, Faizal Shahzad, a Connecticut man of Pakistani descent, attempted to blow up Times Square, and although his reasons for attacking the US appear to have been more religiously ideological than ethnically-motivated, media reports that Shahzad strongly identified with his Pashtun heritage and received bomb-making training in Pakistan's Pashtun-dominated Waziristan region underscore the degree to which ethnic identity may have played a role in his radicalization (Elliott, Tavernese and Barnard 2010). Beyond cases of Islamic militancy, the recent civil war in Sri Lanka provides a noted example of a weaker diaspora reaction to a traumatic event in the form of the Sri Lankan government's escalated campaign against the Liberation Tigers of Tamil Eelam (LTTE), which resulted in that group's defeat in 2008. The Tamil diaspora — perhaps owing to its exhaustion with LTTE strategy and tactics — provided only a restrained response to the escalation of violence waged during that campaign. Future research should aim to flesh out the dynamics of these relationships and examine the role of events, ethnicity and/or religion in mobilizing these individuals. Focusing more intently on intra-diaspora dynamics would also shed additional light on diaspora perceptions and how they work. Along these grounds, it would be useful if comparative research offered a more explicit examination of the relationship between traumatic events on the one hand, and the effects of individuals or groups' financial standing, political influence, degree of assimilation, and status within the diaspora on the other.

This research analyzed the responses of the targeted ethnic minority to traumatic events, but a systematic study of the majority ethnic group — including its diaspora — and justifications for armed action would amplify the literature on the majority or power-holding parties embroiled in ethnic conflict as well as the "under siege" mentality these societies often assume. In addition, future research should examine the evolving relationship between diasporas and movement entrepreneurs in the homeland, the latter of who have unprecedented access to the global ethnic community but must take into account and somehow include the diaspora's sometimes distinct political views and demands in order to gain any influence in these overseas communities. Of course, it would have been deeply enriching if this research could have conducted interviews with Irish and Uyghur diaspora members as well as the Sikhs, or to include another relevant diaspora response such as the Tamil diaspora reaction to events in Sri Lanka, but these choices would have expanded the scope of the project beyond feasibility. These various data nodes offer worthwhile starting points for future case study research of diaspora perceptions of traumatic events. A final suggestion for future study regards the capacity of traumatic events to revitalize the diaspora population's commitment not just to the ethnic group's political goals, but also (and relatedly) its cultural traditions and religious practices. In this research, several Sikh participants suggested that contrary to their expectations, the occurrence of a traumatic event the magnitude of Operation Blue Star led to a renewal of interest in the diaspora in Sikh history and the Sikh faith. These discussions underscore the need for future research on the relationship of culturally significant and threatening events on existing values and identity in the diaspora community.

One discussion stands out in particular and provides a useful ending note for this research: a joint interview I conducted with a young Sikh couple living in the Washington DC area. During the interview, I asked them what they thought had been the purpose behind Operation Blue Star. Without hesitation, the husband, who in 1984 was a child in Punjab, replied that the main reason behind the operation was to "break the spirit" of the Sikhs, not an uncommon answer among respondents. However, his wife then remarked that Operation Blue Star had had the opposite effect. I asked what she meant, and the wife responded: "It did the opposite for the people. Not as much in India, because there is so much propaganda there. But for me, *it made me want to understand more about who I am.*" Her reflection was poignant because a number of other respondents had identified Blue Star as a moment that rejuvenated interest in their own culture and religion. I asked how the Sikhs' perseverance during the traumatic episode served as a source of strength, and the husband in quick succession linked the courage of the Sikhs to several other historical events, including the Mogul attack on Amritsar in the mid-eighteenth century, Maharaja Ranjit Singh's 40-year empire, the military feats of Sikhs who in the nineteenth century defended Punjab against the British, and the Sikhs' defense of the Indian state during two wars with Pakistan. For this young couple, Operation Blue Star was the historic and mythological moment that intersected their own parents' generation with the previous chapters of suffering and triumph scattered across the long history of the Sikhs. Yet, the renewal of Sikhism in response to the dark episode belonged to the next generation — the children of the survivors.